T0246001

Praise for *Keith Urban*

"Keith Urban has done just about everything in country music that anyone could ever imagine. This biography by Jeff Apter reveals the highlights and struggles in getting there. I loved looking at the pictures, not just the celebrations that he's had, but the pictures of his youth really caught my attention. The look in his eyes had the look of destiny. To use one of Keith's quotes, 'Nashville's not my dream. It's my destiny.'"
—**Ricky Skaggs, 15-time Grammy Award–winning musician**

"Jeff Apter's Keith Urban had dreamed of Nashville stardom ever since he was a young, guitar-pickin' boy from a working-class home in Australia. It didn't happen easily or quickly but came through hard work and tenaciousness. In lively prose, Apter takes us on every happy twist and frustrating turn that Urban faced on his way to the top."
—**Elizabeth J. Rosenthal, author of *His Song: The Musical Journey of Elton John* and *The Master of Drums: Gene Krupa and the Music He Gave the World***

"He ain't just that Aussie cowboy with the golden locks and godly good looks who seemingly came out of nowhere in the early 2000s, set the country and pop charts ablaze with his honey-sweet songs, and married a movie star. No, ma'am. There's more than that to Keith Urban—*much* more. From his humble beginnings in blue-collar Brisbane to crooning for swooning swarms in rhinestone-studded Nashville, overcoming addiction, and filling stadiums and tabloid covers around the world, Urban has ridden a long, rocky road to the top, a road full of breathtaking highs, heartbreaking lows, and everything in between. Jeff Apter's long-awaited biography of this beloved modern troubadour is a riveting read that no music fan will want to miss."
—**Peter Aaron, author of *The Band FAQ* and coauthor of Richie Ramone's autobiography, *I Know Better Now: My Life Before, During and After the Ramones***

Carl Perkins

The King of Rockabilly

Jeff Apter

CITADEL PRESS
Kensington Publishing Corp.
kensingtonbooks.com

CITADEL PRESS BOOKS are published by

Kensington Publishing Corp.
900 Third Avenue
New York, NY 10022

All Kensington titles, imprints, and distributed lines are available at special quantity discounts for bulk purchases for sales promotions, premiums, fund-raising, educational, or institutional use. Special book excerpts or customized printings can also be created to fit specific needs. For details, write or phone the office of the Kensington sales manager: Kensington Publishing Corp., 900 Third Avenue, New York, NY 10022, attn Sales Department; phone 1-800-221-2647.

10 9 8 7 6 5 4 3 2 1

First Citadel hardcover printing: December 2024

Printed in the United States of America

ISBN: 978-0-8065-4352-9

ISBN: 978-0-8065-4354-3 (e-book)

Library of Congress Control Number: 2024940939

This one's for the EHBHS vandals.
You know who you are.

Contents

Foreword

By Slim Jim Phantom of the Stray Cats

"I've done more versions of that song than you boys have had hot meals," Carl drawled softly in his whispery Dixie-fried voice.

"And that was the best one ever!"

I never wanted to believe anything more.

We had just finished blasting through "Blue Suede Shoes." Lee Rocker and myself were Carl's rhythm section and Dave Edmunds was producing the recording session. The song was to be for the soundtrack of the cinematic triumph that is *Porky's Revenge.* How or why the film producers arrived at the conclusion to have a new version of "Blue Suede Shoes" in their film, I don't know. Rockabilly was still a little trendy and as close to mainstream as it ever was from the recent success of *Stray Cats*, and Dave was a hot producer, again. The soundtrack is excellent, probably better than the movie.

The *Porky's Revenge* soundtrack includes songs from Dave Edmunds, George Harrison, the Fabulous Thunderbirds, Clarence Clemons, Willie Nelson, and Jeff Beck. All of them I remember. I do not remember any of the actors.

We had finished the track in about ten minutes and all sat around the control room listening to Carl tell a few stories. Some of the stories I had heard before. We met him a couple of years earlier when he came up and played a few numbers with the Cats at a gig in Nashville, where he brought Johnny Cash with him. We had stayed in touch, which still amazes me. I didn't have a cell phone or computer.

The studio was the old Record Plant on 3rd Street near La Cienega in West Hollywood. The date has got to be around late

1984. It was the site of a thousand sessions and numerous hit records—some of the most successful albums of all time were recorded there. It was a luxurious, high-tech joint with all the 1970s rock star splendor and technology associated with a studio of the era. There's a nondescript mini-mall there today. We were probably using eight channels of the forty-eight tracks available on the mixing desk. The input list was probably three mics on the drums, one for the bass, one for the guitar amp, and one for the vocal. We could have been doing this session at Sun Studio in 1955. Dave came up with the idea to keep rolling the tape and do a few more songs. We had only used one hour of studio time and I'm pretty sure we had it booked for all night. Somewhere, among my things, is a cassette copy of that night's recording.

Someday we should get it together and put it out so the world can hear us plowing through quite a bit of Carl's early catalog. Somebody remind me, please. I bet it's amazing.

Carl was definitely what everyone would call a beautiful guy. I call him a "beautiful and rockin' guy." We would work together again in 1985, on a TV show, *Blue Suede Shoes: A Rockabilly Session,* with a lineup of performers aptly called Carl Perkins and Friends. His friends were George Harrison, Ringo Starr, Eric Clapton, Rosanne Cash, Lee Rocker, and Earl Slick, with Dave Edmunds and his excellent band backing everyone up. Lee and I were flown to London and met the group for a couple days' rehearsal in a very regular rehearsal room. Our live set was filmed at a no-frills television studio. The show was a 100 percent pro production but was truly laid back and quite under-the-radar considering the major talent that was involved. It's caught on in a cult fashion, but to this day it's still not as well known as a few other similar shows from the era that coupled original American rock and roll stars with those they'd influenced.

This show has one extremely unique feature. In one segment, we pulled up our chairs in a circle. Carl said it was "like sitting around a campfire." Playing mainly acoustic guitars, we listened as Carl walked everyone through his technique and swapped stories. Ringo and I played tambourines and shakers and joked around in a respectful way. This part of the show was kind of quiet and let everyone's personality shine through and the obvious, shared love for Carl be heard. There's a touching duet with Rosanne.

Lee and I were accepted quickly by George because Carl vouched for us. Eric Clapton had seen Stray Cats, and Ringo, even though he was my hero, was a drummer, so I knew we'd get along. I was a bit too young to be nervous. If Carl said you were okay, then that was good enough for everyone. We had to be good, but that part I knew we could handle. I was a little starstruck. We had been around the block a few times, but Beatles were different.

Like Carl, the show was understated and super cool. He quietly influenced every following generation of guitar players and singers, not just rockabilly types. He influenced the Beatles and as a result influenced everybody since, even if they didn't know it. Go find the show and watch and listen to the poignant and touching moments between George and Carl. You'll get it right away!

We all continue to be amazed by Carl Perkins's *Dance Album*. Do yourself a favor and pick up a copy. You may even already have it in your records. You'll know every song on it and wonder why you haven't been listening to it more often. I recorded some of his songs when Lemmy and I made an album. We were comparing our favorite songs and a few of Carl's matched up. It was very important to Lem to get the beginning of "Blue Suede Shoes" played correctly. Listen to the original—it's a little different from how most musicians would do it.

On a personal level, I loved Carl. He's responsible for much of how my life turned out.

I first discovered him when I was consumed by rockabilly music and style in 1979. After all, he wrote and had a hit song about the most rockabilly article of clothing. You gotta have a good pair of blue suede shoes to be taken seriously. Meeting him, getting to know him, and playing with him as a peer was something that is still beyond my imagination, but it happened and I have the pictures to prove it. He was gentle and forceful at the same time. He wrote and recorded some of the greatest rockabilly and rock and roll songs of all time and quietly backed up Johnny Cash for many years as a shredding guitar picker. We saw each other over the years, and I loved talking with him when I was a little older and appreciated it more. He never expressed even the least bit of resentment, and from what I can tell, he was completely comfortable in his own skin.

I found him to be a Rockabilly Buddha.

As a result of knowing Carl, I maintained a very nice relationship with George. I visited Friar Park a number of times, and he'd call out of the blue when he was in LA and sometimes we'd meet up. I still see Ringo around and have run into Eric a few times over the years. The conversation inevitably comes back to the *A Rockabilly Session* show and how we're all still thrilled to have been a part of it.

Carl's influence and impact on the whole ball of wax cannot be overstated.

His contribution to the style side of music is cemented.

He wrote the song about the most famous article of rock and roll quality footwear.

His contribution to music and musicianship will live forever.

He launched 1,001 ships.

I'm honored to have known the Cat and to have been asked to write the foreword for this fine biography by Jeff Apter. *Carl Perkins: The King of Rockabilly* really does justice to Mr. Blue Suede Shoes!

Well, it's a-one for the money . . .

Prologue

Limehouse Studios, London, England,
October 21, 1985

Carl Perkins wasn't too tough to cry. He might have been raised dirt poor, the son of a sharecropper, and learned his craft in the rowdy honky-tonks of rural Tennessee, but that didn't mean he'd hardened his heart. Tonight, in a TV studio in London, he'd been celebrating the thirtieth anniversary of the song that made his career, in an event known as *Blue Suede Shoes: A Rockabilly Session with Carl Perkins and Friends.* Carl had spent the past couple of hours sharing a stage with true believers, die-hard fans of his music—among them two Beatles, together for the first time in over a decade, and a British blues guitar legend—playing to an audience packed with Perkins devotees. And now, as the cameras finally stopped rolling, having just performed his signature song one more time, he couldn't hold back the tears.

"I have never in my life enjoyed singing that song like I did tonight with my friends, my rockabilly buddies," the fifty-three-year-old said from the stage, wiping his eyes. "God bless you. Thank you."

For the man born Carl Lee Perkins, it had been a hell of a night, spent surrounded by Ringo Starr and George Harrison, Eric Clapton, Dave Edmunds, Lee Rocker and Slim Jim Phantom from the Stray Cats, and Rosanne Cash, the daughter of the Man in Black, one of Carl's closest friends. All were huge admirers of the man known deservedly as the "King of Rockabilly."

Together this mighty ensemble had played the songs that built Perkins's career—not just "Blue Suede Shoes" but "Matchbox," "Honey, Don't," and "Everybody's Trying to Be My Baby" (all covered by the Beatles)—as well as the odd chestnut from Carl's lengthy back catalog. The stage was alive with energy and musicianship and genuine affection for a humble man who'd never really shaken off his blue-collar roots.

"This is the greatest thing that could ever happen to me," Carl said early in the evening. "This is my night with my friends." This wasn't showbiz speak or false humility; he meant every word.

What Carl didn't mention—but was fully understood by everyone present—was the long, hard road he had traveled over the past thirty musical years. His career—and his life—had been a rollercoaster ride. Several years back, he had been forced to fire his bandmate and brother, Clayton, a sometimes wild boy, after he'd thrown one too many punches. He'd lost another musical sibling, Jay—"a jewel of a brother," in Carl's words—to cancer when Jay was just twenty-eight. And in 1956 Carl had been laid up in a hospital bed after a car wreck, his body broken and bruised, looking on as Elvis Presley, his friend and former Sun Records labelmate, launched himself into the stratosphere in a TV studio in New York City, leaving Carl and many other peers in his wake. Carl had also seen many of those close to him—including Elvis—crash and burn. Carl himself had struggled with, and then finally overcome, alcoholism.

But tonight was a celebration, an affirmation that Carl was one of the greats, a true founding father of rock and roll. George Harrison put it simply when he looked over at his friend and spoke to the audience as applause washed over them: "Carl Perkins, everybody."

CHAPTER 1

The little chill bumps stood up on my arms

The first time Carl Perkins heard music, *really heard music*, it didn't come from a phonograph or the radio. It was during the late 1930s, at the time of the Great Depression, when Carl was a kid, barely school age, working with his family on a four-hundred-acre cotton plantation in Tiptonville, Tennessee. They were the only white family in a predominantly black environment. It would be midafternoon and the sun would be beating down on Carl and a group of forty, maybe fifty, workers when he'd hear a voice from someone picking cotton nearby. Soon enough another voice would join in, and Carl would almost explode with joy, knowing what would happen next—they'd all be singing in unison. "My blood would start boiling," he recalled many years later, his excitement still palpable.

More often than not, the first voice Carl heard belonged to a man called John Westbrook, known to all as Uncle John, while the second would usually be another cotton worker called Sister Juanita (whom Carl would one day name-check in his song "Cane Creek Glory Church"). She would be "singing that real high part," recalled an adult Carl, while John Westbrook would be "hittin' the bass note—it was beautiful, man." Others would join in, singing gospel songs, what Carl would call "those old-time hymns." Anyone who didn't know the words hummed along in harmony. As their voices rose, Carl responded in a very physical way: "The little chill bumps stood up on my arms." He was particularly delighted by what he described as "that rhythm thing" the black workers could create vocally, the "ba-dum, ba-dum, ba-dum." Unable to take instruments out into the field, they were forced to improvise vocally, and Carl loved what he heard. Music seeped deep into his DNA; he described the cotton field singers as "a big orchestra" of voices. "[Those songs] just bled into my country soul," said Carl.

Carl Lee Perkins, born on April 9, 1932, was the middle child of three Perkins boys. Carl's big brother, James, known as Jay, was two years older, while his younger brother, Clayton, was born in 1935. Jay was quiet and gentle but strong, while Clayton was more rambunctious, the kind of kid who didn't mind a scrap. (Of the Perkins brothers, "Clayton was the funniest and the wildest," noted family friend Johnny Cash.) Carl loved his siblings equally and would eventually make music with both. On Carl's birth certificate, the surname of his father, who was known to all as Buck, was misspelled as Perkings—Buck was illiterate. His real name, Fonnie, was also misspelled as "Fonie." Carl's mother's name was Louise (née Brantley). They'd married in August 1928.

"My daddy," Carl said in 1977, "was a sweet little fella who knew about three chords on the guitar and could guess the weight of cotton in a wagon by looking at it."

Buck's brother Ernest, one of his six siblings, had married Louise's sister Nell in 1929. When Carl was born, Ernest, Nell, and their baby daughter, Martha Lee, shared a shack in Tiptonville—a rural town roughly halfway between Memphis and Nashville—with Buck and Louise and their family. Carl's birth was traumatic; while his mother was deep in labor, aided only by a black midwife named Mary, Buck was lying nearby, suffering the effects of double pneumonia. No doctor was available for the Perkins family, and while Carl's father was fortunate enough to survive, his health was never good—the downside of too many cigarettes and a bout of scarlet fever when he was younger. He needed to have a lung removed, which only weakened him further. As a release, Buck didn't mind a drink; he would go on weekend benders, frequented pool halls, and carried a knife in his back pocket. Sometimes, while drunk, he'd dish out a little rough justice on his sons, but no more than most other parents of those times.

Still, as Carl grew older, he clung to mainly good memories of his parents. "I just know I had a mighty good Mum and Dad, and I knew I loved my two brothers as much as I possibly could."

When Carl was a child, the population of rural backwater Tiptonville, which was in the Lake County region of Tennessee, wasn't quite fifteen hundred. Most Tiptonville families like the Perkinses would attend Baptist church services every Sunday. "I went to church just to sing," admitted Carl, "because that's all I was really getting out of it. It wasn't until I was ten years old that I started getting the real meaning of it." Sometimes, Carl's enthusiasm for singing got the better of him, especially during the ageless hymn "I'll Fly Away," a favorite. "I felt the sound and the beat all the way to the bone," said Carl. His mother would pinch his ear. "Carl," she'd whisper to him, "you're singing too loud and too fast. Slow down!"

At home, Carl's mother taught him stories from the Bible and made it clear that he should adhere to the beliefs of the Ten Commandments. "Just keep prayin'," she'd tell Carl whenever he found cause to question the Good Book. Though a virtual dust speck on the map by comparison with Memphis, which was ninety miles away to the south, Tiptonville itself had a lively past: Confederate forces had surrendered nearby in the 1862 Battle of Island Number Ten—so named because it was once the tenth island in the Mississippi south of its junction with the Ohio—during the Civil War. Almost forty years later, in 1901, the entire town was destroyed by fire. It was most likely the result of payback after a black man, Ike Fitzgerald, had been lynched by a mob of white townspeople after being accused of rape. "Burning of Town Follows the Lynching of a Negro," reported the *Chicago Daily Tribune*.

Carl and his family lived on the plantation in a wooden shotgun shack, which comprised just three rooms, with no electricity or running water. Carl and his two brothers slept squeezed together in the living room. Newspaper, not wallpaper, lined the walls, while there were cracks in the floor where cold air poured through in winter and likewise the heat in summer. Rainwater would drip from a hole in the roof during wet spells, and to heat the house, the family was forced to burn wood in an old oil drum. Sometimes dark, ominous clouds would roll down the Mississippi toward their house—their official address was Rt. 1 Ridgely—and Carl's mother would call him and his brothers inside. She'd drop to her knees, wrap her arms around her children, and pray out loud: "Lord, please don't let the storm hurt my babies!"

Buck was hampered by the aftereffects of his double pneumonia, and to help, Carl started working in the fields when he was six years old, usually putting in twelve- to fourteen-hour days, sunrise to sunset, what the pickers called working "from can to can't." "It was pick or starve," Carl would say of his childhood. Sometimes Carl would miss school—and his lack of formal education would provide a funny backstory when he came to write his most famous song. Carl understood that he and his family were a long way down the social scale. "We picked cotton," he once said, "but the cotton belonged to somebody else."

The work in the cotton fields was backbreaking, but by the time Carl was ten, he could pick a staggering 300 pounds a day, even bettering his brother Jay, a renowned picker who could manage 250 pounds in a shift. Carl's younger brother, Clayton, however, had no interest in working the cotton fields, despite threats of a thrashing from his father. He figured that a day in the searing heat was more uncomfortable than a whipping by Buck, and he rarely lasted a full shift.

Carl's parents earned a dollar each for a day in the field; Carl and his brothers were paid fifty cents. A five-cent bag of candy was a rare indulgence for Carl, Jay, and Clayton. Each Christmas, they considered themselves lucky if they received oranges and peppermint sticks as gifts. When not picking, Carl would play football with the black kids from the plantation by using old socks stuffed with sand. No one could afford an actual ball.

Just across the Mississippi from Perkins and his family, in Dyess, Arkansas, an equally poor sharecropper's son named John Cash (known as JR to his family), one of seven children, was undergoing the same kind of tough upbringing as Carl and his people. John also lived in a shotgun shack, and he, too, was an impressive cotton picker, having started work in the fields at the age of five.

"Going at it really hard for ten hours or so," he wrote in *Cash: The Autobiography*, "I could pick about three hundred pounds." Born less than two months apart, Carl and Cash would eventually cross paths, and the world of music would never be the same again. They also became very close friends.

"The Mississippi River divided us," Carl said of Cash, "but our lives were so much alike."

"We'd been raised on the same music, the same work, the same religion," Cash wrote in his autobiography. "We were just in tune with each other. Friends for life." They even had identical (and permanent) scars on their fingers, a painful by-product of handling the sharp needles of cotton bolls. "Can't get blood out of that," the adult Carl would say of their calluses.

It was his fellow picker Uncle John Westbrook that helped Carl take his first clumsy musical steps. Carl had begged his father for a guitar, and Buck had fashioned one out of a cigar box, attaching a broom handle and two strings made from baling wire. Uncle John had invited Carl to his shack to show him how to play the guitar. Buck, although initially resistant—he figured that Westbrook would be too tired to host Carl and was just being polite—eventually allowed Carl to head over after dinner, something he began doing regularly. They'd burn straw grass stalks to keep the mosquitoes at bay, then pick up their guitars and play for hours.

"He couldn't play very much," Carl admitted in 1977, "but I thought back then that he was Chet Atkins." Carl described the music Westbrook played as "black blues."

Carl was especially impressed by the way in which Uncle John made the strings of his own guitar "quiver" (Carl's words) and hoped to do the same himself. Uncle John's advice to the boy was simple and priceless: "Just make it vibrate, Carlie," he said. "*Just make it vibrate*." Westbrook showed Carl how to rest his head close to the sound hole of the guitar and listen closely to the sound he was making. Carl's relationship with music, especially the guitar, deepened.

Carl once told a reporter that his father bought him his first proper guitar "as a bribe so I would go to school." And Carl would take his guitar to school along with his books, "[as] sort of a security blanket, I guess." He received some very confused stares from his fellow students when he boarded the bus holding his beaten-up six-string. "I didn't want to spend the day without it," he explained. "I loved guitars all my life," Carl said in a 1978 interview. "Ever since I can remember, I wanted me a guitar as a little kid, and finally got me a little cheap one and I just lived with it in my arms. I loved it."

That "little cheap one" Carl referred to was a hand-me-down acoustic guitar that had done some traveling when Carl's father saved enough to buy it from a neighbor. Because he couldn't afford a pick, Carl found a substitute in the one comb that the family shared for their hair. "I'd break me out a couple of the big [teeth] and put 'em in my short pocket for spares."

As Carl explained to fellow musician Ricky Skaggs in 1997, in a conversation about his first guitar, it was an "old Gene Autry [signature model] that weighed about forty pounds. It had been painted every year." In another conversation about the same guitar, with a writer from *Rolling Stone*, Carl noted that it had been painted so many times that it was almost indestructible. "You could throw it against a wall and not make a dent," he said, laughing. In yet another version of this story—and Carl did love spinning a good story—he insisted the guitar was given to him by John Westbrook, his first tutor, because his father couldn't afford to buy it, and Westbrook died just days later. The poignancy wasn't lost on Carl; the guitar had been passed along from teacher to student. "There was something that was meant to be there," he explained. During one of their final conversations, Westbrook said to Carl, "That guitar can take you miles away from these cotton fields, boy, if you work on it. There's somethin' about you, chile."

Carl's public debut was as humble as his guitar. His fourth-grade teacher at Tiptonville Elementary, Miss Lee McCutchen, was putting together a marching band and was aware that Carl was learning guitar. She asked if he wanted to join the band. "I don't know, Miss Lee," Carl replied, "I'm not that good. But I'll try." Carl had another problem—his family was so poor that they couldn't afford to buy him the marching band uniform of white cotton pants, cap, and red satin cape with gold satin lining. "I was the poorest white boy in my school," Carl admitted in a 1968 interview.

When he revealed this to his teacher, she told him not to worry, and a week later Miss McCutchen discreetly handed him a package containing his complete uniform. He was deeply moved by the gesture, so much so that whenever Carl related the story in future years, tears would well up in his eyes. "I think a lot of boys knew she got them for me," Carl said. (Miss McCutchen would one day drive Carl seventy miles to a radio station in Jackson, Tennessee, WTJS, where he performed "Home on the Range" and "Billy Boy," a traditional folk song that dated back to the early twentieth century. In 1969, when Jackson staged "Carl Perkins Day," she remembered him as her "star pupil . . . a wonderful little boy.")

Playing in the marching band was a big step for Carl, who by his own admission was a painfully shy child, fully aware of his family's poverty and low social standing. "I'd have another kid sharpen my pencil," he said, "because I was too scared to get out of my seat." When Miss McCutchen asked him to perform with the marching band at school assembly, he was too scared to say no but was so nervous that he almost threw up beforehand. And Carl did look awkward in a rare photo from his youth, posing with the school ensemble, which also included a xylophonist and accordion player, and numbered more than a dozen players. They were standing on the steps of what was then the Jackson Free Library (and today is the site of the Legends of Tennessee Music Museum, which houses a Carl Perkins exhibit).

Yet even before he reached the age of ten, Carl had started to wonder if there was a life beyond Lake County. It was a feeling that he'd later express in a song called "I Got Tired." Maybe music was a possible outlet—if nothing else, it would be an escape from the grind of picking cotton. When Miss McCutchen asked her students to write something about themselves, Carl revealed that he liked oranges, had no intention to "grow up and be a man like Hitler" and dreamed about becoming "a big radio star."

"This guitar will get me on the Grand Ole Opry," Carl bragged to his brother.

"You don't really think you'll sing on the Grand Ole Opry, do you?" Jay replied.

"Sure," said Carl. "I am."

Jay remained unconvinced and told Carl he'd best learn how to drive a truck.

In 1939, the Grand Ole Opry, staged on Saturday nights at the War Memorial Auditorium in Nashville, was being broadcast by local radio station WSM, with an hour of the program heard nationally on the NBC Red Network across twenty-five stations in the South. The Opry was hosted by Roy Acuff, a native of Maynardville, Tennessee, known to his many admirers as "the king of country music," who'd once featured in a group known as the Tennessee Crackerjacks. Legends like Hank Williams—who joined the cast in 1949 and was encored six times after his debut performance—were regular features of the Opry, and Carl became a big Hank Williams fan. But there was more to the Opry than great singers, as *Time* magazine reported on January 29, 1940: "Grand Ole Opry is no ordinary hillbilly show. It is opportunity night for all the balladeers, jug players, mouth-organists, fiddlers, washboard knucklers, accordionists, comb-hummers, etc. It is a weekly fiesta, Southern style, for hill folk from the Great Smokies, croppers, tourists."

When Carl's family were able to afford a radio battery, having delivered their annual cotton crop in the fall, he was finally able to tune in to the Opry, with his hound dog, Bildo, nearby. The battery would be good for about three months. "I remember how sad I'd get when the battery started to fade," Carl said in 1968. He'd keep the volume low because his father convinced him that it prolonged the life of the battery. "Daddy used to tell us the radio needed more juice when it was turned up," explained Carl.

After staying up on Saturday nights until nine to hear the Opry, Carl would then try to replicate the music he heard on his paint-heavy guitar. Carl used a simple playing style he called "picking out," plucking one string at a time, clearly influenced by Ernest Tubb's guitar man, Tommy "Butterball" Paige. Carl liked the way Tubb would turn to his guitar player onstage and say, "Pick it out, Butterball."

"I was tryin' to be my own Butterball," explained Carl.

In order to get to know the songs better—and with no way of recording them to play back—Carl and his brother Jay would listen closely to the songs on the radio and transcribe them, Jay taking the first line of the lyric, Carl the next. "And the melodies were very simple," Carl said in a 1989 interview. "That's really how I learned my first songs." On the front porch of their house, Carl showed Jay how to play rhythm guitar. In time he'd borrow a homemade bass fiddle from a neighbor and introduce Clayton to the basics of the instrument, despite his younger brother's resistance. "That bass fiddle's bigger than I am!" Clayton protested.

The bluegrass great Bill Monroe was a country boy like Carl, raised on his family's farm outside of Rosine, Kentucky. His father, like Carl's, was known as Buck. Monroe had successfully auditioned for the Opry in 1939, impressing its founder George D. Hay with his revved-up rendition of Jimmie Rodgers's "Mule Skinner Blues." A wizard on the mandolin, and renowned as a tough bandleader and stickler for the best possible musicianship, Monroe quickly became an Opry regular and a favorite of Carl. (Monroe had a record deal with RCA Victor and scored a hit in 1936, as part of the Monroe Brothers, with the gospel song "What Would You Give in Exchange for Your Soul?") Elvis Presley, a spotty, slick-haired kid from Tupelo, Mississippi, currently driving a truck for Crown Electric, was another rusted-on fan of both Bill Monroe and the Opry broadcasts. Like Carl, Presley wanted music to play some kind of role in his life.

"I liked Bill Monroe, [especially] his fast stuff," said Carl, looking back. "His country was bluegrass but kicked up faster." Carl particularly admired Monroe's song "Footprints in the Snow." Carl began to wonder how Monroe's music would sound if it had the added muscle of bass and drums. He was also a fan of Robert Lunn, a left-handed guitarist and former vaudevillian, whom he'd heard perform "Talking Blues" on the Opry. It was a song Carl would tackle when he began playing live.

At the same time, when his country music purist father, Buck, was out of the house, Carl would twist the radio dial in search of new sounds. "You did not dare touch that radio when the old man was in!" said Carl. Carl particularly loved the music that he stumbled upon at KLCN, a station that played the blues. They broadcasted from Blytheville, Arkansas, about fifty miles from Carl's home. Another was WLAC, based in Nashville, which played rhythm and blues, mostly on an after-dark program called *The Midnight Special*.

Life was changing for Carl and his family. In January 1946, with manual plantation work rapidly becoming mechanized, Buck moved his family moved to Bemis, in Jackson, about seventy miles outside of Memphis. There they joined the other members of Buck's family that had already relocated. Bemis was known as a "company town," established at the turn of the century by the founders of the Bemis Brothers Bag Company. It was a place that Carl's people believed offered better work opportunities. They moved into a four-room house with a roof that didn't leak, which was quite the step up. Jackson would fast become home for Carl and would remain so for the rest of his life.

The repeal of Prohibition in 1933 created a boom time for musicians. It resulted in the opening of hundreds of clubs, especially in the South, where hopefuls like Carl got to learn their trade as musicians—and where people came to drink, fight, and shake it to live music. Honky-tonks, or simply "tonks," as Carl came to know them, were usually located on the outskirts of town, where tax rates were lower, police supervision was not so diligent, and neighbors were fewer than in the bigger towns and cities. These were ideal places for working-class people to shed the drudgery of their day jobs or escape whatever problems awaited them at home. But they could also be downright dangerous—"Rhinestone Cowboy" Glen Campbell once referred to them as "the fightin' and dancin' clubs." In some tonks, the chairs and tables were secured to the floor so that they couldn't be used as weapons in a brawl. The second half of the 1940s was probably peak period for violence in the honky-tonks, as servicemen and defense workers, liberated from the pressures of World War II, descended on these venues in search of the kind of big night out that they would tend to forget the next day. What happened in the honky-tonks normally stayed there—or sometimes in the surrounding car parks and fields, late at night.

"People went to the honky-tonks for a wide variety of reasons," author Bill C. Malone wrote with admirable restraint in his exhaustive study *Country Music, U.S.A.*, "but many working-class folk looked forward to the weekend, when they might move from club to club, drinking, dancing and socializing (this is still described as 'honky-tonking')." Most "tonks" were simple structures, with neon lighting, a tiny stage, a sawdust-covered dance floor, a jukebox in the corner, a few tables and chairs, and—crucially—a well-stocked bar.

Carl began his musical apprenticeship in the tonks when he was still a teenager, in late 1946, at first playing alongside brother Jay on guitar. (Carl, like Jay, had left school after the eighth grade.) Clayton eventually joined them, on a two-string stand-up bass that he didn't so much play as slapped. At the same time, Carl held down day jobs, working (and living) on a dairy farm in Malesus, in Madison County, but it was in the tonks that he really learned his trade. And Carl wasn't alone in getting his start in the tonks; such future greats as Loretta Lynn, Patsy Cline, and Merle Haggard would also learn their craft playing them. Honky-tonks would also inspire plenty of famous songs, everything from Ernest Tubb's "Walking the Floor Over You" to Hank Thompson's "The Wild Side of Life" and Kitty Wells's "It Wasn't God Who Made Honky Tonk Angels." Carl would write his own tribute to the tonks, called "Honky Tonk Gal." Texan native Al Dexter was not only one of the forefathers of the style of music that would simply be known as honky-tonk—he wrote and recorded the legendary "Pistol-Packin' Mama"—but he owned a honky-tonk, in eastern Texas.

The first regular gig for Carl and Jay—calling themselves the Perkins Brothers—was a Wednesday nightspot at the Cotton Boll

Tavern, on Highway 45, a cinder block building situated smack-dab in the middle of a cotton patch (hence its name), not far from Jackson. There was no microphone, not even a stage; instead, they played in a small space near the jukebox. On opening night, to calm his nerves, Carl, still seven years shy of legal age, downed a few complimentary beers and found drinking almost as natural as playing the guitar. Carl would later describe to his friend Tom Petty how he looked on with amazement as patrons at such rooms as the Cotton Boll swilled beer straight from the jug. No fancy glasses or bottles for honky-tonkers. When Hubert Miller, the Cotton Boll's owner, hired Carl and Jay, he told them that their merit as players would be judged by the amount of beer that the patrons drank while they played. As it transpired, they drank enough for the Perkins boys to be invited back the following Wednesday. Carl and Jay earned four dollars in tips on their first night.

Their mother, however, was less than thrilled when she learned where they'd been spending their nights. "Don't waste your music in there," she told them. "Sing in church."

"We tried that," Carl replied, "but they won't pay us."

"I don't want my boys in there," his mother continued. "They fight."

"They fight," Carl accepted, "but they don't bother us."

Carl's mother was also horrified when she learned that Carl and Jay were drinking while they played the honky-tonks. She'd seen up close the effects that the demon drink had on their father, and prayed they wouldn't become boozers like Buck. "It'll ruin your music," she warned them, "and it'll ruin your lives!"

CHAPTER 2

The harder they fought, the louder we played

The set list of the Perkins Brothers' shows at the Cotton Boll consisted mainly of songs Carl had heard while listening to the Opry on the radio, but considerably souped-up versions. As Carl's technique as a guitarist improved, he did not forget Brother John's advice to "make it vibrate" when he played. Among the songs in their set was the hymn "The Great Speckled Bird," first recorded in 1936 by Opry host Roy Acuff, occasionally known as "The Great Speckle Bird" because of a typo on the original label. But when Buck heard his son's rendition, he wasn't quite sure what to make of it. It was much harder and faster than the beloved original. The same went for Carl's renditions of Ernest Tubb's "I'm Walkin' the Floor Over You."

"Carl, you're not singing that song right," Buck would tell him. "You're singin' it too fast."

Carl was apologetic but determined. "I'm sorry, Dad, I like it fast."

Carl's mother would sometimes intervene; she didn't think Carl was doing anything disrespectful. "Buck, let the boy play," she'd say. Carl would admit that he thought a lot of country music "was just too slow and lonesome, [songs] about wrecks and deaths and mamas dying." He wanted to add a little rhythm to the formula, and it resulted in his juiced-up take on these popular "hillbilly" songs. "I liked the country songs," Carl once told a writer from *Vintage Guitar* magazine, "but . . . I just felt them in another gear."

During the first few gigs that Carl and Jay played, some of the regulars got up and walked out, but after a few shows the mood changed and the crowds slowly grew. As Carl recalled, "It wasn't really that long before people started coming around to hear this new music." Carl didn't know he was breaking the established rules by being both the singer *and* lead guitarist—although Jay did take his share of lead vocals—but simply had no idea that was an unusual thing. "I got mixed up," he admitted in a 1989 interview. "I didn't know any difference." And while the songs were mostly familiar—another Roy Acuff number they played regularly was "Wabash Cannonball," a huge hit for Acuff in 1936 (which over the years sold a staggering ten million copies)—Carl and Jay delivered them with extra muscle. They also covered Bill Monroe's "Blue Moon of Kentucky," reinterpreting what had originally been a waltz as a hillbilly blues shuffle. Jay was a huge admirer of Ernest Tubb and would sing some of his hits, which usually got a few dancers up on the floor. They also played favorites such as Hank Williams's "Lovesick Blues"—Carl was a big Hank fan—and "Jealous Heart," a hit in 1944 for Country Music Hall of Famer Tex Ritter.

The more Carl played the honky-tonks, the quicker he realized that in order to maintain the audience's attention, they needed to play hard and fast—and as loud as possible. Because their hiring was dictated by beer sales, keeping the audience on their feet and sweaty—and thus thirsty—was paramount. Beer, thankfully, was usually free for the musicians. "We made a little money," Carl said, looking back, before adding with a chuckle, "just enough to go into debt for better instruments." Carl bought a black Harmony Stratotone electric guitar on a payment plan from Hardeman Music in Jackson (a guitar that is now displayed at the Tennessee Music Museum in Jackson), along with a small Fender amp. It cost Carl about fifty dollars altogether. "But," as he explained, "it did what I wanted." While playing his new guitar in the tonks, Carl stuck a piece of tape over the maker's name, in the hope people would think he was playing a Fender, a much more expensive instrument. Carl soon realized there was no need. "The drunks can't read no way," he said with a laugh.

The Perkins Brothers had no name for what they were playing—the term "rockabilly" hadn't yet been coined. Carl simply referred to it as "feel-good music," music with roots in country and the blues, delivered with a strong beat and enough energy to power a small city. Carl also learned how to move while playing—again, it was an essential tactic in venues such as the Cotton Boll Tavern and the Sand Ditch Tavern, near the western boundary of Jackson, where the Perkins Brothers had begun playing on Friday and Saturday nights about a month after starting out. Carl explained that he stayed lively onstage to avoid being hit by projectiles thrown by the audience. "You were on your toes playing those places." Carl's exaggerated stage movements were also a by-product of the moonshine he slyly sipped while playing. Bar girls ran a lively side hustle in bootleg whiskey, dispensed in fruit jars, which Carl found that he preferred to beer.

The Sand Ditch's owner, Earl Mills, was a colorful character who occasionally settled disputes with a blow from the ax handle he kept behind the bar. He'd bored out several inches of the handle and filled it with hot lead. It was a hefty weapon. "I tell you," Carl once said, "when they said, 'That's it, get out,' you had just enough time to do it, or you'd lose an ear, because they'd swing!"

The Perkins brothers knew how to take care of themselves physically, and soon developed a reputation as the type of people who wouldn't walk away from trouble. Clayton rarely passed up the opportunity of a fistfight. Quite often in the tonks, as Carl revealed, at the first sign of trouble, "Clayton would slam that old [bass] fiddle down and jump out in the middle of it."

"You're gonna get hurt!" Carl would yell at him from the stage. "And we need to keep playing!" This rarely stopped him.

Jay, who stood just over six feet tall and had a strong build, typically ended fights with one punch. Carl's usual reaction to a brawl was more practical—he'd turn his amplifier up just a little louder and hit the strings of his guitar hard. "Then the crowd would usually settle down." There were times, though, when Carl accepted an invitation to fight, and just like his brothers, he usually ended things quickly.

One night at the Cotton Boll it was Clayton who asked Carl to step outside. He'd taken offense at the way Carl had jiggled and moved as he played a guitar solo—to Clayton it was a classic case of what he called "showin' out," and he wasn't impressed. As far as Clayton was concerned, Carl was showboating, and it needed to stop. Once outside, Clayton threw the first punch, and the crowd spilled out of the Cotton Boll, curious to see who was fighting. After a few blows were landed by both Carl and Clayton, Jay stepped in to break them up, primarily because they were needed to get back onstage. They were due to play their next set.

Another night, while playing at the Hilltop Inn, Carl spotted a couple arguing at a table close to the stage. The woman then pulled a .22-caliber pistol out of her handbag and shot her date square between the eyes. In the ensuing melee, a regular—they were known as "tush hogs"—told the staff not to rush calling for the ambulance. "Ain't no need to hurry—he's dead." When the owner promptly installed chicken wire in front of the stage, Carl suggested they put up a sheet of steel instead. As he pointed out, chicken wire wasn't going to stop a bullet. Clayton took to stashing a pistol in his back pocket when they played, at least until Carl intervened—and Clayton threatened to shoot him. Fortunately, Jay stepped in, and Clayton was disarmed.

During a break between sets at yet another show at the El Rancho, Carl was outside smoking a cigarette when he was mistaken for someone else and suddenly had a switchblade held to his throat. Thankfully, a voice yelled, "That's the wrong one," and his would-be attacker ran off. But for a moment, Carl thought he was as good as dead.

Many years later, TV host David Letterman asked Carl about these honky-tonks: just how rough were they? Carl smiled knowingly before he replied. "Rough? That's a mild name for it. The harder they fought, the louder we played. I learned to move pretty quick."

The tonk where Carl and his brothers played the most was probably the El Rancho (formerly known as the Roadside Inn). Like many honky-tonks, it was a simple wooden-framed building, painted white, located just the right distance out of town—it was about five miles east of Jackson, at the intersection of Old Jackson and Spring Creek Roads and US Highway 70. But unlike most tonks, the owner, Truman Jones, had instituted a no-fighting policy in an effort to make the establishment a little more upscale than rival clubs. He even went as far as to use tablecloths and, to dress the Perkins brothers in style, dispatched them to Nashville, where they were fitted out with matching Western-style outfits to wear while playing.

Most nights, admission was between $1.50 and $2 for a couple. Jones would sometimes hire as many as five bands to play on a Saturday, when they'd be open until late, usually about twelve thirty a.m. The capacity of the room was, at a squeeze, around four hundred. Revelers would leave their cars on the roadside around the venue, and on busy evenings, parked cars could stretch for miles around the El Rancho. One night, Elvis Presley, the Opry-loving kid from Tupelo, who'd recently moved with his family to Memphis, snuck in to see Carl and his brothers play.

Carl also began developing bonds with other musicians doing time in the honky-tonks. Among them was Ramsey Kearney, a player from Hardeman County, Tennessee. He was a regular at the Nick Nack Café, near downtown Jackson, a club described as "one part greasy spoon and three parts beer-drenched honky-tonk dancehall." Carl and Kearney jammed at the Nick Nack in 1949, and a photographer captured the moment. Kearney was also a popular DJ on the recently established WDXI Jackson, and Carl would sometimes play live on his program. Carl also got to know mandolinist Benny Coley and guitarist Lindsey Patterson, both from McNairy County, which was about fifty miles from Jackson. McNairy County was the site of a lot of musical jams, which Carl quickly gravitated to, some hosted by the Latta Ford Motor Company.

These three local pickers, along with Jay Perkins, would play with Carl at the opening of a hardware store in Jackson sometime in the early 1950s. In a photo taken on the day, Carl stood out front of the others, looking sharp in a dark jacket and light-colored shirt, his hair swept back, his name CARL hand-painted in block letters on the scratch plate of his acoustic guitar. The image made something very clear: of all his peers, Carl appeared to be the leader, the one destined for greatness.

Carl came to understand that he needed his own material; after all, there were only so many times you could pick "Wabash Cannon-ball" or "The Great Speckled Bird," particularly given that he was now playing several nights a week. When he was about fourteen, Carl had stumbled onto a possible original song idea while still at school. He'd been smitten by a girl from a well-to-do family whose father was known to be so protective of his daughter that he kept a shotgun in the family home, which sounded like a clear warning to potential suitors like Carl. It struck Carl as good material for his first song. In the plainspoken lyric, Carl sang about how he hoped to invite her to the movies on a Saturday night, primarily so that he could hold her hand, but also out of self-preservation. He hadn't for-gotten about her daddy's shotgun (which he mentioned in the song).

"I struck on a little girl named Martha Fay Johnston and I knew that her dad did have a shotgun behind the door," Carl explained to a fascinated Paul McCartney in 1993, pointing out that he knew his crush was destined to lead nowhere. "She was kind of wealthy and I was a poor boy." Carl would work on the song for several years before he had the chance to commit it to tape. The lyric, for one thing, would undergo some revision when he grasped that "Magg" sang far better than "Martha." But given that it was his first stab at songwriting, it wasn't that bad a beginning. His mother liked the song enough to describe it as "cute," and when Carl played it to Jay, he looked at him and asked, "Are you sure you wrote it?"

Stanton Littlejohn was a longtime resident of Eastview, Tennessee, in McNairy County, where he ran a farm and worked in a shoe fac-tory as well. His true passion, however, was sound recording. Little-john was a popular local figure and a regular at the Latta jams—he played the fiddle—and this was where Carl first made his acquain-tance. Around 1947—the exact date isn't known for sure—Littlejohn bought a secondhand recording console, which he set up in the front room of his small timber frame home near the Mississippi state line. Using the console, he was able to produce one-off acetate (lacquer) discs, quite a novelty for the time, and he began recording family and friends, from southwest Tennessee and north Mississippi, who performed everything from old-time fiddle instrumentals to gospel music straight out of church. When Carl learned about this service, he paid Littlejohn a couple of visits—and the fact that Littlejohn asked for only the few cents it cost to produce the disc made it even more attractive to Carl, who was barely surviving on the money he made playing honky-tonks and working his various day jobs.

In 1951, Carl cut several songs with Littlejohn across two sessions; these were his first actual recordings. Not quite ready to try out an original like "Movie Magg," Carl instead took a shot at a few popular hits of the day. Among them was "Good Rockin' Tonight," a hit for writer Roy Brown in 1947, and again a year later for blues belter Wynonie Harris. Both Carl and Elvis Presley would record this later on official releases, but the version Carl cut at Eastview was much rootsier. As writer Trevor Cajiao noted when these recordings were finally made available, Carl's take "retains a hillbilly edge to it, leading this listener to think it's how the song would've sounded had Hank Williams recorded it."

Carl also covered "There's Been a Change in Me," a big hit in 1951 for the country crooner Eddy Arnold, as well as "Drinkin' Wine, Spo-Dee-O-Dee," a number one R&B hit in 1947 for Henry "Stick" McGhee, the brother of bluesman Brownie McGhee. In his version, Carl name-checked the Nick Nack, the honky-tonk where he'd played with Ramsey Kearney. Carl may have been raised in an environment where African Americans rode separate buses, used different bathrooms, and even drank from their own water fountains, but musically he was color-blind and saw no issue in crossing race lines by mixing urban blues with hillbilly tearjerkers.

It's not clear how many recordings Carl completed at Eastview—although it is likely that he also played acoustic guitar on a recording of the instrumental "The Devil's Dream"—but only about twenty minutes of music ever officially saw the light of day. Yet, as

Cajiao rightly stated, these songs offered "a whole new perspective to the early career of the bopcat known as Carl Perkins." Shawn Pitts, writing in *Southern Cultures*, recognized Carl's Eastview recordings, especially "Drinkin' Wine" and "Good Rockin' Tonight," for what they were: snapshots of how he must have sounded in the tonks, "where the band hammered out its signature songs between brawls."

As Pitts also pointed out, "These tracks unquestionably demonstrate that Perkins had a penchant for merging blues and country at an early age." It's hard to know, however, what Carl thought of his first recordings, because he never mentioned them during interviews; nor, curiously, did they rate a single sentence in his 1996 memoir, *Go Cat Go!*

By the time Carl made his first recordings at Eastview, he was doing more than playing the local honky-tonks. In these postwar years, radio remained the key form of entertainment, especially for struggling families like Carl's who couldn't afford a television set. And as Carl and his brothers' reputation grew, radio was already providing a useful outlet for their budding musical career.

Local guitarist Edd Cisco was an old friend of Carl who'd attended school with the Perkins brothers and played with Carl at the Nick Nack. With his help, in 1949 Carl had been welcomed as an occasional member of the Tennessee Ramblers, a loose-knit outfit that had a Saturday-morning radio spot on WTJS, which broadcast out of Jackson. (Edd also helped Carl find a job at the Colonial Bakery in Jackson.) Carl then secured another radio gig, playing solo this time, on a Saturday-night program called *Hayloft Frolic*, where he'd often perform Robert Lunn's "Talking Blues." The host of that show, known to listeners as Uncle Tom Williams, also invited Carl to appear on his WTJS program *The Early Morning Farm and Home Hour*. Soon after, Carl, now with Jay and Clayton, agreed to their own fifteen-minute morning segment, sponsored by Mother's Best Flour. It was there that he occasionally tried out originals on the radio audience. No one seemed to object; Carl would boast that whenever he performed, as many as eight fan letters were sent to the station.

Carl also took advantage of the facilities at WTJS to record a few of his original songs. Not having a thorough understanding of the mechanics of the music business, he would package up tapes of his recordings and post them to "Columbia Records New York City," thinking that was all that was required. He couldn't understand why he didn't receive a response, apart from a few returned tapes. "I could tell half the time they hadn't even been opened," said Carl. But he wasn't put off; in fact, he'd just found his biggest supporter.

Valda Crider was a native of Bemis. Born on April 29, 1931, the youngest of seven, she was almost a year older to the day than Carl. Unusual for the time, Valda's father, Bedford, and her mother, Lillie, were virtually seniors when she was born—they were forty-five and forty, respectively. Bedford had been a farmer for most of his life until he found more reliable—and somewhat less taxing—work at the Bemis Brothers Bag Company.

Carl had first met Valda in 1949. They were introduced by Carl's cousin, Martha Bain, who knew Valda from Bemis Elementary School—they were in the same class—and the pair went for a drive. At the time, Carl owned a beat-up 1934 Ford, and when he wasn't preoccupied with trying to keep the car on the road, he couldn't help but notice something about the striking, red-haired Valda. "Gosh," Carl said when he turned to her, "you smell good." Carl was pleased to learn that Valda and her family lived in the New Town section of Bemis, which was part of the route in his current job delivering milk.

"When I first saw her," Carl would say of that meeting, "there was something special about her. She wasn't the prettiest girl in the world, but she was so sweet." Carl, who sometimes didn't let the truth intrude on a good story, would one day insist that when he first met Valda, he sang to her, which, while entirely possible, might have been challenging while at the wheel of his rust bucket of a car. In a 1968 interview, Carl revealed that he would have liked to marry

Valda right away but couldn't "because I was supporting Mommy and Daddy." Family always came first for Carl.

Unlike Carl, Valda did well academically, with a particular strength in math, and graduated from J. B. Young High School. Rather than go on to college, she took a succession of full-time jobs, eventually landing a position with a Jackson firm that processed utility bills, where she got to use her skill with numbers. Valda was musical, too; she played piano and sang and sometimes took part in a duo with Martha at a local café called Coffee Time.

Despite an obvious attraction to Carl, Valda initially went out with his brother Jay, having been set up by Martha. But Valda made it clear that she was more interested in Carl, and they began dating and eventually Carl proposed to her. (Jay soon married a local girl named Pauline Helton.) But as his relationship with Valda developed, Carl was also seeing an older woman on the side, a divorcée called Betty Mayo. Somehow, by 1952, Carl was engaged to two different women. He was almost heading down the aisle with Mayo when he realized his huge mistake—he duly left her, proposed (again) to Valda, and they were wed at Corinth, Mississippi, on January 24, 1953. They were married on Saturday, and the following Monday Carl was laid off from his job at the bakery. For the next year, the newlyweds were forced to live in a single room with Carl's people in Hicksville, the poor side of Jackson.

There were many reasons why Carl chose Valda—her looks, her intelligence, but perhaps just as crucial was the fact that she supported his career. "When my wife married me," Carl admitted, "she knew I was good for nothing but music. . . . She was a good listener and she'd brag on my singing."

CHAPTER 3

I'm Carl Perkins and I want to make a record for you

Although their paths hadn't yet crossed by 1953, the careers of Carl and Elvis Presley were both developing in their own gradual way. Carl continued playing the tonks, now full-time, six nights a week, a move supported by Valda. Speaking in Carl's 1996 memoir, Valda believed that he deserved his shot at a career in music. "I felt he had been denied so much," she said. Elvis, meanwhile, was taking his first steps toward making music of his own. And Carl and Elvis's most important booster was also establishing himself.

In January 1950, Memphis native Sam Phillips—a man that *Rolling Stone* magazine would one day describe as "the South's first genuine hipster"—had converted an empty shop front at 706 Union Avenue into a studio and founded the Memphis Recording Service. His business card read, "We record anything—anywhere—anytime." A former radio engineer and DJ, Phillips had been fascinated by sound since he was a young man, when he learned sign language to communicate with his deaf aunt, a woman named Emma. Phillips, like Carl, had once played in the school band, and in another interesting parallel, had grown close to a black sharecropper, a man named Silas Payne, just as Carl had with John Westbrook. As he explained in the biography *Sam Phillips: The Man Who Invented Rock 'n' Roll*, "He taught me how that even when you're feeling bad, you can be feeling good." Music was crucial to that.

Phillips had started out by recording local rhythm and blues acts such as Rufus Thomas and Junior Parker. In March 1951, Phillips recorded Jackie Brenston's "Rocket 88," which became a huge jukebox hit and topped the R&B charts. It would be widely regarded as the first rock and roll release. Phillips certainly thought so. "I have no doubt in my mind that this was the first true rock and roll record," he said. "[And] not because I cut it."

In a move that would have an impact on Carl's future recordings, Phillips, while recording "Rocket 88," had improvised by stuffing some newspaper into the torn cone of a bass amplifier—and he liked what he heard. "The more unconventional it sounded," Phillips said to *Rolling Stone* in 1986, "the more interested I would become in it." In February 1952, Phillips launched the Sun Records label and promptly put in thousands of road miles trying to establish his company. "I'd sleep in my car and carry the records in my trunk," he once said. "No one drove more in a three-year period than I did."

Phillips wasn't at the studio when a nervous eighteen-year-old Presley turned up on the doorstep at 706 Union Avenue in 1953. Instead, Presley was greeted by Marion Keisker, who, when not helping Phillips run the studio, hosted a radio program on WREC, which was where she'd first met Sam.

Keisker asked Presley to describe the type of music he performed, and he replied, "I don't sound like nobody." That day, for the princely sum of $3.98, Presley recorded the Ink Spots' "My Happiness" and "That's When Your Heartaches Begin," and left Sun with an acetate tucked under his arm. Keisker was sufficiently intrigued by the kid to tape his singing and play it to Phillips. These were baby steps, but Presley was on his way.

The same couldn't be said for another of Carl's soon-to-be friends and labelmates. John R. Cash, as he was still known, was currently serving Uncle Sam and had been stationed at Landsberg am Lech in West Germany since 1951, where he worked as an Air Force radio officer, intercepting messages sent by the Soviet Union's forces. ("If you ever need to know what one Russian is signaling to another in Morse Code," Cash wrote in his autobiography, "I'm your man.") When not eavesdropping on the Soviets; writing to Vivian, his American sweetheart; or listening to the Grand Ole Opry on an Air Force radio, John was rehearsing in a trio with two fellow servicemen, Reid Cummins and B. J. Carnahan. They called themselves the Landsberg Barbarians and played at local bars.

While in Germany, where he was stationed until 1954, Cash also wrote songs, which he recorded on a cheap tape deck. And it was while in Germany that Cash befriended C. V. White, an African American whose flashy dress sense—his suede shoes were colored blue—would come to play a bit part, at least according to some reports, in Carl Perkins's most famous song. When John asked him what the C. V. stood for, he replied, "Champagne velvet."

It was July 1954, and Carl and a very pregnant Valda, along with their baby son, Carl Stanley, a sickly child born two months premature in September 1953, were now living at Parkview Courts in Jackson in apartment 23D. They were a working-class family of almost four squeezed into a government project house, which they rented for $32 a month. It was a very basic dwelling, as Carl described it: "Two rooms up, two down, concrete floors and not even a window fan." On hot nights they'd sprinkle water on their sheets to cool themselves down. The Perkinses were getting by—just—on the money Carl earned playing the honky-tonks.

One day, Carl and Valda had their radio tuned to DJ Bob Neal. He broadcast from the Memphis station WMPS and promoted concerts in and around the city. "I've got a brand-new record," Neal announced. "The boy's name is Elvis Presley." Neal then played Elvis's recording of Bill Monroe's "Blue Moon of Kentucky."

Seconds later, Valda looked at her husband and declared, "Carl, that sounds just like you."

Carl could barely believe what he was hearing—he'd been playing "Blue Moon" live for seven years, pretty much in the style that Presley recorded. But rather than feel anger toward Elvis, hearing "Blue Moon" was a revelation for Carl: "I knew it was pretty close to what I'd be struggling with all these years," he'd admit. Right then Carl understood that he needed to get to Memphis, to this place called Sun Studio, where he learned that Elvis had cut "Blue Moon." Valda was completely in support; she knew Carl had to give it a shot.

What Carl didn't know at the time was that Bob Neal had seen him play at the El Rancho and had attended the gig with Elvis. Neal was a big fan, as was Presley. "We were both struck by the sound Perkins was getting," Neal said. "It was very similar to Elvis's own."

It had been a steady rise for Presley since he walked out of Sun with an acetate of Ink Spots covers. He'd been back in the studio in January 1954 and then again in early June. A few weeks after the latter session, Sam Phillips introduced Elvis to guitarist Scotty Moore, who duly introduced the singer to bass player Bill Black ("the best slap bass player in the city," Phillips declared). At his next Sun session, in July, Elvis and his two new bandmates began playing around with an arrangement of Arthur Crudup's blues song "That's All Right (Mama)," which they played faster than the original. "What are you doing?" asked an intrigued Phillips from the control room, as he captured the recording on tape.

Elvis, Moore, and Black also recorded "Blue Moon of Kentucky," which became the B-side of "That's All Right," the first single Presley would cut for Sun. By a pure stroke of luck, the DJ Neal had flipped the record over and played "Blue Moon" on the day that Valda and Carl tuned in and recognized a musical kindred spirit.

One Thursday afternoon in October 1954, Carl decided to take a trip that would change the direction of his life. He, Jay, and Clayton rose early and packed up Carl's 1941 Plymouth, strapping Clayton's bass to the roof, inside a cotton sack. Their destination was Memphis. They were joined by their drummer, W. S. "Fluke" Holland, so called because of his tendency to overuse the invented word *flukus* (as in "What the flukus is that?" or "Where is that flukus?"). Born in 1935 in Saltillo, Tennessee, Holland was a friend of Clayton; he'd joined the band the year before, having stepped up onstage one night at the El Rancho—without drums—and tapping out a solid rhythm on the side of Clayton's bass. ("Man, hit it harder!" Carl called out to him. "I like it.") Standing over six feet tall; his fair, wavy hair carefully styled; and with a tendency to wear sunglasses at night, Holland cut quite a stylish and imposing figure onstage and off. A nonsmoker and a teetotaler, he also owned his own Cadillac, which was both impressive to the Perkins brothers and very handy for a working band. Soon enough, the side of Holland's Caddy was emblazoned with the words, THE PERKINS BROTHERS BAND. For the trip to Memphis, Fluke borrowed a set of drums.

Carl's plans were vague at best. He figured they would roll up to the studio—still known as Memphis Recording Service—play some songs for this man Sam Phillips, and walk out of there with a record deal. Easy. Not surprisingly, that wasn't quite how it worked out. For one thing, Phillips wasn't there when Carl, his brothers, and Fluke arrived. Instead, Carl was greeted by Marion Keisker, who took one look at him, his crew, and their instruments and understood immediately what their purpose was. She had some bad news. If they were hoping for an audition, she informed Carl, they'd wasted their time.

She explained that Sun Records was investing all its efforts (and what little money it had) in Elvis Presley's budding career. As if to prove her point, a cardboard replica of Presley stood in the foyer of the studio. They had high hopes for the kid from Tupelo, whose debut single, "That's All Right," was receiving strong support in and Memphis.

Carl, however, had no intention of giving up and driving back to Jackson without at least meeting Sam Phillips. He asked Keisker if they could sit outside the studio until Phillips arrived. Keisker shrugged and got back to work.

Within minutes, Phillips arrived, driving a two-tone Cadillac Coupe de Ville, the latest model. It was quite the contrast to Carl's battered Plymouth, which he'd unintentionally parked in Sam's spot. When Phillips stepped out of his car, Carl noticed that his dark blue trousers and light blue shirt matched the color of his Cadillac. Carl was seriously impressed and thought to himself, *Wow, that has to be the cat that owns this place!*

As Phillips entered the studio, Carl began talking at hyperspeed. He knew this was his one chance to impress the man who might just give him a shot at a recording career.

"Mr. Phillips," he said, "I'm Carl Perkins and those are my brothers out in the car, and I want to make a record for you."

"Sorry," Phillips said over his shoulder, walking as he spoke. "I'm too busy, man."

Carl refused to give up, reminding himself, for one thing, that he couldn't let Valda down. He'd come a long way and he just had to find a way to get inside that studio. At that precise moment, Carl shot Phillips such a sorrowful look that the producer couldn't ignore him, and they continued talking. Phillips later told Carl, "You was the most pitiful-looking boy I had ever seen. You looked like you'd have cried"—if he'd been turned away—"or your whole world would have ended." Phillips just didn't have the heart to say no.

Phillips reluctantly gave Carl and his band a few minutes to impress him. But their first move was a mistake. Jay loved the music of Ernest Tubb and could imitate his vocal style pretty well. So rather than try out one of Carl's originals—and Phillips was very much in the market for good original songs—they started off by playing a couple of Jay's Tubb-inspired numbers. Phillips, who was in the control booth, spoke to Jay over the microphone. "Son," he said, "you need to forget about Ernest Tubb, there's already one of him on the radio." Phillips told Carl and his crew that while he admired their playing, he had no use for them.

With that, Fluke, Clayton, and a seriously vexed Jay accepted their fate and started gathering up their gear. Carl would later say that Jay muttered to him, "That little son of a bitch don't like us," a comment Phillips overheard. (He laughed.) As far as they were concerned, they'd given it a shot and failed, so it was back to the tonks. Carl, however, was having none of it. He told them that he was going to try one of his own songs.

Phillips overheard this and walked back into the studio, as Carl began playing "Movie Magg" and the band joined in. Phillips stood and listened, and when it became clear he was not making any effort to stop them, Carl began jiggling around on the spot, just as he did when he played the honky-tonks. Phillips was intrigued: There was something about Carl's voice and the way he played guitar that caught his attention. Carl reminded Phillips, just a little, of Hank Williams.

"That's a good song," Phillips told Carl when they finished playing. "But can you stand still and sing?"

"Yes, sir," Carl replied, clearly thrilled. "I'll do whatever you tell me to do."

Phillips explained that if they were to make music together, Carl needed to remain in one place while they were recording, otherwise the microphone might not pick up his voice. Phillips also explained that while having one original was a solid start, Carl needed at least two good songs to make a record. Carl played Phillips another original, "Honky Tonk Gal," but Phillips wanted something in a style similar to "Movie Magg." Phillips also pointed out to Carl that though he may be a rocker at heart—something Carl had made clear to him—he already had Elvis on the label, "and I can't have two of you cats sounding a lot alike in singing this up-tempo music."

However, Phillips told Carl, if he could write another "Movie Magg," something sentimental and story-driven, he was welcome to return and cut a record. Carl was so excited by the possibility of working with Phillips that he began scribbling out some ideas in the passenger seat of his Plymouth, leaning against the dash, as he and the band drove back to Jackson. The whole experience had been a thrill for Carl. Years later he would admit to Phillips that the Sun Studio, although tiny by comparison with most studios, "was the biggest room I ever saw in my life."

When Carl got back to Parkview Courts, Valda answered the door and asked him how things went in Memphis. Carl didn't say anything; instead, he started sobbing with joy.

"Didn't I tell you?" said Valda as she comforted her husband.

"You were sure right," said Carl, wiping his eyes. "You were sure right."

Carl wrote a song that he titled "I'll Be Following You," which was not too far removed from "Movie Magg" in style. It was another song that came to him while he was playing the El Rancho. Occasionally a face in the crowd or an incident on the dance floor would spark an idea, and between sets he'd scribble down some notes. However, the key inspiration for the song was his relationship with Valda. "I wrote it," he told a reporter in 1972, "because I felt that way about the woman I married. If ever she was in trouble or ever she felt lonely, she'd just turn around . . . I'd be there."

When Carl returned to Sun a little later in October 1954, Phillips suggested that he change the song's title to the far punchier "Turn Around." Carl had no objection. "If you like it," Carl told him, "I don't care what you call it."

Although Phillips produced the "Turn Around" session, he also brought in three additional musicians to help flesh out Carl's sound: a local steel guitarist named Stan Kesler, plus Bill Cantrell on fiddle and guitarist Quinton Claunch. Phillips knew the latter pair very well, from the time that Sam worked as a presenter at WLAY in Muscle Shoals, Alabama, and Claunch and Cantrell were in a band called the Blue Seal Pals, which would sometimes play at the station. Both had relocated to Memphis a few years earlier. Phillips invited them to help not only with this second Carl Perkins session but with other sessions he was producing at Sun with such artists as Maggie Sue Wimberly and the Miller Sisters. He figured, rightly enough, that having these experienced players in the studio would help people like Carl, who were relatively new to recording.

The session gave Carl the chance to record with his recently acquired Gibson Les Paul guitar, which had been all but gifted to him by John Towater, the proprietor of Hardeman Music in Jackson and a fan of Carl's music. Carl would frequently stand outside the store, his face all but pressed to the window, admiring the guitar. Towater, knowing how much Carl craved the guitar, allowed him to pay it off for the bargain price of $5 a week. Carl was convinced it would help him play like Les Paul, whose sound he loved. He'd have a conversation about Les Paul with Scotty Moore, Elvis's guitarist. "The only thing I know, Scotty," Carl told him, "is you gotta have . . . fifteen fingers on that left hand [to play that way]."

While everyone involved was pleased with the end results of "Turn Around," which required only a couple of takes, Phillips put Carl's debut release on hold, and it would be another nine months before Carl returned to the studio. Phillips's main focus remained on Elvis Presley, whose single "That's All Right" had been a local hit, with a little help from the Perkins clan, who'd call radio stations requesting the song. "All my kin did," Carl said. Elvis had also started to play shows in and around Memphis that were well received. But there was also a financial reason for putting Carl's record on ice— Phillips was struggling to keep Sun solvent, owing money to his artists, pressing plants, various benefactors, and others. "I have been making every effort possible to keep it out of bankruptcy," Phillips wrote in a letter to his brother Jud.

"I first [saw] Elvis . . . in a little town called Bethel Springs, Tennessee," Carl told a *Rolling Stone* reporter. (Funnily enough, drummer Holland thought that it was Elvis who first saw Carl play at Bethel Springs, at a spot called the YN Club, which just went to show what a peculiar thing memory could be.) As impressed as Carl had been by "That's All Right," it was the way Elvis moved onstage and, especially, the way he looked, that floored him when he saw him play in early 1955, in a half-empty school gymnasium.

Whereas Elvis's band, Bill Black and Scotty Moore, dressed down, in understated sports coats and trousers, Elvis positively glowed: He wore a dazzling pink shirt, a white sports coat, and jet-black tailored trousers that matched the color of his dyed hair. And the way Elvis looked wasn't the only thing that captured Carl's attention—as soon as he hit the stage, young girls, barely in their teens, rushed to the front, screaming their lungs raw. That certainly didn't happen to Carl when he played the El Rancho. Voices were raised in anger, sure; but no one had ever screamed for him as he played. That was new.

After Presley's thirty-minute bracket, Carl caught up with the singer as he and the two musicians packed their gear for the return trip to Memphis.

Carl couldn't help but notice how well turned out Elvis was; his fingernails were neatly filed, his hair swept back—he even wore what looked like a little makeup around his eyes. (Once they got to know each other, Elvis persuaded Carl to give it a try, but he gave up after poking himself in the eye. He'd laugh about the incident. "I had to face the world as I was.") Presley was undeniably handsome; it was hard not to look at him. But Jay, who was with Carl, thought otherwise. He turned to his brother and whispered, "He's a sissy."

"Jay, you're wrong," Carl told him. "This boy has got it."

Jay wasn't sold. "But he's not as good as you. He don't play lead guitar."

"But he don't look like I do, either," said Carl, who was the first to admit that he wasn't anywhere near as good-looking as Presley. Carl had, by his own account, "come out ugly" at birth and his hair had recently started to thin. (The writer Tom Graves would describe Carl as "gaunt, jug-eared, and as country as corn bread and collard greens.") And Carl was a married man, a father of two, hardly the ideal CV for some kind of rock and roll matinee idol. Elvis was resolutely single.

"Sure enjoyed the show, man," Carl told Elvis, politely overlooking the fact that at the end of his set, Presley had gotten tangled up in Moore's guitar cable and fell on his backside. "Well, thank you," Elvis replied. And then he and the others drove off into the night.

From the very beginning, Carl never saw Presley as a rival, despite Sam Phillips's divided loyalties. As he explained to TV host Tom Snyder in 1996, "I knew when I first saw him that there never would be, because of the way he looked, and his musical abilities were amazing. He was a wonderful guy. There was never any rivalry or animosity between Elvis and I."

"Presley meant more to kids than just a guy singin' a song," Carl said in 1978. "He was a sex image, a good-lookin' cat who didn't really have to sing at all when he walked out on the stage."

Carl's debut single, "Turn Around," was released in February 1955, but not on the Sun label. Instead, Phillips released it on Flip, a brand-new "audition" label that was distributed purely to local radio and markets in and around Memphis. This enabled Phillips to reduce his costs; he was testing the record's commercial potential before—potentially—splashing out on a larger promotion. Carl's debut release was the second on Flip (which Phillips was forced to wind up soon after, when a West Coast label with the same name threatened to sue).

Once again it was through the good graces—and good taste—of

the WMPS DJ Bob Neal that Carl came to hear his own music on the radio. As Carl would recall with a laugh, dramatic things happened at the Perkins household upon hearing Neal introduce "Turn Around." "Valda, she dropped the baby"—their daughter, Debra Joye, who was born in November 1954—"and I like to fainted."

It wasn't a hit, and despite strong support from Neal and WHBQ's fast-talking, ad-libbing DJ Dewey Phillips (no relation), it didn't get much airplay beyond Memphis, but the song was a keeper. It would still be part of Carl's live set some forty years down the line.

Carl didn't actually receive a copy of the record until after he'd heard it on the radio, and even then, the 78-rpm disc Phillips sent him had cracked in transit, rendering it unplayable. Carl had to buy a copy from Hardeman Music, and because he didn't own a record player, was forced to play it on a friend's turntable. But that didn't detract from the otherworldly experience of hearing his voice on the platter or the poignancy of the moment when he returned home and showed the vinyl to Valda. "I'm a crier," he said, "and Valda cried with me."

CHAPTER 4

I thought, "You fool, that's a stupid shoe, and that's a pretty girl, man"

Sam Phillips somehow managed to keep Sun afloat, so much so that, not long after releasing Carl's first single, he began working with another new artist. John Cash had been hanging around the Sun Studio since early 1955, soon after his return from Germany. He'd studied radio announcing in Memphis until he worked up the courage to audition for Phillips. Like Carl, Cash was ill prepared, arriving at Sun with his acoustic guitar and fifteen cents in his pocket, which he gave to a panhandler outside the studio. And Cash, like the Perkins Brothers, made a big mistake—he played gospel songs at his audition, which Mr. Phillips (always "Mr. Phillips" to Carl, Cash, and Presley) pointed out were not part of the Sun sound. Allegedly—although Cash later denied this—Phillips told him to "go home and sin, then come back with a song I can sell." Cash's debut single for Sun, an original titled "Hey, Porter," was released in May 1955, three months after Carl's "Turn Around." John was now referring to himself as Johnny, on Phillips's suggestion.

When Phillips introduced Carl to Johnny, he was interested in one thing in particular. "Is that your real name?" he asked him. "*Johnny Cash?*" It struck Carl as totally unique. Carl would grow very close to Cash; he became one of his closest friends.

"When I got to know John in '55 I really liked the dude," said Carl. "He seemed a lot like a brother to me. He was a quiet, manly, nice fellow." And he admired Carl's music enormously—according to Carl, one of the first things Cash said to him was, "Man, I love your singing." When Cash made his debut on the Louisiana Hayride, rather than play his popular song "Cry, Cry, Cry," the first number he played was Carl's "Movie Magg." "It was John's favorite song," Carl told a Dutch writer in 1972, even though the record had only sold a few thousand copies.

Carl and Cash played their first concert together at a theater in Parkin, Arkansas, to a crowd of about two hundred. Before the show, having discovered that there was no toilet in the venue, they relieved themselves on the grass behind the theater, like typical country boys. When Cash and his band—christened the Tennessee Two by Sam Phillips—took the stage, Carl stood in the wings, giving them the thumbs-up as they played.

Elvis, whose "That's All Right" had sold around twenty thousand copies, joined his Sun peers for shows at Amory, Mississippi, and Helena, Arkansas, during the summer of 1955. Acting on a suggestion from Sam Phillips to upgrade his stage wardrobe for the trip, Carl had gone clothes shopping with Presley at a popular store on Beale Street in Memphis called Lansky's, whose customers were typically African American. Presley shopped there so often that the sales staff knew him by name. This impressed Carl, who bought a shiny blue shirt and a pair of smart black pants, on Elvis's recommendation. "There'd be a big table full of slacks," Carl said of shopping with Presley, "and he'd just scratch through them." Carl had Valda sew some pink ribbon down each pant leg, which, in turn, impressed Elvis when he first saw them during the tour. "That ain't nothin' but a piece of ribbon, man," Carl told him, but it didn't stop Elvis from customizing his own pants, too.

Carl was better known in Amory, having played there before with his brothers. During his set, which went over well, he performed the Platters song "Only You," which had been requested by a member of the crowd. When Carl came offstage, he spotted Elvis sitting nearby, a woebegone look on his face. Only hours before, as they set up for the gig, a playful Elvis had been shooting at Carl with a water pistol. "Uh-oh, man—this thing's electric," Carl told him, pointing at his guitar. "I might get killed!" (Presley fired at a nearby wall instead.) But now Presley's mood had changed. It turned out that he, too, intended to perform "Only You" but had been unintentionally upstaged by Carl. When Presley pointed this out to Carl, he told him to go ahead and do it anyway, adding, "Hell, the Platters are singing it somewhere tonight."

But things grew worse for Elvis not long after he began his own set, when the crowd began chanting, "We want Carl!" As Carl later remembered it, this inspired Elvis to dig deeper and try to win over the crowd. "Sweat popped out of him and was drippin' to the floor," Carl recalled, "and he had that hair flyin' and his legs movin'." In 1997, Carl stated that the crowd's reaction on what would be their last gig together "really hurt me. I stood beside the stage and said, 'Please don't do that. This boy's never heard that in his life.' It didn't make me feel that good." Carl insisted that there was a camaraderie between the artists involved with Sun. "Everybody was for everybody, you know."

Yet Johnny Cash, who opened the show, had a different version of events that night at Amory. He said that when the crowd began calling for Carl, Elvis "did one more song before giving up. He left the stage and Carl came back on to thunderous applause."

One thing, however, was very clear, as Cash documented in his autobiography. He had a telling conversation with Carl after the show.

"You did really good tonight, Carl," Cash told him. "I never thought I'd see anyone outshine him."

"Yeah," Carl replied, "but there's one thing missing. He's got a hit record and I don't."

Carl had continued working with Sam Phillips at Sun, searching for the hit that would make him more than a local favorite. In July 1955, again with Claunch, Kesler, and Cantrell helping out in the studio, Carl recorded a few more originals, including "Gone, Gone, Gone" and "Let the Jukebox Keep On Playing." The latter was another song inspired by an event Carl witnessed at the El Rancho, when a "tush hog" became angry at Carl when he unplugged the jukebox before beginning a set. "Jukebox" became Carl's next single for Sun, released on August 1, the same day as the release of Elvis's last single for Sun, "I Forgot to Remember to Forget" (backed with "Mystery Train"). Presley's single was a hit, reaching number 1 on the *Billboard* Hot Country Songs chart, whereas Carl's latest, while popular locally, made no impression beyond state lines.

"Jukebox," however, could have been given a second life. Carl was a big fan of Webb Pierce, a country crooner from Louisiana; he and his brothers covered Pierce's "There Stands the Glass." Pierce's people approached Sam Phillips about his possibly recording "Jukebox," but with one caveat: He was to receive a slice of the publishing. Carl was so keen to hear Pierce sing his song that he offered to give him a cut of his writing credit, but Phillips refused to budge. The deal was never done.

As for "Gone, Gone, Gone," it captured a different aspect of Carl—it was more urgent and dynamic than the Hank Williams–inspired country of "Jukebox." To Carl, the music he was playing was simply "country [music] with a black man's rhythm." Soon enough, though, millions of people would be calling this music "rockabilly."

In November 1955, Sam Phillips sold Elvis's contract to RCA Victor for $35,000, which at the time was considered an astronomical sum. Phillips had no qualms, as he later told the press. "We had two up and coming stars in Carl Perkins and Johnny Cash. I haven't regretted selling Presley's contract because I figure that you can't be sure of an artist's life for more than six months." "Selling" Elvis achieved two things for Sun. It gave Phillips the financial lifeline he always seemed to need—smartly, he bought Holiday Inn stock, which would make him richer than Sun ever did—and it opened the door for Carl to be truer to himself musically. Phillips made that very clear to Carl, telling him—depending on which version of the story Carl was in the mood for telling—"Now you can rock," or perhaps, "You're my rockabilly cat now." Either way, it meant that Carl could ease up on the hillbilly twang, cut loose on his guitar, and rock a little. All he needed was the perfect song.

And the inspiration for that song—one that would change the course of Carl's life, not just his career—came to him during yet another gig, in late October 1955. Carl, in at least one telling of the story, said he was performing for a sorority at Jackson's Union University, though that changed when he spoke with Tom Snyder in 1996. "I was playing one of the tonks near my hometown," he explained to Snyder, "and I'd been watching this boy and girl jitterbugging. They were really good." When Carl took a break, the couple stood in front of the stage—Carl then saw the man take a step back and say quite clearly: "Uh-oh, don't step on my suedes." He was referring to his suede shoes, which were very popular at the time. "Oh, I'm sorry," the girl told her date. Carl couldn't get his head around what he was witnessing: "I thought, *You fool, that's a stupid shoe, and that's a pretty girl, man.* I could not get that out of my mind."

Carl got home to Parkview Courts early in the morning after the gig and lay in bed, unable to sleep, the image of the honky-tonker and his precious shoes swimming in his head. "My soul was torn up," said Carl. He really felt bad for the pretty girl who was taking second place to a pair of snappy suedes. At that moment, Carl thought about the old children's nursery rhyme, "One for the money, two for the show," and knew that he'd found the spark for a song.

So as not to wake Valda and the children, Carl snuck downstairs, picked up his guitar, and started to strum a simple melody. Unable to find any writing paper, he scribbled down some words on the back of a bag used for storing potatoes, misspelling *suede* as *swade*—or *swaed* in another telling of the story. (Carl was savvy enough to hold on to those original lyrics, which would one day hang proudly in his den.) In the morning, he sat with Valda and played her the song, which he referred to as "Don't Step on My Blue Suede Shoes."

"I really like that," she told him. And then she corrected his spelling.

There was, however, a twist to this tale. According to Johnny Cash's biographer, Robert Hilburn, Cash had lit the spark for Perkins in the fall of 1955, when he told him about C. V. White, the sharp-dressed man he'd met while serving Uncle Sam in Germany. Hilburn stated that it was White who had warned Cash, "Don't step on my blue suede shoes." In his 1997 autobiography, Cash backed this up, writing that he'd mentioned White to Carl when they played at the theater in Parkin, Arkansas (and watered its lawn when they couldn't find a bathroom). "Later that night," Cash wrote, "I told Carl about CV White and the blue suede shoes."

Regardless of the hard facts about the origins of "Blue Suede Shoes," things quickly fell into place for Carl. The morning after committing his ideas to a potato bag, Carl borrowed a neighbor's phone to call Phillips at Sun Studio.

"Mr. Phillips," Carl told him, "I wrote me a good song last night."

"What is it?" asked the producer.

Carl explained that the working title of the song was "Don't Step on My Blue Suede Shoes."

Phillips thought about this and then asked if it was anything like the late-nineteenth-century minstrel song, "Oh, Dem Golden Slippers!"

"No," Carl explained, "this cat don't want nobody *steppin'* on his blue suede shoes."

Carl sang the song to Phillips over the phone and made it very clear this was absolutely nothing like "Oh, Dem Golden Slippers!"

"Hmm. Sounds interesting," said Phillips, who recommended shortening the title.

Carl and his band rehearsed the song tirelessly for the next few days and played it something like eight times during a weekend concert. They wanted to have it absolutely right before returning to Sun.

The session to record "Blue Suede Shoes" took place during December 1955, and it couldn't have come at a more crucial time for Carl. He was as good as broke—in fact, Carl had been so desperate to buy Christmas presents for his children that he'd returned to work the cotton fields for a day. "My hands bled," he told the writer David McGee. He'd also had a cautionary word with God. If he couldn't get better gifts for his children next Christmas, Carl said in a quiet prayer, "You're gonna have a thief on your hands to deal with. I need your help."

This time around it was strictly Carl's band working at Sun—Clayton, Jay, and Fluke Holland—with Phillips in the control booth.

During the first of three takes, Carl sang "go, man, go" per the "baa baa black sheep" nursery rhyme, but during the next take he sang "*go, cat, go.*" It was unintentional, purely an accident, as was the line about drinking liquor from an old fruit jar. During a break, Carl spoke with Phillips. He confessed that he'd made a big mistake. "I called that man a cat."

"And he's gonna stay a cat!" replied Phillips, who had a great ear for a catchy hook. Phillips was convinced that soon enough the words "go cat go" would be spoken fluently by every rock-and-roll-loving teenager in America. When Carl pointed out that he'd also made a mistake with his guitar, Phillips told him not to worry: "No one's ever going to hear the mistake but you." Carl insisted on a third take, and after hearing the playback, it was apparent to everyone that they'd just created his first great song. As far as Carl was concerned, Phillips was "a genius at work" and here was the proof.

"When we recorded 'Blue Suede Shoes,'" drummer Holland told a writer from *Rock & Blues News*, "we were hot in the clubs. So I had a lot of confidence in the song. We just went in and set up and cut it . . . it was something special."

The second track they recorded at the session was "Honey, Don't." It was a song that Carl had first played with the band during a gig at a small Jackson club called Tommy's Drive In, a venue that, according to drummer Holland, "was no bigger than a living room." (Or perhaps, according to another interview—in typical Carl fashion—it might have been the Pine Ridge Club.) Carl reshaped the song on the fly while inside Sun, and his improvised and unusual arrangement—and the flip-flopping lyric—confused Jay. "Have you been drinking?" he asked his brother.

Jay wasn't the only one to find "Honey, Don't" a little peculiar. Soon after the session, Carl was talking about the song with Elvis's guitarist, Scotty Moore, who questioned Carl's chord progression on the track. Songs just don't work that way, Moore explained. "Well," Carl replied, "it don't sound that bad!"

As an unschooled musician, Carl did nothing by design. "I didn't know what the hell I was doing," he'd admit. "I was just trying to hook something together to sound a little different." And Carl was proud of his efforts with "Honey, Don't." "That song was a little ahead of his time," he'd note when asked about it in 1996.

Phillips, too, was excited by what they'd just created. "Blue Suede Shoes," in particular, was fresh, original, and catchy—and it packed enough energy to light a small city. It also seemed to have the potential to win over a very broad audience, across different formats and charts. "I think it was the record that did so much for everything that Sam been trying to do," said Sally Wilbourn, a new employee at Sun, "which was to get black radio stations to play the white man's music, and the white radio stations to play the black man's records. 'Blue Suede Shoes' was one of those records that bridged the gap."

Typically, Phillips would send records to Chicago to be mastered, but not "Blue Suede Shoes." Instead, he did it himself, later that day, in the studio. He also requested that the pressing of the record be a rush job. Phillips swiftly provided acetates to local DJs such as the wildly popular Dewey Phillips, who broadcast six nights a week on WHBQ, and they began playing the track frequently during the weeks leading up to its official release in the first week of January 1956. Everyone seemed to love "Blue Suede Shoes."

Orders for the record quickly overwhelmed Sam, Marion Keisker, and nineteen-year-old Wilbourn. In one day, Phillips's Memphis distributor, Music Sales, ordered a thousand copies, while twenty-five hundred copies were sold in Dallas in about the same amount of time. By the end of January 1956, "Blue Suede Shoes" was a bona fide hit. Phillips described it as a "three-way smash," meaning it was blitzing pop, country, and R&B radio—and selling in vast quantities.

Carl didn't have a telephone and one day his neighbor called him to the phone. He had a long-distance call from Sam Phillips in Memphis.

"Carl," Phillips told him, "you know what happened? Chicago has ordered twenty-five thousand copies." Phillips explained to Carl that he'd never dealt in such large numbers—he thought the order was only for twenty-five hundred.

Phillips gave Carl some great news: "You got a hit on 'Blue Suede Shoes.'"

CHAPTER 5

I remember the Chesapeake Bay Ferry
and it's the last thing I remember for three days

By late February, the *Memphis Press-Scimitar* was reporting that "Blue Suede Shoes" had sold 250,000 copies with another 75,000 on order. It quickly hit the number 1 spot on the Memphis Country chart (and would stay there for the next three months). The phones at Sun rang constantly as hopefuls who'd heard "Blue Suede Shoes" called and asked the million-dollar question: "How do I make a record?" Phillips, meanwhile, placed an ad for the record in *Billboard* that put it simply: "A tremendous hit—rock and roll, pop, and country & western!!!" Everyone suddenly wanted a piece of "Mr. Blue Suede Shoes." A review of the record in *Billboard* magazine declared that his red-hot song was "fine for the jukes," but Carl was soon to graduate to much bigger venues.

By March 1956, with "Blue Suede Shoes" continuing its assault on the charts and airwaves, cover versions began to emerge, a handy by-product of writing a hit song. There was a rendition from Delbert Barker and the Gateway All-Stars, then another by Sid King & the Five Strings (who also dabbled in the as yet unnamed style of rockabilly), as well as a version by Sam "The Man" Taylor, a jazz tenor saxophonist. There was a cover by a Texan country singer calling himself Thumper Jones (who'd become better known as the hard-living George "Possum" Jones). Even the accordionist and easy-listening maestro Lawrence Welk had a crack at "Blue Suede Shoes."

"There was every kind of cover," noted Carl.

There was also another, more troubling rendition of "Blue Suede Shoes" in the works, by Carl's friend and former Sun peer Elvis Presley, whose new hit-in-waiting, "Heartbreak Hotel," reached the charts on March 3, the same week that "Blue Suede Shoes" entered the *Billboard* Hot 100.

But before Carl had a chance to take all this in—or look into moving Valda and the kids out of Parkview Courts—he hit the road. In mid-February, he performed for the first of four times at the Big D Jamboree, which was broadcast on the local AM station KRLD from the Dallas Sportatorium. The Big D, promoted as "the Southwest's biggest, oldest, boldest & best country music show!," was a stepping-stone to more prestigious events such as the Grand Ole Opry and the Louisiana Hayride. Carl, billed as "the hottest three-field newcomer in years!", headlined the show each Saturday night, playing to a full house of about four thousand fans. He was paid $350 per show, the most money he'd earned in his life. The rest of the band was enjoying the high life, too, especially Fluke Holland and Clayton, who spent much of their offstage time seeking out female company. "I was just a good old boy having fun," said Holland.

Sam Phillips flew to Dallas on the first night of the Big D and presented his new star with a pair of honest-to-goodness blue suede shoes. It was a neat publicity stunt for both Carl and Sun. "You know, Mr. Phillips," Carl said quietly backstage, "I've never been in a city this size." He was still country through and through.

Phillips had another, more significant gift in mind for Carl— he'd negotiated a deal for him to buy a Sixty Special from the Southern Motors Cadillac dealership, which was run by Phillips's friend Joe Canepari. It was one of Cadillac's most luxurious sedans, valued at around $5,000. While awaiting delivery, Carl was given a loaner, an eight-seater 1953 Chrysler Imperial, which Carl said was built like a "railroad car." That would prove to be a saving grace for Carl and his brothers in time.

Carl, meanwhile, splurged on an automatic washer for Valda, a first for the Perkins household. "I'm going to buy her a lot of things," Carl told a writer from the *Memphis Press-Scimitar*—as soon as he received some of the proceeds from his record sales, he clarified. Just to show how far Carl's star had risen, a man had begun doing the rounds of such Memphis nightspots as the Cotton Club, insisting that he was Carl, hoping to get free admission and drinks. "This boy is an imposter," roared Sam Phillips, "and we've got the police after him."

Carl returned to the Sun Studio three times in March. One of the standouts from those session was "Boppin' the Blues," a cowrite with Howard "Curley" Griffin, a partially sighted DJ whom Carl had met at WDXI in Jackson who lived in the same housing project as Carl. "He had a tape recorder," Carl recalled, "and was good with lyrics. He had a little poem called 'Boppin' the Blues.' The title will always be his, but I wrote the song."

Carl also recorded "Everybody's Trying to Be My Baby," delivering the facetious lyric, in which he bragged about how women found him simply irresistible, with his tongue wedged so far in his cheek that he almost choked. Carl was, after all, the first person to admit he came up a little short in the looks department. One night, as he watched from the wings as Elvis Presley played and his audience swooned, Carl said to himself, *Perkins, you gonna have to go out sideways hoppin', son, or they ain't gonna look at you.* He'd also joke that if Elvis resembled him, "this music might never have started." Looks mattered.

He also cut "All Mama's Children," which he wrote with his buddy Johnny Cash. As he'd done with "Blue Suede Shoes," Carl took inspiration from a nursery rhyme; in this case, it was "there was an old woman who lived in a shoe." He even managed to name-check blue suede shoes in the lyrics, just in case his fans forgot the name of his biggest hit. (Carl did the same again with another song, "Put Your Cat Clothes On," which he recorded later that year.)

Rather than rush-release something new from Carl, Sam Phillips wisely held off until every last drop had been wrung from "Blue Suede Shoes." When Carl staged a concert in west Texas, he played his hit seven times in a row, the crowd refusing to let him leave the club, despite a raging blizzard. When Carl played in Richmond, the *Richmond Times-Dispatch* referred to him simply as "Carl ('Mr. Blue

Suede Shoes') Perkins." "Perkins's own blue suede shoes are now part of his regular costume for performances," they noted. "He has had them sprinkled with glitter."

Elvis Presley, meanwhile, was being pressured by his new label, RCA Victor, as well as his producer Steve Sholes, to cut his own version of "Blue Suede Shoes." Elvis agreed with Sholes, who knew it would be a hit song (again), but went on to explain that the song belonged to Carl. "That's a Sun record." Interestingly, Sholes had called Sam Phillips as "Blue Suede Shoes" climbed the charts and asked him point-blank, "Did we buy the wrong guy?" (Phillips said no.)

Elvis reluctantly agreed to record the song—he required thirteen takes, whereas Carl needed only three—but asked that it not be released until April, long enough, he figured, to let Carl's original gain the traction it deserved nationwide. Fortunately, RCA Victor agreed to his request, and even then it appeared on an EP, not as a standalone single. The ever-modest Carl appreciated the gesture. "He could have recorded it first and nobody would have known Carl Perkins existed. He wanted me to have success with it." (Elvis, however, did perform it on CBS TV's *Stage Show* on February 11 and again on March 17.)

On March 17, Carl's "Blue Suede Shoes" hit number 3 on the R&B charts, a first for a country artist. And Carl kept working, making his TV debut performing the song that night on ABC TV's *Ozark Jubilee*. The show was hosted by Red Foley, a handsome Kentucky-born singer with a baritone voice and a personable manner who'd been recording hits since 1941's "Old Shep," which was one of Elvis Presley's favorite songs.

While *Ozark Jubilee* had a viewing audience of several million, it was essentially a country music program. What Carl needed was a spot on a national mainstream TV show, which would ensure that his song became known across America. By late March, Presley had appeared five times on *Stage Show*, which was produced by the superstar Jackie Gleason, and these national TV spots—Elvis's first—boosted his profile enormously. Carl needed something similar.

Finally, Carl's ascent to stardom seemed certain when he was invited to New York City to appear on NBC TV's *The Perry Como Show*. Como's weekly program had huge ratings—it was also one of the first TV shows to be broadcast in color. Carl, who'd never been to the Big Apple, was booked for March 24. Sam Phillips made plans to travel to New York and present Carl with a gold disc while a TV audience of millions looked on. Everything seemed to be in place.

Carl, along with Jay, Clayton, "Fluke" Holland, and Stuart Pinkham (also known as Dick Stuart or Poor Richard, a DJ), set out on March 20 for New York. Back at home in Jackson, Valda was pregnant with their third child. Around six thirty on the morning of March 22, having just played a show for two thousand fans with Gene Vincent and the Burnette brothers in Norfolk, Virginia, Pinkham fell asleep at the wheel while driving on Route 13 between Dover and Woodside, and their car, the 1953 Chrysler "loaner," plowed into the back of a truck. Carl and Jay were stretched out in the back seat. The car rolled several times and landed beside a bridge. Carl was thrown from the vehicle and lay in a watery ditch, unconscious until drummer Holland turned him over and saved him from drowning. Jay, meanwhile, was trapped in the back of the Chrysler. Clayton and Holland were shaken but unhurt.

"I remember the Chesapeake Bay Ferry," said Carl, "and it's the last thing I remember for three days." Their injuries were severe: Carl broke his right shoulder in three places, suffered numerous cuts and abrasions, and also broke four ribs. Jay was in even worse shape; his neck was broken, and he'd suffered terrible internal injuries. The accident was front-page news in the *Memphis Press-Scimitar*: "Memphis Singer Hurt in Crash," reported Robert Johnson, a staff writer. "Carl Perkins, the Rags-to-Riches Singer from Jackson . . . Was Hospitalized with his Entire Troupe." Carl's injuries were listed as a "deep scalp cut and a possible fractured skull," while it was noted that Jay was the "most seriously injured." The crash, reported the *Press-Scimitar*, would prevent Carl from keeping his "engagement on the Como show, the most important appearance so far in his career."

Carl lay in a bed in the Dover hospital, drifting in and out of consciousness. He remained in traction for eight days. When he overheard someone say that a person had been killed in the accident, Carl, thinking it was Jay, screamed for a nurse. It was then that he learned that the truck driver, a man named Thomas Phillips, had died in the crash.

"The sad part of it was that the truck we hit killed the man," Carl said in 1967. "For a good while it took the good feeling out of the fame the record had." Carl spent most of his time in traction looking over at Jay, praying that his brother would return to consciousness. "When he woke up and opened his eyes, man, we were happy boys."

Elvis Presley, who was in New York, heard about Carl's crash and quickly dispatched a telegram on behalf of himself and his band that read: "We were all shocked and very sorry to hear of the accident. I know what it is for I had a few bad ones myself. If I can help you in any way, please call me. I will be at the Warwick Hotel in New York City. Our wishes are for a speedy recovery for you and the other boys." (Presley's name was misspelled as "Alvis," sloppy work on the part of Western Union.) Elvis decided against performing "Blue Suede Shoes" on *Stage Show*, which had been planned, in deference to Carl's situation. He sang "Money Honey" instead. While Elvis was still in Manhattan, Carl was visited in the hospital by Scotty Moore, Bill Black, and D. J. Fontana, who had recently joined Presley's band. All the while, Carl's "Blue Suede Shoes" and Presley's "Heartbreak Hotel" competed for the top spot in the *Billboard* chart. "Blue Suede Shoes" eventually hit a chart peak of number 2 and sold more than one million copies, but for the moment, Carl's career was stuck in neutral.

Carl spent a good deal of his time in the hospital reflecting on the state of things. Missing out on the Perry Como program was a huge loss—if he'd made it to New York, he would have appeared on the show before Elvis, and, as he later stated, "It doesn't hurt to be first."

To their credit, the Como people contacted Carl while in the hospital and assured him that the booking remained open.

Carl understood that he'd just lived through a remarkable few months but also knew that the accident had stopped his momentum—and in a business such as rock and roll, which had hit boom time, momentum was crucial. The shrieking, pomaded Little Richard, the third of twelve children from a Macon, Georgia, family, whose father was a deacon (and sometimes bootlegger), had just breached the *Billboard* Top 10 with "Long Tall Sally." Chuck Berry, from St. Louis, who'd done hard time at the age of eighteen for armed robbery, had already charted highly with "Maybellene" and "Roll Over Beethoven," with such classics as "School Days," "Too Much Monkey Business," and "You Can't Catch Me" set to follow. Vincent Craddock, aka Gene Vincent, a twenty-one-year-old rocker (and closet Beethoven fan) from Norfolk, Virginia, had hit it big with "Be-Bop-a-Lula," also a top 10 hit in the *Billboard* charts. Even Bill Haley (and his Comets), who'd been kicking around since 1947, had exploded with "Rock Around the Clock," a song so popular, it had featured in two hit movies: 1955's *Blackboard Jungle*, and then a film called *Rock Around the Clock*, which reached theaters in March 1956. At age thirty, the kiss-curled Haley seemed positively ancient to much of his audience, but the song resurrected his career. (Haley would cover Carl's "Blue Suede Shoes," in 1960.)

As he slowly recovered, another report of Carl's wreck appeared in the *Memphis Press-Scimitar*, featuring a photo of his badly smashed-up car. The headline read: "Crash Taught Carl Perkins: Don't Drive When Tired." "I've learned a lesson—all the boys in the band learned a lesson," Carl told reporter Robert Johnson. "We're lucky to be here at all." He also told Johnson that he was overwhelmed by the public's reaction to his misfortune: "I had no idea how wonderful people could be. Letters were coming in by the hundreds [to the hospital]." Carl had survived a similar wreck a couple of years earlier, en route from a honky-tonk to the emergency room at the Jackson hospital, but this was far worse.

Some of Carl's peers felt that if it wasn't for the crash, he might have achieved the same kind of acclaim as Presley, perhaps even surpassed him. Johnny Cash certainly thought so. "I believe that without the accident," he wrote in his 1996 memoir, "Carl would have become a real superstar in the pop/rockabilly world." Producer Bob Johnston, who worked with Cash and Bob Dylan, agreed. "Instead of Carl being the one to go up, Presley was," he said. "Carl would have been the first one, but he was in the hospital while his record was selling a million copies." "The only reason Carl is not recognized [as broadly] for 'Blue Suede Shoes,'" said Sam Phillips, "is that Elvis became so mammothly [*sic*] big."

Yet Carl, despite his disappointment, wasn't so sure that he had what was required to emulate Elvis, let alone surpass him. He'd witnessed Elvis-mania at a Louisiana Hayride concert, when Presley was mobbed by young women after a show, and understood that it was no place for a married man. "Elvis had the looks on me. The girls were going for him for more reasons than music. Elvis was hitting them with sideburns, flashy clothes, and no ring on that finger. I had three kids."

Still, Carl admitted to having some serious discussions with his God as he slowly recovered. "Is this it?" he asked the man upstairs. "Am I going to get well? Is my brother going to die?"

Carl knew for sure that he'd been left behind when he lay in his hospital bed and watched Presley perform "Blue Suede Shoes" on *The Milton Berle Show* on TV on April 3. Elvis's version was slightly different from Carl's; he played it faster and Scotty Moore took two separate guitar solos (quite an achievement given that the song ran for barely two minutes and change). Carl tried his best to be philosophical; in fact, he liked Presley's version so much that when he did return to playing live, he edged closer to the Elvis treatment. And when asked about Presley's take on his hit song, Carl replied: "I was real proud." So was Sam Phillips, who'd hold on tight to the publishing rights to "Blue Suede Shoes" for the next twenty years. He made two cents from each and every sale of the record, regardless of who recorded it, which amounted to a handy nest egg over time.

Carl may have been a physical wreck, but demand for his presence remained strong. As he later said, even while he was in the hospital, booking agents "were screaming at me to get back to work.

There were new show dates coming in every day and the bookers advised me to take them." It didn't matter, Carl was told, if all he could do was stand there and sing "Blue Suede Shoes," he should take the work. His major concern, though, was Jay, who was in no shape to return to the road. When Carl finally agreed to a concert in Beaumont, Texas, on April 21—again as part of the Big D Jamboree—he'd be joined by his old friend Edd Cisco on guitar; Jay was still unable to perform. Carl would be paid $1,500 for his performance. The money came in handy because Carl and Valda had finally left Parkview Courts and moved into a pricier rented duplex in East Jackson. But Carl had bigger plans; he hoped to buy their first home. Valda, meanwhile, had just given birth to a third child, a son named Gregory.

If there was an upside to Carl's misfortune, it was that he had some songs in the bank from recording sessions prior to the accident. "Boppin' the Blues" was released as a single in May 1956, with "All Mama's Children" on the flip side. While it fared reasonably well in *Billboard*'s Hot Country Songs and Western Best Sellers chart, reaching number 9, and would become one of Sam Phillips's two favorite Perkins recordings—the other was "Movie Magg"—"Boppin'" barely dented the Hot 100, only making it to number 70. It was a huge disappointment after the multichart success of "Blue Suede Shoes," which had become the first Sun release to sell one million copies.

As writer Colin Escott commented in the liner notes for *The Classic Carl Perkins* box set, "Boppin' the Blues" "was meant to capture the essence of the new [rock and roll] music but instead it showed how closely tied Perkins was to the country tradition." It definitely wasn't "Blue Suede Shoes Revisited." Elvis Presley, meanwhile, continued to mess with the formula: both "Hound Dog" and "Don't Be Cruel," destined to become two of his signature songs, would be released in the ensuing months, and neither sounded like his early Memphis recordings.

"Boppin' the Blues" may have been a flop, but Sam Phillips did his utmost to talk up Carl and his fellow Sun artists, a roster that currently included Johnny Cash, Eddie Bond (who rejected a teenage Elvis when he auditioned for his band), Warren Smith, and Jack Earls, who worked with Bill Black's brother, Johnny, also a guitarist. Roy Orbison, a softly spoken Texan native who'd been playing the guitar since he was six years old, was now also with the label. He'd played Phillips his song "Ooby Dooby" over the phone from New Mexico and within three days he was in Sun making a recording.

Along with Bob Neal, Phillips organized live shows for his acts under the banner Stars Incorporated. Phillips ran an ad in the May 12 issue of *Billboard* featuring photos of his artists, and a blurb that proclaimed: "These are the biggest drawing stars in the rock 'n' roll business." It was a bold statement, but the truth was that Cash, whose "I Walk the Line" reached number 1 on the Country chart in May, was currently the only charting artist among the group.

Finally, on May 26, Carl made his belated appearance on *The Perry Como Show*. His fellow guests included the TV stars Ozzie and Harriet Nelson. The always amiable Como spoke with Carl prior to his performance, trying to put him at ease. "The record has sold, what, one million, one million two hundred thousand copies, right?" Como asked. Carl politely nodded in the affirmative, looking about as awkward as you'd expect a country boy to be on national television.

"I'm sure you're very happy about it, Carl," Como continued. "Is your trio ready?"

"I can get them ready," Carl replied. Joining Carl onstage was his brother Jay, who was still wearing his neck brace two months after the crash. (Carl had asked that they not do the show until Jay was physically able.) Despite a spirited performance, and some concerted knee jiggling on Carl's part, it was impossible to overlook the fact that the Perkins brothers were still very much on the mend.

"I knew that Jay wasn't well," said Carl. "Even when we did *The Perry Como Show*, and that old soldier stood there with his brace around his neck, with that twisted smile, you'd never know he was in so much pain." But Jay insisted on helping Carl on the show because he wanted "Blue Suede Shoes" to sound as close to the record as possible. According to Carl, Jay's gesture represented "the kind of love you cannot buy." But Jay's health was of great concern; he'd been suffering constant headaches ever since the wreck, which would worsen over time.

Carl, frankly, wasn't in great shape himself. "I was a mess, a wreck, for years," he would admit. He was drinking harder than he ever did when he was playing the tonks. "When you're a country boy just a month from the plow," Carl explained, "you can't take the strain without a crutch."

Still, Carl's belated appearance on Como's shows did spread ripples—newspaper reports of his subsequent shows, in Birmingham and Montgomery, Alabama, in late May, highlighted his national TV spot and made a point of mentioning Carl above his fellow guests, Johnny Cash, Roy Orbison, Warren Smith (whose "Rock 'n' Roll Ruby" was having some success), and Eddie Bond and the Stompers. A story in the *Angola Herald* described Carl as "the new recording sensation of Sun," whose hit "Blue Suede Shoes" "has won him literally hundreds of thousands of fans, and especially among the teenagers, who find just the precise beat that's right for bop in this rock and roll number." Sam Phillips couldn't have said it better himself.

Yet some reporters didn't quite know what to make of this new music—rockabilly, rock and roll, whatever you chose to call it. A writer from the *Pittsburgh Press* mentioned Carl's latest release, "Boppin' the Blues," referring to him as a "rock 'n' roll specialist," whatever that was. "Like it or not," wrote Pittsburgh's William K. Trosene, "you just can't fight this rock 'n' roll craze that has swept the country . . . eight of the top 15 tunes on the bestseller lists are ones with that solid beat." Another writer, from the *Guthrian*, an Iowan newspaper, was less subtle. "Carl Perkins seems to have taken his blue suede shoes for a long walk on a short pier and he won't be bothering the public with noise much longer." And Elvis? "Whenever Elvis shouts, 'Hound Dog,'" sniffed the same critic, "it sounds as though someone punched him in the stomach."

The specter of Elvis seemed impossible for Carl to avoid, be it in snooty dismissals of the rock 'n' roll "craze" or while he was out on the road. On June 1, Carl, Johnny Cash, and Roy Orbison played an outdoor show at the Overton Park Shell in Memphis before a crowd of five thousand fans. It was the "first big popular music show of the summer," announced the Memphis daily the *Commercial Appeal*, that was going to "rock and roll around in the Overton Park Shell." Elvis wasn't on the bill, but he was side stage, looking on. In theory he was just a face in the crowd, there to support his buddies and peers. But at the end of the night, after each Sun artist played their set, it was Elvis who was called up onstage by the audience. He took a couple of bows and then stayed for some time afterward signing autographs. In a photograph taken after the show, Carl could have been mistaken for an Elvis fan as he stood beside the star while young admirers swarmed around them.

Away from the stage, Carl and Roy Orbison would sometimes go driving together, and Orbison would sing parts of his new songs to Carl. "Do you think I should go up another octave?" Orbison would ask. Carl couldn't believe what he was hearing. "How high can you go?" he'd ask. "You're just about through the car roof now."

Carl finally received his first royalty check from Sun in August, around the time of the release of his next single, "Dixie Fried," an original he'd recorded back in March. It was his second cowrite with Howard "Curley" Griffin and one of Carl's best tracks to date, with a lyric that drew on his recent past in the tonks. But, as Colin Escott pointed out in the liner notes to *The Classic Carl Perkins*, the record was doomed. "It was so determinedly rural in content," he wrote, "that Phillips could not have entertained serious hopes for it in the pop market." While it fared well in the country charts, reaching the top 10, it gained no traction at all on the mainstream list. But like so many of Carl's early recordings, "Dixie Fried" had a long life span, being covered in later years by George Thorogood and the Destroyers, the Kentucky Headhunters, and Chris Isaak, among others.

Carl could take some solace in his check from Sun, which was for $12,000, a not insignificant amount. Sam Phillips certainly thought so, telling a reporter that people like Carl "hadn't seen that much money in their lifetime—or their daddy's lifetime," which was undeniable. Carl also received $14,000 from Hi-Lo Music, which was Phillips's publishing company. Fully aware that he wasn't working in isolation, Carl gave his brothers $5,000 each and gave "Fluke" Holland $2,000, for their help with "Blue Suede Shoes" and so much more.

Carl set up his first bank account—he'd not had enough money to bother in the past—and also put down a deposit on the Perkins family's first real home, at 308 Park Avenue in Jackson, where they would live for the next twelve years. It was nothing flashy, just a single-level, two-bedroom, one-bathroom home in a neighborhood populated by young families like Carl and Valda's. Their kids would play in the woods near their home; every evening Valda would stand at the front door and call out, "Time to eat," and their children would emerge from their various hidey-holes. Valda loved to cook; breakfast was always biscuits and gravy. "There's no toast in my house," boasted Carl.

Carl and Valda were good hosts. "You all will stay for supper, won't you?" Valda would ask their guests, and over many years the foldout bed in the Perkins den would be used by Johnny Cash, Roy Orbison, Charlie Rich, and their families, among many others. "They'll all tell you," Carl once said, "'Carl's got one of the greatest little women ever lived.' She's a good country girl, Valda." Singer-songwriter Roger Miller, who, like Carl and Cash, came from cotton-picking stock (Erick, Oklahoma, in his case), once stayed for so long that the tires on his car, out in the street, had gone flat and there was a parking ticket tucked under his windshield, which was covered in leaves. Sometimes Valda would call Carl into another room and gently suggest that it was time for their latest guest to leave. They had children to care for, after all.

There were other acknowledgments of Carl's success. When he returned to play Amory, where he'd once upstaged Elvis, he was mobbed by young women at the end of his set, his clothes torn from his back. But, as the *Huntsville Times* reported, Carl "escaped with undamaged blue suede shoes." Sam Phillips staged a party in Carl's honor, to mark the moment when sales of "Blue Suede Shoes" surpassed one million copies, Carl was carried out into the street and dumped into the back seat of his brand-new Cadillac, a gift from Sam Phillips. "Carl says he'll drive it mighty careful," read a report in the Memphis press the next day.

Sadly, Carl didn't. He totaled it on US 70 in late August. "Blue 'Swayed' Cadillac," reported the *Jackson Sun*, alongside a picture of Carl's front-ended car. No one was hurt in the crash, but the Caddy was a write-off.

This generous gesture from Phillips didn't sit so well with Johnny Cash, who even years later would write, "I'm still annoyed that he never gave me a Cadillac." Cash's first royalty check wasn't quite as big as Carl's—he received the grand sum of $6.42.

Cash had concerns about Phillips's fiscal dealings. "I'm not sure he treated me properly in a financial sense," he'd write in his autobiography. Carl was more diplomatic, as was his nature. "I did not feel right to question [Phillips] about too much of anything, really," he said when asked. "I trusted him."

CHAPTER 6

Put four Cadillacs in his yard, and 200 singin' girls trying to climb the fence, and you got some trouble

Post-"Blue Suede Shoes," Carl's relationship with "Mr. Phillips" remained strong, but he would grow wary of any new signing to the label. He was concerned that Sun's latest act, whoever that was, would be getting the bulk of Phillips's attention. The most recent addition to the Sun stable was twenty-year-old Jerry Lee Lewis, a piano player and singer. Like Carl, he was born poor—in Ferriday, Louisiana—but, personality-wise, he and Carl couldn't be more different. Lewis was cocksure and opinionated; his long, fair hair would flop into his eyes as he pounded the keys of his piano with all the fervor of some fire-and-brimstone backwoods preacher. It was a world apart from Carl's country manners, slightly rigid playing style, and gently jiggling right leg. Carl referred to Jerry Lee as a "wildfire Louisiana boy . . . always cocky." When Sam Phillips was asked to describe Jerry Lee's "madness," he replied, "It's a type of insanity that almost borders on . . . genius."

Lewis's people had strong religious roots—his cousin was the evangelist Jimmy Swaggart—and he freely stated that rock and roll was the devil's music.

"How can the devil save souls?" he once said when arguing in the studio with Sam Phillips. "What are you talking about?"

Carl, however, didn't agree. "It would hurt when I read or heard that preachers were breaking our records and calling it the devil's music," he said. "I never felt that we were spreading evil."

Sam Phillips had a more deadpan take. "Rock and roll," he would tell a writer from *Rolling Stone*, "probably put more money in the collection boxes of the churches across America than anything the preacher could have said."

Jerry Lee, who would become known as the Killer, may have been just a kid, but he had no problem voicing his opinion. Before he caught the ear of Phillips in 1956, he'd auditioned for executives in Nashville, who asked him if he'd considered switching to guitar. "You can take your guitar and ram it up your ass," he replied.

Before releasing his own material, Jerry Lee helped out on sessions at Sun—he played piano on Carl's recordings of "Matchbox" and "Your True Love" on December 4, 1956 (for all of $15, his studio fee). And it was that Carl Perkins session that spawned what came to be known as the Million Dollar Quartet.

Carl wasn't too sure what to make of the loudmouthed, arrogant Lewis—"You can't predict today what he'll be like tomorrow," he said—but as he got to work on that Tuesday afternoon in December, he began to sense some magic in the making. "I mean, Jerry Lee played the piano like he wanted to play it and you didn't tell him," said Carl.

Carl's father, Buck, was in the studio that day. Carl was discussing what song to record with his band when Buck piped up and said, "What about that old 'Match Box Blues'?" He was referring to a Blind Lemon Jefferson song that dated back to 1927, called "Match Box Blues" (which had roots in an even earlier song, Ma Rainey's "Lost Wandering Blues," recorded in 1924). Carl said that he'd never heard it, but once Buck recited a few of the lyrics from memory, Lewis quickly found a groove on the piano and transformed a slow blues into what would end up a rockabilly classic. While it became a very different song, the simple message behind it—poverty was no fun—remained essentially the same.

"I didn't have an opening or anything," recalled Carl. "I started with that rhythm riff and Jerry Lee said, 'Yeah, I like that, man' . . . The song just happened."

Toward the end of Carl's session, in which he also cut "You Can Do No Wrong," "Put Your Cat Clothes On," and "Her Love Rubbed

Off"—all originals—as well as a cover of Chuck Berry's "Roll Over Beethoven," there was a visitor to Sun. Elvis Presley dropped by the studio, fresh from Las Vegas and about to leave for Hollywood to shoot the film *Love Me Tender*. He was accompanied by a dancer named Marilyn Evans.

After listening to "Matchbox" in the control room and voicing his approval—he described the songs as "killer"—Elvis joined Carl and his band, who by now had finished recording. They started swapping stories, discussing, among other things, Chuck Berry, with whom Carl had just played a few dates. While on the road, rather than use the tour bus, the two musicians traveled together in Carl's Cadillac. ("He always wanted to ride in that," Carl recalled, chuckling.) Gathered around the piano inside Sun, they played parts of Berry's "Too Much Monkey Business" and "Brown Eyed Handsome Man." Everyone agreed that Berry was a great lyricist and fine songwriter.

Inside the control room at Sun Studio, meanwhile, Sam Phillips sensed the gravity of the occasion and put in a call to Johnny Cash, whose "I Walk the Line"—a title suggested by Carl—was riding high in the charts, on its way to selling 750,000 copies by the new year. He soon arrived at Sun with his wife, Vivian. In the control booth, the always-alert Phillips decided to let the tape keep rolling from Carl's session. He told his engineer Jack Clements, "Man, let's just record this ... We may never have these people together again." (When Carl learned about this, he acknowledged that it was no accident that Phillips decided to record the session. "He was a very intelligent man." Fluke Holland, however, thought that Clements had simply gone to get a sandwich and left the recorder running by accident.)

Phillips also put in a call to the *Memphis Press-Scimitar* newspaper, which swiftly dispatched writer Robert Johnson to Sun. He was joined by George Pierce, a photographer for news agency UPI. As Johnson would report, Presley sat down at the piano and began playing Fats Domino's "Blueberry Hill," and "the joint was really rocking before they got through." Elvis, too, was a Jerry Lee convert, this being the first time they'd met. "That boy can go," he enthused to Johnson between songs.

Someone produced an acoustic guitar and Elvis took a run at "You Belong to My Heart," a 1945 hit for Bing Crosby. Then, with Carl and the band locking into a solid groove, they sang a few gospel songs, including "Just a Little Talk with Jesus" and "There'll Be Peace in the Valley for Me." Everyone knew the material well, as writer Dave Marsh would observe: "One after another, from memory, one man starts to sing, and after a pause of a couple bars, the others click in and join him, effortlessly." Elvis then tried out some impersonations, first Bill Monroe, then Ernest Tubb. The congregation also took a crack at "No Place like Home" and "When the Saints Go Marching In." Carl sang lead on "Keeper of the Key," a stark country weeper cowritten by Nashville great Harlan Howard, and then tore off a blazing rockabilly-styled guitar solo in the middle of "Down by the Riverside." During a run-through of Little Richard's "Rip It Up," everyone cheekily sang, "It's Saturday night and I just got laid," which sounded much better than the original "paid."

The mood among the group that was gathered inside Sun was lighthearted, upbeat, collegial. There was no pressure to make a hit record; this was simply music being played for music's sake. As Carl would recall, "It was everybody playing a feel and just getting in the groove and really enjoying it." As one future reviewer would note when the recordings of the day were finally released, "This is just a tape of some Southern good old boys—and when Elvis sits down at the piano to start jamming with the others, and Sam Phillips rolls the tape for posterity's sake, it's some good old boys having one hell of a good old time."

"What key is this in, Carl?" Presley asked before they tried "That's When Your Heartaches Begin," an oldie made popular by the Ink Spots in 1941, which was also one of the two songs Elvis recorded on his original Sun acetate. He then nailed the vocal, definitive proof of just how good a singer he truly was.

"The wrong man's been sitting here at this piano," Elvis noted, and Jerry Lee asked him to "scoot over" so he could play. Lewis duly launched into "When I Take My Vacation in Heaven." Lewis also took the opportunity to play his new single, "Crazy Arms," for the gathering, which was due to be released in a few days' time. Cash, like Elvis and Carl, had never heard him play before. "I was bowled over. He was so great."

After a couple of hours, an end was finally called to the impromptu session, a jam that started as a happy accident but would one day launch a Broadway show. Carl, Presley, Lewis, and those lucky few who stayed right to the last note—"I'm always the last one to leave," Elvis told the others—soon headed to Taylor's, a nearby diner, for cheeseburgers and coffee.

The next day, a picture of Carl, Cash, Presley, and Lewis, singing while standing around the piano, appeared in the *Press-Scimitar*. The headline read: "Million Dollar Quartet." (Elvis's girlfriend, Marilyn Evans, was cropped from the published shot.) It seemed that reporter Johnson wasn't aware of the rolling tape, because, as he wrote in his story, "If Sam Phillips had been on his toes, he'd have turned the recorder on. . . . That quartet could sell a million." His words would prove to be prophetic.

In mid-January 1957, Carl was profiled in the *Chicago Tribune*. When asked about life before and after "Blue Suede Shoes," Carl put it precisely: "It's the difference between having something on the table, and nothing on the table." The song had brought some creature comforts for Carl and his family, as the writer noted: "Now they have a fine brick house on Park Avenue and two large expensive cars in the yard."

The conversation, inevitably, shifted to the all-conquering Elvis, whom Carl described as a "good boy," despite the temptations of superstardom. "I'll tell you," said Carl, "you take a 21-year-old singin' boy, put four Cadillacs in his yard, and 200 singin' girls trying to climb the fence, and you got some trouble." Carl managed to laugh at a recent mishap of his own when he played Chicago. He'd parked his car in front of the Garrick Theater, and when the show was over, he couldn't find it anywhere on the street. Carl asked a passing cop if he'd seen a blue-and-white Cadillac, and he replied, "Sure did. They towed it away." Carl had to fork out $32 to retrieve his ride. So much for being a big name in the rock and roll biz.

The article mentioned Carl's children, including three-and-a-half-year-old Stan, who had taken to answering the phone at home by saying: "Carl Perkins, Blue Suede Shoes," before promptly hanging up. As for six-month-old Stephen, whenever he heard one of Carl's songs, he "began to gurgle, bounce up and down, and laugh . . . He might follow in his father's footsteps." That would turn out to be true.

From March to May 1957, in between recording sessions, Carl hit the road with Cash and Lewis for a tour promoted as "the biggest country rock 'n' roll show ever." When asked to describe Lewis's early playing style, Carl said that "he'd sit at the piano with just one corner of his face showing, playing Hank Williams tunes." But this was about to change. When the roadshow reached Calgary in Canada—it also traveled through the American Midwest, the South, and Texas—Lewis spoke with Carl. He admitted that he was envious. Being a piano player, he explained, was physically restrictive—he was sitting down all the time. He just didn't think it was fair.

"You guys with the guitars," moaned Lewis, "you can all move around."

"Well, Killer," Carl replied, "can't you stand up and play that thing?"

Lewis thought it through and figured that maybe Carl was right. That night onstage, while playing, he kicked his piano stool over and, as Carl recalled, "shocked the audience." After the show, Carl turned to Cash and said, "He took me by my damned word and he tore them all to pieces!" That night, as Carl would one day relate to TV host David Letterman, "A legend was born."

But there were problems behind the scenes. Carl found Lewis's arrogance hard to take—this was, after all, a man who'd name-check himself in his lyrics, as he did in "Lewis Boogie"—and challenged him to a fight one night on the 1957 tour. Their relationship grew worse when Lewis insisted that he go onstage after Carl, even though he was the least established artist on the bill.

The press coverage of the tour didn't help to ease Carl's mind. A writer from Toronto's *Leader-Post* reviewed the show at the Exhibition Auditorium; while Carl was praised for "getting things off to a foot-stomping start" with his songs "Boppin' the Blues," "True Love," and "Blue Suede Shoes," it was the newcomer Lewis who received the biggest praise. "In a class all by himself was Jerry Lee Lewis, who gave the Auditorium piano a trouncing such as it has never had before." Interestingly, the critic used the term "rockabilly" when describing the two shows that the troupe played, proof that the phrase was now pretty much in common use.

As for Johnny Cash, he was busy cutting it up with Carl's brother Clayton, who was always on the lookout for a good time. Cash nicknamed him "Floyce." During a stop on the tour, they agreed that their hotel room needed a makeover and spent the day painting the walls black. They also tied up various doors with rope, preventing hotel guests from leaving their rooms. On one occasion, they moved most of the furniture from Johnny's room and set it up just outside the lift door. As guests exited the lift, they found Johnny asleep in the hallway, tucked up in bed. In the time it took for the house detective to be summoned, Johnny and Clayton somehow managed to clear away any evidence of mayhem. "Floyce" also had unusual talents. He could open a Coke bottle with his teeth and had a thing for biting people's ears—which didn't impress Sam Phillips. "Better watch that boy," Phillips told Carl, after Clayton tried to chomp on the producer's ear.

Fun, however, wasn't what Jay Perkins had in mind; his headaches worsened as the tour rolled on. Carl was deeply concerned for his brother, and for his own uncertain career. He hadn't had a hit since "Blue Suede Shoes." And his boozing hadn't abated any. Early Times whiskey was his drink of choice, although, as he admitted, "I'd take anything."

Jerry Lee Lewis's second single for Sun, "Whole Lotta Shakin' Goin' On," was released just before the tour with Carl and Cash. The song was originally recorded by Mabel Louise Smith (aka Big Maybelle) but given a full-tilt boogie makeover by Lewis. It made its way to number 3 on the *Billboard* Hot 100 and reached number 8 on the UK singles chart. It was Sun's biggest hit since—of course—"Blue Suede Shoes."

As for Carl, his latest, "Your True Love," with "Matchbox" on the flip side, came to him while he was in the studio. As he worked on it, Sam Phillips asked him, "Whose song is that?" Had he heard it somewhere else? When Carl replied that it was his, Phillips suggested he write it down, "because you're singing it different every verse." Carl, however, didn't like the end result. Phillips increased the speed of the tape to make it more up-tempo, but as far as Carl was concerned, "I sound[ed] like Mickey Mouse."

"Your True Love" didn't make it beyond number 67 on the *Billboard* Hot 100 pop chart upon its February 1957 release, despite Sam Phillips's best efforts. He placed an ad in *Billboard* for the single that proclaimed, "That Sensational Carl Perkins Boy Has Done It Again," and produced a press release that described Carl as "that torrid 'Rockabilly' sensation who's currently settin' the scene on fire." But Carl had been eclipsed by "Whole Lotta Shakin'." Carl confronted Phillips about this, telling him, "You got Jerry Lee Lewis on the brain." Carl took offense that Phillips had given him the tag "Jerry Lee Lewis and His Pumping Piano" but hadn't given him a tag. Phillips duly christened Carl the "Rockin' Guitar Man," but it was clear that their relationship was starting to fray.

Three months after the Million Dollar Quartet session, in late March 1957, Carl was back at Sun. He had a new song to cut called "That's Right," another cowrite with Johnny Cash. During the playback, Elvis Presley dropped by the studio. He'd had a banner year in 1956, selling more than twelve million singles and almost three million albums—the type of numbers that Carl could only dream about. Presley had also signed a three-year movie deal with Paramount Pictures and starred in *Love Me Tender*, which had premiered in mid-November and became a huge hit. (Carl and Valda saw the film in Jackson and were photographed afterward outside the Malco Theater, standing in front of a life-size poster of Elvis.)

Presley was currently in the process of buying a property named Graceland, a fourteen-acre spread about ten miles south of Memphis, which was a castle by comparison with Carl and Valda's modest two-bedder in Jackson. Presley had become a nationwide star;

his world was exploding at a furious rate. As for Carl's other peers, Jerry Lee Lewis's "Whole Lotta Shakin' Goin' On" continued to burn up the charts, while Johnny Cash's 1956 hit, "I Walk the Line," was tracking its way to global sales of about 2.5 million.

Carl, meanwhile, was once again searching for the spark that he and Phillips had generated with "Blue Suede Shoes." In early September 1956, still riding the wave of the song's success, Carl stood outside the Steel Pier on the boardwalk at Atlantic City, where he was playing some shows—billed as "Famous Recording Star Carl Perkins"—and looked into the sky as the Goodyear blimp flew overhead. It spelled out his name in vivid lights. Tears streamed down Carl's cheeks; he'd made the big time. Six difficult months had passed since then—but for Carl it felt like a lifetime.

Still, as Carl related, Presley loved "That's Right." While it played, he danced across the Sun Studio floor and declared that it was a hit in waiting. "Man, I'd kill for that song," Elvis told Carl. It was high praise from a man whose songs were now crafted by the best writers that money (and his very persuasive manager, Colonel Tom Parker) could buy, including Brill Building hitmakers Jerry Leiber and Mike Stoller, and whose subsequent five singles would all race into the Top 10.

Carl and Presley, along with Sam Phillips, who had a tape of the track tucked under his arm, went straight from Sun to the WHBQ studio. Dewey Phillips was on the air, and as the trio entered the studio, he ripped the platter he was playing from the turntable and made a typically hyper announcement: "Somebody lock the door! Don't let 'em out! Got 'em both down here, burning down jukeboxes." He then queued up "Hound Dog."

As Presley's song was playing, Phillips handed him the tape of Carl's "That's Right." "I think this is one of the best records that will ever come out of Sun," the producer declared. Dewey asked Presley to introduce Carl's song, and he made it very clear how he felt about it. "Well, ladies and gentlemen," Presley stated, "if this ain't gonna be a hit record, I'm gonna be fooled." Dewey devoted the rest of his program to Carl and Elvis. When they finally left the studio, the street outside was lined with kids who'd been tuning in. Carl and

Phillips looked on as Presley drove off at high speed, with numerous cars in hot pursuit.

Despite all the praise, "That's Right" was destined to be Carl's next flop when it was released later in 1957. But there was a line in another song Carl cut in late 1957, called "Lend Me Your Comb," in which he used the word *booger* that caught the ear—and the imagination—of a UK group about to set out on their own musical journey. They'd come to play an enormous part in the second act of the Carl Perkins story.

CHAPTER 7

Mr. Phillips, it ain't gonna do me no good to stay down here

In the wake of the smash hit films *Blackboard Jungle* and *Rock Around the Clock*, which both cashed in on two new phenomena—teenagers and rock and roll—there was a steady flow of new movies trying to capture the mood of the moment (and bring in the teeny-boppers). Storylines were pretty much secondary in these films—what was crucial was a music-heavy soundtrack and a stream of on-screen cameos from rock-and-rollers, DJs, and pretty much anyone else currently in the spotlight.

Released in 1956, *Don't Knock the Rock* featured performances from Bill Haley & His Comets and Little Richard, as well as a star turn from high-profile DJ Alan Freed, who was acknowledged as the pioneer of these "rock and roll movies." Freed, who also appeared in *Rock Around the Clock*, starred in the imaginatively titled *Rock, Rock, Rock!* and—proof that you *could* get blood from a stone—1957's *Mister Rock and Roll*, which featured Chuck Berry, Frankie Lymon, and the hugely popular Little Richard. Alan Freed was pretty much everywhere, or at least he was until a payola scandal derailed his career and effectively ruined his life. (He died of alcoholism in 1965, at the age of forty-three.)

Released in 1957, and interesting for little more than the cameo from Carl and his band (for which Carl received $1,000), *Jamboree* was the latest in this conga line of zeitgeist-riding jukebox movies. As Carl would later reveal, the film company behind *Jamboree* had part ownership in a music publishing firm and offered two songs to Carl, one titled "Glad All Over," the other "Great Balls of Fire." Carl chose the former—which he would one day describe as "junk"—to perform in the movie. Jerry Lee Lewis was given the second track.

Originally titled *The Big Record*, the Warner Bros. film was the work of expat Roy Lockwood, who was better known for directing radio soap operas in his native England. The movie's musical director was Otis Blackwell, who had written Elvis's hits "Don't Be Cruel" and "All Shook Up." The storyline, such as it was, centered on an offstage couple (actors Paul Carr and Freda Holloway) who became singing sensations but ran into trouble when their managers decided to turn them into solo stars. *Jamboree* was no *Casablanca*, that was for sure, but it was a precursor of the music-on-film genre that would, many years later, lay the foundations for the commercial giant that was MTV.

A reporter from the *Akron Beacon Journal* put it bluntly in the review of the film: "[*Jamboree* is] still another musical free-for-all . . . there is a bit of a story but this is used only as an excuse to tie together the sounds that come forth from 17 of today's most popular recording artists." Tellingly, when some of those stars were named in the same review, Carl was way down the list, well below Jerry Lee Lewis and sandwiched between the Four Coins and Lewis Lymon and the Teenchords. (Although the "local boy" Carl did get higher billing when the film screened at Jackson's Jaxon Drive-In.) Another reviewer, from the *Buffalo News*, rightly figured that the central storyline simply propped up the appearance of "a procession of today's popular musical recording stars."

Future *American Bandstand* host Dick Clark appeared in the film, along with eighteen prominent DJs from all over America. Fats Domino performed, as did the country star Slim Whitman, "Party Doll" singer Buddy Knox, Frankie Avalon, and Connie Francis, but the DJs in the film in fact outnumbered the musicians. As for Carl, he appeared in a recording studio sequence with his brothers Jay and Clayton and drummer Fluke Holland. Carl pulled off a few slick moves as he sang "Glad All Over," but behind him, the rest of the band, most likely spooked by the camera crew, barely moved a muscle. As far as acting went, there was no doubt that they were all skilled musicians.

However, it was the ubiquitous Jerry Lee Lewis who stole everyone's thunder on *Jamboree* when he performed the electrified "Great Balls of Fire" soon after the opening credits. Rolling his eyes and singing and playing at a frantic speed, Lewis came on like a man with the devil inside. Cowritten by Otis Blackwell, "Great Balls" would soon become his biggest and most controversial hit when it was released in the winter of 1957. It hit number 2 on the *Billboard* Hot 100 chart and number 1 on *Billboard*'s Hot Country Songs chart—it also reached number 1 in the UK. Yet again, Carl had been outgunned by his younger and far brasher Sun labelmate.

Carl seemed a little more at ease during his next appearance, also in 1957, performing two songs as a guest on *Ranch Party*, which screened on KTTV-TV in Los Angeles. It was a televised form of the country music radio show *Town Hall Party*, which had been broadcast on the West Coast since 1951. The show's genial host Tex Ritter, who along with Gene Autry was one of the original "movie cowboys," was country through and through, from the soles of his cowboy boots to the brim of his ten-gallon hat. There were no teenagers, teenyboppers, or songs about great balls of fire to be seen or heard on *Ranch Party*.

Ritter spoke to the audience about Carl: "A very famous guest star on *Ranch Party* must have traveled west in his time and heard the cowboys say, 'Don't you dare step on my patterned leather boots, partner.' Possibly he went back home to Memphis and wrote a song and he's here to sing it. Carl Perkins and his boys—'Blue Suede Shoes'!"

Before performing, Carl smiled and directly addressed the viewing audience. "Hi, friends," he said, "I'm Carl Perkins. I've got my blue suede shoes on and I'm ready." Wearing a fringed, Western-styled shirt, in keeping with the theme of the program, Carl stepped forward to play his signature hit, his legs moving in all directions, while the rest of the band got on with their work, more than happy to let him take the lead. Jay barely moved during the entire performance.

A little later in the show, prior to Carl's second performance, Ritter explained how this rocker came to be on the program. After all, he was not strictly a country act. "You know every now and then we like to vary from our Western songs and bring the youngsters a little bit of be-bopping music. Our guest for today can really be called the king of the be-bop . . . here's Carl Perkins and his boys." Carl and his band played "Your True Love," with Jay and Clayton sharing his microphone as they harmonized on the chorus. It wasn't quite bebop, despite Ritter's comment, but just one of Perkins's guitar solos—generously acknowledged by the studio audience—had more juice than the rest of the undeniably earnest *Ranch Party* lineup combined. This show's cast included comic Smiley Burnette and the Collins Kids, Larry and Lorrie, who sang a Hank Williams song about a cigar store Indian named "Kaw-liga," a performance notable mainly for the impressive double-necked Mosrite guitar played by fourteen-year-old Larry. (Carl would later perform "Kaw-liga" in concert.)

Following the *Ranch Party* rehearsal on Saturday afternoon, Carl was approached by an unfamiliar figure who asked him what kind of guitar he used. "I play the only kind there is," Carl replied. "A Gibson Les Paul."

"You're sure about that, ain't ya?" the man replied. He went on to ask Carl if he was free for a few hours and, if so, if he wanted to take a ride. "I promise you," he said, "you won't go wrong." Only when they pulled into the parking lot of the Fender guitar factory—and the mystery man parked in a spot marked, simply, LEO—did Carl realize he was in the company of the guitar-making legend Leo Fender. Once inside his factory, Fender handed Carl a Jazzmaster guitar.

"See how that feels," he said.

"Sure, I'd heard of Leo Fender," Carl said later, "but I'd never owned one of his guitars."

Carl walked away with a new guitar and a bass for his brother— and immediately switched his allegiance to Fender.

≈

Leo Fender wasn't the only man of influence Carl met while on the West Coast in late August 1957. After playing *Ranch Party*, Carl met with Don Law from Columbia Records, who ran the label's country music division. Johnny Cash, who was also out on the West Coast, sat in with them. The Sun recording contracts of both Carl and Cash were due to expire before the end of the year, so the meeting with Law was timely.

The fifty-five-year-old Law, a Londoner now based in the United States, was a true music man; he'd produced the only recordings ever made of enigmatic bluesman Robert Johnson and had worked with Bob Wills, "the king of western swing," as well as the bluegrass duo Lester Flatt and Earl Scruggs, who were also signed to Columbia. Law had recently produced the Flatt and Scruggs's debut album, *Foggy Mountain Jamboree*, a record that more than half a century later would (finally) be inducted to the Grammy Hall of Fame. Carl and Cash's meeting with Law, held at the home of *Ranch Party*'s Collins Kids, had been brokered by Bob Neal from Memphis, who had promoted some of Carl's live shows.

By now, Carl was all but done with Sun; he'd grown bitter at what he perceived as a lack of interest in his career from Sam Phillips. First Elvis, then Johnny Cash, and now Jerry Lee Lewis—Carl felt they'd all taken precedence over him, despite his having produced Sun's first million-seller in "Blue Suede Shoes." And back when he was recovering in the hospital after his car crash, Carl had been visited by Jim Denny, a Nashville music figure who broadcast on WSM and managed the Grand Ole Opry.

Denny told Carl that he didn't think he was receiving a proper share of royalties for "Blue Suede Shoes," which led to Carl switching his publishing from Phillips's Hi-Lo Music to Denny's Cedarwood Publishing, which he'd set up in 1954 with country star Webb Pierce. Denny was one of many industry players who had offered to manage Perkins, but as Carl admitted, he resisted all their overtures because of what he would describe as "the dumb old country boy in me . . . I never thought anybody had ought to get 10 or 15 cents out of my dollar when I was the one doin' the work."

Don Law's pitch to both Carl and Cash was straightforward:

If they signed with Columbia, they'd be paid a 5 percent royalty on every record sold, which, as Carl noted, was a far healthier figure than Sun's 3 percent. That was all the motivation he needed to switch labels.

"Mr. Phillips," Carl told him when they met in Memphis, "it ain't gonna do me no good to stay down here." As Phillips would tell a reporter, "Carl's reason at that time was, see, I'd given each of them a lot of time getting started and then Jerry Lee Lewis was getting a lot of my time. They, Carl and Johnny [Cash]"—who also agreed to move to Columbia—"looked on it that we were petting Jerry."

Phillips warned Carl that while the switch to Columbia might have made sense for Cash, "I'm telling you, it's a mistake for you." He felt that his music was more suited to the rough-and-ready approach that characterized Sun's recordings. But that didn't change Carl's mind. When asked why he chose to leave Sun, Carl simply replied: "Bigger labels paid better money." During his time at Sun, Carl had recorded almost forty "sides"—eight were released as singles and seventeen remained unreleased.

Cash's reasons for shifting labels were different from Carl's (although Columbia's increased royalty definitely appealed to him, too). He wanted to stretch out as a musician and make a gospel album. He'd sung gospel songs on his audition with Sam Phillips back in 1955, when Phillips made it clear that it wasn't a style of music he knew how to sell. Cash was also interested in making a concept record, which Law believed would get Columbia's backing, so Cash saw clear and obvious advantages in signing with the bigger label.

Carl signed a formal contract with the label in January 1958. He was in a Nashville studio with Don Law within weeks, on February 3. But as it turned out, leaving Sun was, by Carl's own estimation, "The biggest mistake I ever made in my life."

In the late 1950s, the vinyl single remained the principal source of currency for musicians such as Carl; the era of the album was still some time off. Carl's first long-player, simply called *Dance Album of Carl Perkins*, was rush-released by Phillips soon after Carl left Sun and was, like so many LPs of the time, essentially a collection of the recordings Carl had made at 706 Union Avenue. Naturally, it opened with "Blue Suede Shoes," and featured "Movie Magg," "Matchbox," "Your True Love," "Boppin' the Blues," "Honey, Don't," and "Everybody's Trying to Be My Baby." While hardly a priority for Sun upon its release, *Dance Album of Carl Perkins*—which was later reissued as *Teen Beat: The Best of Carl Perkins*—would come to resemble a highly impressive greatest hits, even if, over time, the best-known versions of Carl's songs weren't necessarily his own. As a reviewer at Allmusic.com noted many years later, "*Dance Album* is a hits-only album in retrospect, after those tunes became standards."

Sam Phillips had also accumulated a stock of Johnny Cash recordings, which he released on a regular basis after he, too, moved to Columbia. The first of these, *Johnny Cash Sings the Songs That Made Him Famous*, released in late 1958, featured ten of the singles Cash had recorded while with Sun. In 1958, Carl and Cash were, at least in theory, working for two labels at the same time.

Carl's first session for Columbia, with Don Law producing, took place at Nashville's Owen Bradley's Quonset Hut Studio on February 3. The studio was aptly named, because it was actually inside a hut attached to a house on 16th Avenue South owned by Bradley and his brother Harold, a guitarist and entrepreneur. The publicity department at Columbia didn't hold back: "Carl's on a new lick!" roared a press release. "Carl has switched from the Sun Record label to Columbia and even bigger things are expected from him now." Another press release described Carl as "the hottest sound of the fiery fifties." All this before he'd released a song on the label.

This was the first of four separate sessions for Carl during 1958, all with Law producing. On February 3, Carl worked on four originals—"Jive After Five," "Rockin' Record Hop," "Pink Pedal Pushers," and "Just Thought I'd Call"—backed by his usual crew of Jay, Clayton, and Fluke. The Nashville native Marvin Hughes, a Grand Ole Opry regular who'd backed Presley on his 1956 hit "I Want You, I Need You, I Love You," also sat in on the session. It was clear from "Jive After Five" and "Rockin' Record Hop," in particular, that Carl was trying to capture the same raw, live sound he'd conjured up with Sam Phillips. But Carl was never quite sure how Phillips made that magic happen. "It wasn't high priced equipment [at Sun]," he told his biographer David McGee, "but there was always a little roar about the records."

Carl's first session with Law for Columbia lacked that "little roar." The songs were competent, he was playing as well as ever—a blazing guitar solo gave "Pink Pedal Pushers," which was picked as his debut Columbia A-side, some desperately needed muscle—but something elemental was missing. The Columbia press team may have stated that Carl's new record "could very easily put him in the record forefront once again," but that was way off the mark. As was the warning the label attached to the record: "Mr. DJ: Caution. This package is highly inflammable."

A guitar player named Roland James, working in the same Nashville studio as Carl during this first session, noticed that Carl was now playing a Fender Stratocaster, rather than the Gibson he'd favored in the past. (Carl used a 1953 Gibson Les Paul on "Blue Suede Shoes," which went up for sale in 2023 for a cool $150,000.) He believed this was a misstep on Carl's part. "The Gibson had a much better sound for what he was doing," James told writer Colin Escott.

Another problem may have been Carl's new working environment. He'd grown accustomed to 706 Union Avenue and the way players fed off one another during recording sessions, which sometimes stretched for twelve hours and at times could become very freewheeling. (Generous servings of Early Times made sure of that.) There was never any clock-watching while working with Sam Phillips—"he'd let you take all the time you wanted," said Carl—but the Quonset Hut was a very different atmosphere. There was an actual clock on the wall in the Nashville studio, and all the while Carl was fully aware that he had three hours in which to cut four songs. "That put a fear in me when I walked into that studio," Carl told his biographer. The pressure was well and truly on. And in comparison with Sun, the Quonset Hut Studio was like a football stadium; it was at least three times as spacious. The intimacy of Sun was gone, as was the bottle of booze that often did the rounds during sessions there. "It's strictly business," Carl said about recording in Nashville for

Columbia. "When you look through that glass window and see Chet Atkins there . . . it's hard to open up."

The cold, hard truth was that Carl's recording debut with Law and Columbia was only notable for one thing—it would be the last Perkins session to feature Carl's brother Jay. He had been in poor health ever since the 1956 car crash, and Carl had noticed that Jay's usually dependable live playing had become problematic. After a show in St. Paul, Minnesota, Carl asked Jay if he was okay. He could tell that something wasn't quite right. "It's my left hand," Jay answered. "It keeps going to sleep." When he got up to leave the room, Jay all but fell to the floor. "My left side keeps giving way," he admitted. By the time Carl convinced Jay to leave the tour and see his doctor in Jackson, he was pretty much dragging his left leg behind him.

Jay consulted a doctor, who blamed it on a nervous condition, but when his headaches continued, he met with a neurosurgeon named Dr. Tyor. "Jay's trouble is associated with his brain," he explained to Carl. Further tests at the Methodist Hospital in Memphis proved this to be true—they revealed a brain tumor. Exploratory surgery removed part, but not all, of the growth. The surgeon explained to Carl that what remained was malignant and inoperable; he'd done what he could but now could only prescribe morphine to help ease Jay's pain.

Yet in their car on the way home from the hospital, Carl was upbeat; he didn't quite grasp the severity of the word *malignant*.

"Carl," Valda explained, "malignancy *is cancer*."

Now that he fully understood the situation, Carl, who had just received a royalty check from Sam Phillips, gave some money to Jay's family when it became apparent that he couldn't play anymore.

When it was obvious that Jay was very close to death, Carl, Clayton, and Johnny Cash, as well as Luther Perkins (no relation to Carl) and Marshall Grant from Cash's band, took him fishing, hoping to lift his spirits. They went out in two boats, searching for giant catfish near a dam at Peakwood, Tennessee. "Getting those monsters up off the bottom felt like reeling in Sherman tanks," wrote Cash. "For a few hours," Carl would one day write, "Jay was a boy again . . .

dangling his toes in the cool water." They took their catch back to Carl's home in Jackson for a fish fry.

Jay died in hospital in Jackson on October 20, 1958, with Carl by his side. Jay was just twenty-eight years old. He left behind his wife, Pauline, and two children: his son, Jerry, who was six, and his eight-year-old daughter, Gayle. As Carl learned, the last thing Jay said was, "See that Carl and Clayton don't kill each other."

"Jay's death was a sad, terrible thing in [Carl's] life," wrote Cash. "I know how deep that wound goes." Cash had lost a brother, named Jack, who died in a horrific accident when Johnny was twelve—he was almost sliced in two by a table saw while cutting wood—and he felt Carl's pain acutely. Carl, naturally, was devastated. "I lost a jewel of a brother when Jay left." Jay had been in the trenches with Carl ever since they started playing the tonks in the late 1940s. He'd also tasted the success of "Blue Suede Shoes." They couldn't have been any closer. "He was liked by everybody who ever knew him," said Carl, whose mood darkened upon Jay's death. Carl was convinced that their 1956 crash contributed to his brother's demise. "[It was] the car wreck that killed him."

Resting atop one of the wreaths at Jay's service was a card that read, simply, *With love, Elvis.*

In mid-November, Carl appeared at a benefit show in Jay's honor at the Municipal Auditorium in Memphis, which was organized by Johnny Cash. Jerry Lee Lewis performed, as did Webb Pierce, Merle Travis, Porter Wagoner, Lefty Frizzell, the Collins Kids, and many other friends and peers of Jay. They raised $4,000 for his family. Toward the end of the show, Jay's idol, Ernest Tubb—the musician he'd always hoped to emulate—stepped up to the microphone. "In honor of a great man," he said, "I dedicate this song." He then played "Walking the Floor Over You." Carl, seated nearby, sobbed loudly as Tubb sang Jay's favorite song.

Carl was drunk at the benefit concert, as were several other members of the Perkins clan. "Me and my brother Clayton both became hopeless alcoholics," said Carl. "No question about it." But it would be several years before Carl faced up to his demons.

CHAPTER 8

I knew that I was just gonna get drunk

As 1958 turned into 1959, Carl was deep in a very dry commercial spell—his increased royalty rate of 5 percent didn't matter a great deal because his records weren't selling. He could do little more than look on in frustration as his former Sun peers prospered. Johnny Cash, now also with Columbia, finally got to record his gospel album, titled *Hymns by Johnny Cash*, with Don Law producing. At around the same time, Cash recorded another Country number 1, 1959's "Don't Take Your Guns to Town," proof that at least one former Sun alumni was prospering at Columbia Records. Roy Orbison, meanwhile, was in transit from Sun to RCA Victor and finally to Monument Records, a label based in Washington, DC, hardly the center of the musical universe. Yet this was where he'd record his best work, including the epic, aching "Only the Lonely." But before then, a song Orbison had written as an ode to his wife, "Claudette," was the B-side of one of the Everly Brothers' biggest chart songs, 1958's "All I Have to Do Is Dream." Like many of his Sun colleagues, Orbison bought a Cadillac with the proceeds.

The wild child Jerry Lee Lewis, who remained with Sam Phillips and Sun, was still riding high on the global success of "Whole Lotta Shakin' Goin' On" and "Great Balls of Fire," although his third marriage, in December 1957 to Myra Gale Brown, his thirteen-year-old first cousin once removed, was about to upend both his career and his life. As for Elvis Presley, Sun's biggest son, his latest movie, 1958's *King Creole*—plugged as "a story pulsing with the heartbeat of today's youth!"—may well have been his best work on the big screen, although by March of that year he was swapping his black drainpipes and sideburns for the khaki and short back and sides of the US Army. He underwent basic training at Fort Hood in Texas before shipping out to West Germany. But his ever-savvy manager Colonel Tom Parker ensured there would be a steady flow of Elvis releases during his absence, among them the hits "One Night" and "A Fool Such as I." It was as though the King never left the country.

Carl, however, spent much of his time bouncing between home in Jackson and the studio in Memphis, mourning the loss of his brother and boozing too much. He was now drinking when home, something he had not done before Jay's death. Carl found a secluded spot near his house in Jackson, where he'd park, sit, and drink. "I knew when I went that I was just gonna get drunk," Carl told a *Rolling Stone* writer. He'd usually have a "fifth"—a fifth of a gallon—stashed somewhere in his Cadillac, which he'd work his way through over the course of a few hours. Valda eventually found out where Carl was hiding out, and when it got dark, she'd send someone to track him down. "They'd get me and bring me home. It was a terrible time."

Carl was struggling to find just one song that might return him to the airwaves and the charts. He'd often share the rides from Memphis to Jackson with guitarist Edd Cisco, who had taken Jay's place in the band, and bemoan his situation with Columbia. "It ain't right, Ed, it ain't right," Carl would tell him after another unsatisfying recording session. The magic was gone.

Carl endured three more sessions with Don Law in 1958, and the material he recorded grew increasingly bizarre, especially for such a gifted songwriter and a truly original voice. At one of these sessions, in what must have been a particularly bitter pill to swallow—or simply a moment of sheer desperation—Carl agreed to record Jerry Lee Lewis's "Whole Lotta Shakin' Goin' On," along with his own takes on "That's All Right," "Shake, Rattle and Roll," "Tutti Frutti," and "Long Tall Sally," songs that were already closely identified with Elvis, Bill Haley, and Little Richard. His vocal ad-libbing at the end of "Whole Lotta Shakin'" sounded more like a cry for help than some kind of rock and roll celebration.

These tracks were compiled on Carl's first LP for Columbia, November 1958's *Whole Lotta Shakin'*, which featured nothing but covers of rock and roll standards, along with a sloppy production mistake on the front cover that gave the impression that Carl played guitar left-handed. If Carl was looking for a sign that he'd made a mistake changing labels, there it was. *They didn't even know how he played the guitar.*

Curiously, one original from those 1958 sessions was a sharp-edged rockabilly ramble called "Because You're Mine," featuring fine picking from Carl and some smart honky-tonk piano from Marvin Hughes, but it sat in the Columbia vaults and was never released. Another song left in the vaults was 1959's "The Drifter," Carl's more than passable attempt at a wide-screen Western story-song, a style taken all the way to the bank that year by Marty Robbins with his huge hit "El Paso."

Over time, Carl recorded more covers than originals for Columbia—in a stretch between June 1958 and March 1959 he cut just two of his own songs. "I'd always have my songs ready," said Carl, "but [Law] seemed like he always had three or four he wanted me to do." Most of the songs Law presented to Carl were the work of successful country songwriters. While it may have been the established system in Nashville, this way of working wasn't right for Carl. And there were always covers. During his third 1958 session with Law, Carl cut Ray Charles's "I Got a Woman" and Hank Williams's "Hey, Good Lookin'," as well as "Ready Teddy," a hit two years prior for the Georgia screamer Little Richard, who'd recently undergone a religious conversion while traveling in an Australian country town. (Rising from his seat on a train, Richard threw all his expensive jewelry out the window and declared that he was now a man of God. Soon enough he'd enroll in a Seventh Day Adventist church to study theology.)

The single released from Carl's third session for Columbia was called "Levi Jacket (and a Long Tail Shirt)," which came on more like a jingle for clothing than the latest from one of rock's finest. It didn't chart; in fact, only two tracks from the dozens Carl recorded during this frustrating period of his career came anywhere near a chart: 1958's "Pink Pedal Pushers," which made the Country Top 20 and number 91 on the *Billboard* Hot 100, and 1959's "Pointed Toe Shoes," which made it all the way to number 93 on the Hot 100 and then dropped away just as quickly.

"There was a lot of excitement there for a while," Carl said about recording for Columbia, "but it didn't have what the public wanted."

Elvis may have found fame on the big screen with *King Creole*, drawing large audiences right across the Western world, but Carl only managed to find work on B movies such as *Jamboree*. The next film in which Carl appeared, named *Hawaiian Boy*, was so obscure that not a single print remains in circulation today. It hit cinemas in late August 1959 and just as quickly disappeared. Although the film was set in and around Manila, and shot mostly in Hawaii, Carl filmed his parts in Los Angeles, appearing alongside a predominantly Filipino cast that included nineteen-year-old actor and singer Eddie Mesa—known as the "rock and roll king of the Philippines"—as well as Mesa's wife, Rosemarie Gil. Fernando Poe, Jr. and Augusto Valdes Pangan (aka Chiquito), who later in life would have some success in Filipino politics, also appeared. African American gospel singer Roy Hamilton made a cameo as himself. The movie was directed by Cirio H. Santiago, Mesa's manager, who'd enjoy a five-decade-long career in film, yet strangely *Hawaiian Boy* never rated a mention in his lengthy filmography.

The film promised plenty—"A New High! In Entertainment! In Excitement! That once in a lifetime motion picture you'll fall in love with and remember for a long time to come . . ." screamed its theatrical poster—but delivered very little. Carl's role—he was billed as "the sensation that is Carl Perkins"—basically required him trying his best not to appear too uncomfortable while performing a few songs, including "That's All Right," and, yet again, Jerry Lee Lewis's "Whole Lotta Shakin' Goin' On'." To this day, the movie remains so obscure that there is some debate as to whether Carl sang "Blue

Suede Shoes" at some point. Carl insisted that he never saw *Hawaiian Boy*. Who could blame him?

Things grew so difficult for Carl as the end of the decade neared that he could no longer afford to employ his drummer W. S. "Fluke" Holland, who'd been with him since their first session at Sun. Holland considered leaving the music business altogether but found a new home in Johnny Cash's live band—and would remain there for an astonishing forty-four years, until Cash's death in 2003.

Cash always seemed to be able to provide a lifeline for Carl and those around him. He recorded Carl's song about the 1881 gunfight at the OK Corral, "The Ballad of Boot Hill," for his 1959 Columbia EP *The Rebel—Johnny Yuma*. And "Boot Hill" would resurface on no less than ten subsequent Cash studio albums and collections, providing Carl with a handy trickle of royalties.

Back in the tonks, Carl replaced Holland with drummer Tony Moore, while Edd Cisco stayed on guitar. Meanwhile in the studio, Don Law tried surrounding Carl with members of what was known as Nashville's "A-Team," among them pianist Floyd Cramer, harmonica player Charlie McCoy, pianist Hargus "Pig" Robbins, and saxophonist Boots Randolph. They were all fine players, the best to be found in Music City, but as Carl gradually came to understand, "they wasn't rockers." Carl also soon realized that if he was to cut another "Blue Suede Shoes," Nashville was the wrong place. "I shouldn't have found a reason big enough to take me away from Sun Studio in Memphis," he admitted. "That's the environment I should have stayed in." Carl would come to realize that "the early days at Sun were the greatest recording sessions that I've known. It was so much different to . . . Nashville."

There was still no "little roar" to be heard on his Columbia recordings, which really hit the skids in June 1962, when Carl recorded Otis Blackwell's "Sister Twister." It resembled nothing more than a desperate attempt to hitch a ride on the twist bandwagon, made famous by Chubby Checker. In a *Vintage Rock* article, writer Douglas McPherson said that "Sister Twister" was "so unsuited to the twist craze that it's hard to believe Perkins had heard of Chubby Checker." It didn't chart.

Carl was becoming so disenchanted with music that he sold his classic EchoSonic amp, which he'd bought from the amp's maker, Ray Butts, while driving through Cairo, Illinois, in 1957 with Roy Orbison. The amp had a lot of history, but when Carl got a call from a Cadillac dealer in Arkansas, offering him $1,000—roughly double what he'd paid for it—he didn't think twice. Carl didn't even bother to learn the purchaser's name; he simply accepted his money and waved him goodbye.

"My 'Blue Suede Shoes' money was gone," Carl explained, "I was drinkin' an awful lot and that $1,000 looked really good to me. I was kind of down."

Carl's stocks in America were at an all-time low, but he didn't know that he'd developed a devoted fan base offshore, especially in the UK. In May 1960, a fledgling British band by the name of the Silver Beetles was setting out on a run of dates outside of their hometown of Liverpool, opening for an act by the name of Johnny Gentle, performing at such glamorous venues as Dalrymple Hall in Fraserburgh and the Rescue Hall in Peterhead. Among the group's members was a seventeen-year-old guitarist named George with a wild dark quiff of hair—"like a fucking turban," according to his bandmate Paul McCartney—whose admiration for a certain American and his music was so strong that he was currently using the stage name Carl Harrison. The first record that fellow Silver Beetle John Lennon bought with his own money, when he was sixteen, was "Blue Suede Shoes."

How any of the Silver Beetles—whose other members were Stuart Sutcliffe, and a drummer named Tommy Moore—came to hear Carl's music was a complicated process. It wasn't as though his less-than-stellar recordings with Columbia were on high rotation at the BBC.

Back home in Liverpool, McCartney, Lennon, and "Carl," eager to hear more of Carl's recordings beyond "Blue Suede Shoes," were told about a local sailor who traveled between Liverpool and the United States and sometimes returned home with hard-to-find vinyl records. They tracked him down and asked to borrow some of his collection, which included music of Carl's. They'd then play the records on a stereo—not at the proper speed of 45 rpm, mind you, but at 33 rpm, in order to decipher what Carl was singing, which they'd then transcribe.

But this wasn't just an exercise in fan worship; the three budding musicians were also building their live repertoire. Their strategy was clever and original—rather than simply try to learn the more popular A-sides, they'd flip the records over and tune in to the B-side of each release. That way they were guaranteed to learn new material, unfamiliar to local audiences. The savvy Liverpudlians didn't simply want to recycle what was already out there. This was how the Beatles, as they'd soon be known, came to master such relative Carl obscurities as "Honey, Don't," "Matchbox," and "Everybody's Trying to Be My Baby."

George was particularly fond of Carl's 1957 release, "Your True Love," which the band had introduced to their live sets by the time they played their first shows in Hamburg, Germany, in August 1960. They also covered "Honey, Don't" and "Blue Suede Shoes," as well as material from Gene Vincent, Chuck Berry, and Ray Charles. But Carl's music seemed to register most strongly with the band. John Lennon would wax lyrical about Carl's *Dance Album*, rating it one of the few LPs of which he "really enjoyed every track." "I had only three childhood idols," Lennon told a friend. "Elvis, Carl Perkins, and Jerry Lee [Lewis]." Paul McCartney would go one step further: "If there were no Carl Perkins," he'd state, "there would be no Beatles."

As Carl would discover in due course, "They knew all about me and idolized my songs." In time, The Beatles would also help resurrect his career.

Carl in 1956 at the time of his
breakthrough hit, "Blue Suede Shoes."
Pictorial Press/Alamy Stock Photo.

(center) with his brothers
on (left) and Jay (right) and
mer "Fluke" Holland, 1956.
rial Press/Alamy Stock Photo.

Carl with his friend and Sun Records peer Elvis Presley, Memphis, June 1956.
© *Robert Williams/The Commercial Appeal/ZUMApress.com/Alamy Stock Photo.*

Carl with his first Cadillac and Sun Records founder Sam Phillips, Memphis, 1956.
Pictorial Press/Alamy Stock Photo.

Carl with Johnny Cash and June Carter in the UK, 1964.
© 2024 Brian Smith/Courtesy Easy on the Eye Books.

Carl onstage with the Nashville Teens at the BBC, London, October 1964.
© 2024 Brian Smith/Courtesy Easy on the Eye Books.

Carl playing as part of *The Johnny Cash* Show, early 1970s.
© *J. T. Phillips/ Globe Photos/ ZUMAPRESS.com.*

Carl with (left to right) Roy Orbison, Johnny Cash, and Jerry Lee Lewis, November 1970. *CBS Television/ Wikimedia Commons.*

Carl performing with his son Greg on bass, 1982. © *2024 Linda Matlow/PIXINTL.*

Onstage with Dave Alvin from the Blasters, with Carl's sons Greg on bass and Stan on drums, Chicago, 1981. © *2024 Linda Matlow/PIXINTL.*

The C.P. Express on the roof of the Circus Circus Hotel, Las Vegas, 1989.
© 2024 Dwight Haldeman.

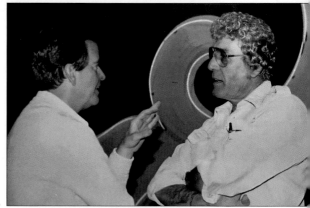

Chatting with
Dick Clark
Academy of C
Music A
April
© 2024 Dwight Hala

Carl with Jeff Goldblum
on the set of the film
Into the Night, 1985.
© Universal Pictures/
Courtesy Everett Collec
Alamy Stock Photo.

...the set of *Blue Suede Shoes: ...abilly Session*, London, ...1985, with (left to right) ...dmunds, George Harrison, ...pton, Rosanne Cash, ...tarr, and Slim Jim Phantom. *...Mirror/Mirrorpix/ ...tock Photo.*

With (left to right) Mark Knopfler,
Eric Clapton, and Paul McCartney
at Carl's final show,
Music for Montserrat,
London, September 1997.
*Rebecca Naden/PA Images/
Alamy Stock Photo.*

Carl in Arles, France, June 1989.
© 2024 Dwight Haldeman.

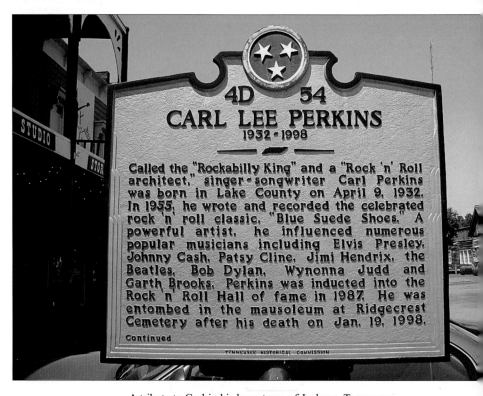

A tribute to Carl in his hometown of Jackson, Tennessee.
Thomas R. Machnitzki/Wikimedia Commons; https://creativecommons.org/licenses/by/3.0/deed.

Another tribute to Carl, in Walnut Ridge, Arkansas.
Thomas R. Machnitzki/Wikimedia Commons; https://creativecommons.org/licenses/by/3.0/deed

CHAPTER 9

I thought they looked like girls,
but I liked their records straight away

Throughout the early part of the new decade, Carl did what he could to provide for Valda and their three children—they'd welcomed another boy, Gregory Jay, who was born on January 15, 1959—but creatively he wasn't so much treading water as drowning.

Carl resorted to playing such out-of-the-way spots as the Saddle Club in Chickasha, Rosa's Western Club in Fort Worth, the Southern Club in Lawton, Oklahoma ("the home of the stars," according to a newspaper ad), or the New Red Barn in Ulm, Montana. He seemed destined to be billed as "Mr. Blue Suede Shoes" for the rest of his career. Or "Mr. Blue Swade Shows," as a flyer proclaimed for a gig at the Lake View Inn at Almonesson, New Jersey, in October 1961. Or perhaps even "Carl Perkins and His Blue Suede Boys" as they were billed at Club Zanza in Hayti, Missouri. "He rocked the world with 'Blue Suede Shoes,'" announced the *Great Falls Leader,* while a poster for his concert at the Southern Club reminded ticket buyers that Carl ("and his sensational dance band") was "famous for his 'Blue Suede Shoes.'" No other song was mentioned.

When Carl played the KRNT Theater in Des Moines during March 1961, he was a glorified opening act, appearing onstage before country singers George Morgan and Hawkshaw Hawkins and headliner Ferlin Husky, best known for the hit spiritual "Wings of a Dove." Promotion for a September 1962 gig at the Country Junction Night Club, just south of Jackson, put more emphasis on the venue's

"Hot Bar-B-Q & Cold Beer," than on Carl's upcoming show. When Carl played Kansas City's Chestnut Inn during Christmas 1960, the "Dancing Girls Floor Show" got higher billing. Politician Carl D. Perkins, the long-serving Democrat from Kentucky, was currently receiving far more press coverage than the other Carl Perkins.

Ticket prices for Carl's solo concerts were rarely more than a dollar.

Carl could take some solace, in his darker moments, that his peers from the previous decade were also struggling. Elvis, after his return from service in Germany, had hit the Hollywood treadmill, and was now pumping out mediocre rom-coms such as 1961's *Blue Hawaii*—described as "not so much a film as a musical travelogue"—with increasingly mediocre soundtracks to match. His place as pop pinup number one had been taken by Ricky Nelson, who'd been inspired to take up music upon hearing "Blue Suede Shoes." He'd recorded Carl's "Boppin' the Blues" in 1957 and was a die-hard fan.

Jerry Lee Lewis, meanwhile, was still in exile, blacklisted after the revelations about his child bride. Over at Columbia, Johnny Cash made regular appearances on the Country singles chart, but hadn't breached the upper reaches of the *Billboard* Hot 100 since 1958's "Don't Take Your Guns to Town." Arguably his best record of the period was 1961's *Now Here's Johnny Cash*, with which Johnny had not been involved. It was another of Sam Phillips's Sun-era compilations.

In between his final Columbia sessions—there were two in 1962, in March and late June—the now thirty-year-old Carl held down a residency in Las Vegas. In 1962 he played a series of four monthlong residencies at the Golden Nugget, one of the city's earliest casinos, established in 1946 when vice cop Guy McAfee—who'd become the Nugget's first president—raised $1 million in seed money from thirty of his friends. (Parts of Elvis Presley's 1964 film, *Viva Las Vegas*, would be shot at the Golden Nugget.) Carl's first residency ran from mid-February to mid-March, the second from May to June, then August to September and November through to mid-December. Typically, he'd play several forty-five-minute shows daily; over time, he'd also work in Tahoe, Reno, and Carson City.

The work was reliable and the money handy, even though Carl wasn't always the main attraction—in August 1961 he was bottom of the Golden Nugget bill to country singer and former Miss Idaho, Judy Lynn.

During Carl's pre-Christmas run of dates, he spent time with country singer (and sometimes yodeler) Patsy Cline, who was making her Vegas debut at the Merri-Mint Theater in the Mint casino, which was just across the strip from the Golden Nugget. Carl had spent time on the road with Patsy in January 1962 as part of a Country Spectacular package tour, which also included Johnny Cash, George Jones, and one of Carl's boyhood musical heroes, Bill Monroe. Carl liked Cline; she was a straight shooter, a forthright and opinionated Virginian who, in Carl's words, "would be accepted on her terms or none at all." She'd recorded a song that Carl sketched out while on the road with her in 1962, and had then handed over to Mel Tillis and Danny Dill to finish in Nashville. It was a lush, heavyhearted ballad called "So Wrong," which made it to number 14 on the *Billboard* Hot Country Songs chart in July. Johnny Cash wasn't the only one recording Carl's songs.

Carl and Patsy, who were the same age, learned that they had plenty in common—much more than their mutual habit of throwing the slang word "hoss" into seemingly every other sentence. (She called Carl simply "Perkins.") In Vegas, after their sets, they'd compare honky-tonk war stories, as she'd also found her voice playing for the "tush hogs" before hitting paydirt with her breakthrough 1957 single, "Walkin' After Midnight" and becoming, in the words of *Rolling Stone* magazine, an artist "that expanded the boundaries of country music." Just like Carl, Cline hadn't made it past the eighth grade before setting out on her musical journey. A road accident likewise briefly curtailed Cline's career. In June 1961 she spent a month in the hospital having broken her wrist, dislocated her hip, and suffered terrible lacerations when her vehicle was struck by another car and two passengers died. In 1961, while still on crutches, Cline recorded what would become her signature song, "Crazy," the work of an up-and-coming songwriter named Willie Nelson.

Carl may have been playing many out-of-the-way venues, but

1962 was one of his busiest years—it wasn't often that his neighbors spotted his Cadillac in the driveway of the family home in Jackson. He traveled to the Continent for the first time, undertaking a series of nine shows in October at the European American Base in Berlin, Germany, playing for troops stationed there. All in all, he played about 150 gigs that year. His recording career was stuck in neutral—he'd finally be cut loose by Columbia in July 1963—but the demand for Carl as a live act was strong.

Carl's Vegas residencies continued into 1963; he pretty much set up shop there for the first six weeks of the year. But in early March he got the shocking news that Patsy Cline had been killed in a plane crash, along with two other performers, Hawkshaw Hawkins—who'd shared some bills with Carl—and Cowboy Copas, as well as Cline's manager, Randy Hughes, who was at the controls of the aircraft. Carl was devastated. He had performed two very unlikely songs during his Vegas residency: "The Lord's Fishing Hole" and "When You're Twenty-One," both spirituals, both his own compositions, on the urging of Cline, and had smiled with her for a photographer, posing with her mother, Hilda.

Carl was so distraught that he drove his car to the crash site in Camden, Tennessee, where he was granted access because of his state government license plates (he was friends with the governor, Frank Clement). But Carl would come to regret his decision to view the wreckage. It was a gruesome scene; body parts and shreds of clothing were scattered all around. Carl would suffer nightmares in which he'd relive memories of what he saw. "It wasn't something I'd rush to see again," he said.

Carl was now a free agent, no longer with Columbia after his frustrating relationship with the label. He'd recorded more than forty songs over four years and ten sessions with Don Law, utilizing a wide variety of players and styles, and he hadn't come anywhere near producing a hit—or even a song that would be considered a Carl Perkins classic. In August 1963 he agreed to a two-year deal with Decca Records, again working out of Nashville. Proving what a little village Music City could sometimes be, Carl would now be recording with Owen Bradley, in whose Quonset Hut Studio he'd worked while he was with Columbia. He'd also play with some of the musicians who'd helped on his Columbia recordings.

Bradley, who'd once been the music director at Nashville's WSM, had played a key role in developing what became known as the "Nashville sound." It was a smoother, more polished take on country music, best heard in the recordings of Kitty Wells and Carl's dear departed friend Patsy Cline. But again, it wouldn't be a natural fit for Carl.

As for Decca, its UK parent label was in the process of gaining unwanted notoriety for rejecting Carl's biggest British admirers, the Beatles. When the band auditioned for Decca in 1962, they were informed that "guitar groups are on the way out" and duly went on to make musical history with Parlophone. They'd just exploded into the UK charts—reaching "the toppermost of the poppermost," as the Fab Four would joke—with "Please Please Me." In America, Decca was better known in recent years for pumping out a series of successful film soundtracks, including *Around the World in Eighty Days*, *The Sweet Smell of Success*, and the Rogers and Hammerstein musical *Flower Drum Song*. It was thoroughly mainstream, wholesome entertainment, nothing more.

Carl knew he was drinking too much to make good decisions but didn't have the willpower to stop. When he began recording with Decca in mid-August 1963, he allowed producer Bradley to choose the arrangements and the players; essentially Carl showed up and did as instructed. "It wasn't a happy period," he'd confess, although he made it clear that he had no problems with Bradley—"Mr. Bradley" to the always-polite Carl. His first single for the label, an original called "After Sundown," was a six-tissue tearjerker awash with Floyd Cramer's sparkling piano, the rich harmonies of the Jordanaires (heard on many of Elvis's hits) and enough pathos to convince a listener to drink every Nashville bar dry. It was an obvious crack at the "countrypolitan" sound that Bradley had taken to the bank with Patsy Cline's huge hits "Crazy," "Walkin' After Midnight," and "I Fall to Pieces," and wasn't a bad song by any stretch, but the smooth, slick production didn't suit Carl. Though it was most likely unintentional, when Carl sang, "I'm left alone with my blue memory," it was hard not to think of the song that made him famous back in 1956—and how far he'd strayed from that classic sound.

Carl recorded two other originals at the session, "For a Little While" and "Help Me Find My Baby." The best thing that could be said of the latter was that Carl's father loved it. When Carl played Buck the recording, he told him: "That's gonna be the best thing you ever recorded." (It wasn't.) During his first session, Carl also recorded a cover of "I Wouldn't Have You," a song written by Ramona Redd and Mitchell Torok, a former member of the Louisiana Hayride and the composer of "Mexican Joe," a big hit in 1953 for country crooner "Gentleman" Jim Reeves. Carl's Decca debut was released in February 1964 and promptly went nowhere on the charts. Another failure.

Yet again Carl was forced to look on while Johnny Cash all but owned the airwaves during 1963 with "Ring of Fire," which remained at number 1 on the *Billboard* Hot Country Songs chart for a remarkable seven weeks. One of the song's cowriters was June Carter, the woman whom Cash would eventually marry, in the process shattering the notion of fidelity that he'd sung about in "I Walk the Line" (a title that Carl had suggested to Cash). Yet despite Carl's many problems, his marriage with Valda remained rock solid.

Carl completed his latest run of Golden Nugget dates in October 1963. He'd only been in the studio once during the year, when he cut "After Sundown" and three other songs, and he had no immediate plans to record again. Carl was still boozing, and his records weren't selling; he was seriously considering some other kind of work. He thought about buying some land and starting a small farm. He'd also clashed badly with his brother Clayton.

In the wake of Jay's death, "just about all the time [Clayton] wanted to stay drunk," remembered Carl, which, given his own drinking, made them a volatile couple. One night in Las Vegas, after a few too many insults from Clayton during a card match, they'd slugged it out, throwing haymakers at each other in a car park at the rear of their motel. This brawl came to a hasty (and costly) conclusion when Clayton swung at Carl, who ducked, and he connected with a brick wall, fracturing his hand. Carl's road manager, Jimmy Martin, took over on bass while Clayton's paw healed.

Their bad blood spilled over again later in 1963. This time Carl and his band were playing a show in Cincinnati, Ohio, sharing the bill with Ray Price and Red Foley, whom Carl respected greatly. (He'd made his TV debut on *Ozark Jubilee* back in 1956, a program hosted by Foley.) They were in Carl's room after the show, and Clayton was drunk, sprawled on the bed, when Foley dropped by. Without provocation, Clayton leaped up and punched him, sending his false teeth flying. Carl reacted quickly and knocked Clayton out with a single blow. Foley wasn't badly hurt, but he had some advice for Carl: "Send that boy home." Patsy Cline had also warned Carl about Clayton, telling him, "That boy is plain mean."

This was one fight too many for Carl. He was done. Carl loaded his brother into his car and drove all the way back to Jackson, a four-hundred-mile trip. Carl parked outside of his parents' house and ordered Clayton from the car, informing him that the days of the Perkins Brothers were well and truly over. "My own brother," Carl would one day recall, shaking his head in dismay.

Carl's fortunes soon changed, however, when he got a call from Bill Denny, the son of his music publisher, Jim. It was a call that would change the trajectory of Carl's life. He offered Carl a spot on a tour of England with Chuck Berry, a tour that would be promoted by Don Arden. Arden was notorious for—allegedly—having dangled a band manager from a hotel room window in order to seal a deal. He'd also pulled a gun during a heated business discussion and, when challenged, shrugged and said, "It's okay, it isn't loaded." Arden was a hard man, known to some as the "Al Capone of Pop," who in his previous guise as a singing hopeful had recorded a cover of "Blue Suede Shoes." (And whose legendary toughness would rub off on his daughter, Sharon Osbourne.)

Chuck Berry, like Carl, had also been doing time on the casino circuit, playing the Walled Lake Casino in Michigan. He'd also recently been doing time in jail, serving a total of twenty months for violating the Mann Act, having driven a fourteen-year-old girl across state lines for "immoral purposes." It was only because of a friendly parole officer that Berry was able to undertake the UK jaunt.

Carl had fond memories of Berry. In an interview, he recalled the first time they met, when they shared some dates around the time of "Blue Suede Shoes." He'd heard a voice calling from outside his dressing room door demanding: "I want to meet Carl Perkins." When Berry walked inside and came face-to-face with Carl, he was dumbstruck. He'd heard "Blue Suede Shoes" and was convinced that Carl was black (as had Fats "Blueberry Hill" Domino). "I thought you were one of us," Berry admitted. "Well, brother, I am," Carl replied. "It's just music that knows no barriers."

In promotional material for the UK tour, Carl was described as "the original recorder of the great rock standard 'Blue Suede Shoes' . . . Many people have awaited this artist's tour for many years." The first date was set for May 9 at the Finsbury Park Astoria in London. Berry would top the bill, preceded by Carl and such local groups as the Animals and the Swinging Blue Jeans. Tickets for the opening show were fifteen shillings (roughly US $24 today). The tour would wind its way through Birmingham, Nottingham, Sheffield, Liverpool, and other major centers, before closing at the end of May with two shows back in London at the Hammersmith Odeon. Carl, fortunately, had grown accustomed in Vegas to playing multiple dates on the same day, because this tour would cover plenty of miles and include more than forty shows. It was a heavy workload.

Carl feared that UK audiences would have no clue who he was. Carl's greatest supporter, however, had a very different opinion. "They're bound to love you," Valda assured Carl, and yet again she was right. For several years, the Beatles had been performing several of Carl's songs in concert—John Lennon originally sang "Honey, Don't" before it was agreed to "give" it to Ringo Starr (although a Lennon-sung version would one day emerge on *The Lost Lennon*

Tapes), while George Harrison regularly performed "Everybody's Trying to Be My Baby" and took inspiration from Carl's guitar playing. The Beatles had also recorded two versions of Carl's "Glad All Over" during a session in 1963, and during various live sets on the BBC had also played "Sure to Fall" and "Matchbox." They'd been performing his "Lend Me Your Comb" since their days (and nights) in Hamburg—Paul McCartney would one day tell Carl that they thought the lyric of "Comb" was "far out." The band had plans to record some of Carl's songs in upcoming sessions with their producer, George Martin. The Beatles also loved Chuck Berry, covering nine of his numbers in their various BBC sessions.

Carl didn't know a lot about this new group from Liverpool, although his son Stan was a convert and had played him their first US release on Capitol Records, *Meet the Beatles*. (A number 1 hit in the States not long before Carl left for the UK.) "I thought they looked like girls," Carl chuckled, "but I liked their records straight away." Carl also recognized a little of his own style in guitarist George Harrison.

And they did have some shared experiences: Carl's musical education in the honky-tonks bore more than a passing resemblance to the rowdy apprenticeship that the Beatles had served on Hamburg's Reeperbahn just a few years earlier. Violence and alcohol ruled the bars of Hamburg, just as they did the tonks of Mississippi. These were the type of places where music occasionally broke out between the sounds of glasses being smashed, voices raised, and furniture upturned. And both the performances of Carl and the Beatles were powered by booze, although the Liverpudlians also survived their hard days' nights with a little help from amphetamines.

Carl wrote to the Beatles before leaving America, opening his letter with a casual, *Hey fellows*. He thanked them for their support of his work and congratulated them on the band's global success. He also enclosed some songs that he hoped they might want to record. *I'll be in your wonderful country in May*, Carl concluded. *Here's hoping I'll get to meet you all in person*. He signed it, *Your friend, Carl Perkins*.

CHAPTER 10

I hadn't seen audiences like that in America for years—I'd almost given up

When Carl arrived in London, his touring partner Chuck Berry was riding high in the UK charts with "No Particular Place to Go," and his former Sun labelmate Roy Orbison was also charting strongly with "It's Over." Carl's name was nowhere to be seen on the Top 40. But apparently, he hadn't been forgotten—he was greeted by the sight of a sign that read: WELCOME CARL "BEATLES CRUSHER" PERKINS. The meaning wasn't completely clear—what was a "Beatles crusher"?—but it felt supportive. Anything that linked his name with the Beatles had to be a good thing. Maybe Valda had been right, after all.

Soon after settling in, Carl sat down for an interview with the *Evening Standard*'s Maureen Cleave, a Beatles insider (who'd pen the unintentionally notorious article that implied that the Beatles were more popular than Jesus). She described Carl as "a calm and kindly man," a farmer's boy, a father of four whose loving wife "knew I was good for nothing but music."

"I worked in the fields with colored people singing and passing the time of day," Carl said when asked about his roots. "Music was a part of my life." He showed Cleave the calluses on his fingers.

When asked by Cleave to explain the mystery that was rock and roll, Carl replied: "Rock 'n' roll is something that causes you to pat your feet and at the same time you are speaking with your mouth. You can't hardly keep still." Cleave was impressed with what she called Carl's "excellent definition." "Long after we'd forgotten Carl Perkins in this country," Cleave wrote, "the Beatles were buying his records and singing his songs." And right now, there could be no better boost for a flagging career like Carl's than to have the Beatles name-checking him.

It certainly didn't hurt that just weeks before Carl's arrival, the band's "Can't Buy Me Love" had been the number 1 song in the UK (one of their three chart-toppers for the year). Just to prove how devoted they were to Carl's music, all four Beatles would agree to become honorary members of the British Carl Perkins Fan Club, which was the handiwork of two Perkins devotees from Manchester, Brian Smith and Dave Waggett. They'd pitched the fan club idea to Carl during the tour, and he readily agreed. "He was wonderful," Smith said when asked about Carl, "such a nice bloke." The first fifty fan club members received a welcome surprise—a matchbox that had been autographed by Carl. Waggett and Smith drove from gig to gig in an old, borrowed Ford with a handwritten cardboard sign stuck in the window: CARL PERKINS FAN CLUB—ON TOUR.

Carl had toured with Chuck Berry before but found him to be a very different person in 1964. It was clear that Berry's stint in jail had left deep scars. "Never saw a man so changed," Carl said. In the past, Carl had found Berry easygoing, always ready to pick up his guitar in the dressing room and jam, or share a joke, but that had all changed. Carl found Berry "cold, real distant and bitter"; tellingly, his lawyer was now part of his entourage. As it turned out later in the tour, Berry's self-imposed isolation would prove to be a huge boon for Carl.

The writer Norman Jopling covered the first London show for the *Record Mirror*. He described the atmosphere of the evening as "tense and dramatic." And expectations were high, for Berry and Carl, who were both making their UK debuts. Carl was set to take the stage after sets from the Nashville Teens—managed by Don Arden—and a female duo known as the Other Two (also signed to Decca). "They went down well," wrote Jopling, "but the audience was already shouting for Carl Perkins." Cries of "We want the king of rock" could be heard even before he took to the stage, with the Nashville Teens as his backing band. Carl proceeded to play a set that juggled crowd favorites—"Matchbox," "Let the Jukebox Keep On Playing," and, naturally, "Blue Suede Shoes"—with some unexpected numbers, such as "Mean Woman Blues," which Elvis had recorded for his 1957 film, *Loving You.* "His voice was rather country-tinged," noted Jopling, "owing to the years he has spent singing C&W." The night was a success, judged Jopling, "and if the rest of the shows are as good as this one, then British audiences are in for a wow."

The early dates were so well received—"they were dancing in the aisles," reported Carl—that he was booked for two appearances, on ITV's *Ready, Steady, Go!,* where he shared the bill with Little Richard and the Animals, and the BBC Radio's *Saturday Club.* A planned Granada TV special with Berry, however, didn't happen, although a surprise late-night show at Manchester's Twisted Wheel Club on June 6—for members only—provided hard-core fans with bragging rights for years. Squeezed onto a tiny stage with the Nashville Teens, Carl blazed.

"[It was] probably the nearest we would ever get to a Tennessee juke joint and the days of the Perkins Brothers Band," wrote Brian Smith. "He gave us the lot [including] some of the longest and most blistering guitar solos I ever heard him play."

During another concert, devotees unfurled a banner that read: CARL PERKINS—KING OF ROCK, while some fans, eager to get close to their hero, invaded the stage. One London show was cut short when "a handful of delinquent imbeciles," as a reporter from *Blues Unlimited* magazine noted, broke through the barriers and forced Chuck Berry to retreat backstage as he tried to close the concert. Every night, Carl said from the stage, "You don't know just how happy you've made this ol' country boy feel"—and he meant every word. "I hadn't seen audiences like that in America for years," Carl pointed out. "I'd almost given up."

Even a brief dispute over money didn't disrupt the upbeat nature of the tour. Carl and the other members of the tour killed time in a local pub, Carl loudly cracking jokes about how the families of his fellow musicians were "close to starvation," until the required funds were finally delivered by a driver. "Gentlemen, I believe we have a show to do," said Chuck Berry, who'd instigated the "strike," and with that, the troupe headed to the next venue.

When the ensemble reached Bolton, prior to the show at the Odeon Theatre, Carl and the Animals' Alan Price settled in around a piano and played country songs for almost an hour. Carl's fan club president, Brian Smith, who was looking on, said it was "one memorable afternoon." Carl's rail trip to Manchester was, bizarrely, only the second time he'd ever traveled on a train.

Decca, Carl's record label, capitalized on the feverish response to the tour and booked him into their West Hampstead studio on May 22 to record some material. It even rated a mention in the music press, with the announcement, "Carl Perkins to Record Here." He was backed by the Nashville Teens, while Mike Smith was at the desk—he was the man who'd produced the Beatles session that Decca rejected. (Smith redeemed himself, to some degree, by producing Brian Poole and the Tremeloes' "Do You Love Me," a number 1 hit in 1963.) Teaming Carl with some hungry young rockers, rather than slick Music City musicians, turned out to be a masterstroke; it was his best session in years. "Those boys knew the music better than the Nashville people did," Carl would tell writer Colin Escott. "There's no question about it."

Together, Carl and the Teens cut six of his songs, including a revved-up remake of "Blue Suede Shoes"—"let's rock again, cats, let's go now!" yelled Carl, sounding like a man about to explode— and another take on his 1957 single "Your True Love." They also recorded an aching-hearted ballad, "A Love I'll Never Win," where Carl laid bare his soul, singing, "I'm waiting for a love I'll never win / It's like waiting for a ship that don't come in." Strangely, the song was never released during Carl's time with Decca. (The Nashville Teens was a band in demand; they also worked with Jerry Lee Lewis in 1964, cutting *Live at the Star Club, Hamburg*, which would be recognized as one of the great in-concert albums. "[It's not] an album, it's a crime scene," gasped *Rolling Stone*'s Milo Miles. "Jerry Lee Lewis slaughters his rivals.")

Carl had the Beatles in mind with one new track from the

session, "Big Bad Blues," and he was hoping they might record it, as he admitted to a reporter during the tour. But the hot-blooded song, which featured great riffing and soloing from Carl, was earmarked as his next single, on Decca's UK imprint Brunswick Records. Carl, meanwhile, performed another new song called "Lonely Heart" on Granada TV's *Scene at 6:30*, surrounded by regulars from a nearby club, who'd been invited to the shoot and clapped along enthusiastically.

Carl played his final UK date at the Hammersmith Odeon at the end of May, and during the show, police raced to the venue, after a report of gunfire. They feared he'd been shot. But rather than find a wounded rocker, they discovered a broken window—"and a very much alive Carl Perkins," as a report in the *Shepherds Bush Gazette* pointed out. "It looks like someone was playing a joke," said a policeman on the scene.

With his obligations fulfilled, Carl was preparing to catch a flight back to the United States but was asked to stay for just a little longer. There was a party, he was told, that he really should attend. "Man, I'm a little too tired for that," Carl replied. After being told he *really* should go, Carl said, "Okay, I'll go to the party, but I can't stay long. My plane leaves at nine in the morning."

On the Sunday night, May 31, the Beatles were playing a show at the Prince of Wales Theatre in London, as part of the *Pops Alive!* series of concerts organized by their manager, Brian Epstein. Post-show, they'd arranged for a reception at which their guests of honor would be their American visitors, Carl Perkins and Chuck Berry. But soon after Carl arrived, he learned that Berry was a no-show. As he'd tell a reporter in 1997, "I can never thank Chuck enough. So, I had all four of them cats asking me questions about my music. I made really good friends with those guys."

The "four cats" Carl referred to were, of course, the Beatles, who finally got to meet one of their biggest musical heroes. In one version of the story, Carl said that upon entering the room, Ringo Starr stood up on a chair and told the gathering, "Ladies and gentlemen—he's here!" In a slightly different telling of the story of his first meeting the Beatles, Carl said that it was George Harrison who broke the ice. He walked over to Carl and asked what the correct key was for "Honey, Don't."

"It's in the key of E," Carl replied.

Harrison turned and addressed his fellow Beatles. "I told you we weren't doing it right!" They'd been playing it in G.

Talk then turned to "Blue Suede Shoes." Harrison asked Carl why he didn't play it like he'd written it—Carl's live take was now closer to Elvis Presley's version, as far as he could tell. Carl was confused; he genuinely thought he was playing it as he'd written it, but Harrison was adamant. "No, you're not." On Carl's original, there was a distinct pause after the opening "one for the money," whereas Elvis had powered on without stopping for a breath. Harrison seemed genuinely upset; he couldn't understand why Carl would change the way he played his own song. (Years later, Carl had a similar situation while playing "Blue Suede Shoes" with rootsy English rocker Dave Edmunds, another big admirer. They stopped mid-song and Perkins asked, "Ain't you gonna play, boy?" and Edmunds replied, "Not until we play it the way *you* played it.")

During the party, Carl chatted quietly with Ringo Starr, who addressed him as "Mr. Perkins." Carl grinned at the drummer. "Mr. Perkins?" he laughed, before informing Ringo that he had it wrong; that was his father's name. He insisted that Ringo call him Carl. Just Carl.

The high point of Carl's visit came during the following day, June 1. He was collected in the afternoon by Brian Smith and driven to Abbey Road Studios. There, at the Beatles' invitation, Carl looked on as they recorded his track "Matchbox." It was another of the songs they had learned from the B-sides of Carl's Sun singles (and had most recently played live at London's Paris Theatre a few weeks earlier). It didn't matter that vocalist Ringo, who was keeping the beat on his newly acquired Ludwig drum kit, had a sore throat—Carl loved what he heard. (Two days later, Starr was in hospital with tonsilitis.) When various Beatles asked Carl to give his opinion, he replied: "Why, that son of a bitch sounds like that old Sun record!"

It took the group five takes to nail "Matchbox," George playing his solo on a shiny new Gretsch guitar, a gift from Chet Atkins. "I played one of those a little bit," Carl said admiringly, as Harrison unveiled his new six string. Although it was never officially confirmed, Carl may have played the opening guitar riff on the version of "Matchbox" that found a home on the Beatles' *Long Tall Sally* EP in the UK and on the US-only album *Something New*, which was released in July. "Matchbox" reached number 17 on the *Billboard* Hot 100, the best return for a song of Carl's since 1956. It would be one of three Perkins tracks the Beatles would eventually record. Harrison had also pushed for them to record "Your True Love," as he'd one day tell Carl, but without luck. It was probably George's favorite Carl Perkins song.

During the Abbey Road session, which stretched until well after midnight, the Beatles covered "Slow Down," a 1957 track from Larry Williams (who wrote "Dizzy Miss Lizzy," also covered by the Beatles), with the lead vocalist John Lennon almost shouting himself hoarse. They then cut a new Lennon-McCartney song called "I'll Be Back." Later on, Carl and the band jammed several of his numbers, including "Blue Suede Shoes" and "Honey, Don't," the four Beatles peppering him with questions all the while, asking Carl how he came up with song titles, what his writing process was, and more. They were genuinely shocked that Carl could conjure up a melody and lyrics—*at the same time.* "You must be kidding," said George Harrison, shaking his head.

The memories of his day in Abbey Road with the Beatles never left Carl; he'd happily retell the story for the rest of his life. "It really was a thrill," he said.

Before leaving for the airport, Carl asked if they'd autograph a band photo for his eldest son, which John Lennon signed on behalf of the other Beatles. His inscription read, simply, *To Stan from The Beatles.* Stan wasn't an especially popular kid at school, but on the day that he showed the signed photo to his classmates, he was, in his own words, "the king. I outshined any football player, whatever."

Carl's tour of England had revived, and redirected, his career. "It came along at a dark period of my life," he'd admit. "I was about ready to quit the music business. I came back home and I was a new man, I really was. . . . I knew I had [found] a place that loved me and my music." Rather than deal with diminishing audiences at home, he'd play one hundred concerts in the UK over the course of 1964 and relatively few in America. And his British following remained strong, both among his fans and fellow players: over the ensuing years, Carl returned there no fewer than eighteen times.

And over time, Carl's bond with the Beatles would grow even stronger. "Those boys gave me a shot in the arm, so to speak," he stated. And how did Carl feel about their renditions of his songs? "Their versions are okay," he joked, "but the royalty checks were nicer." Carl said that he earned about $50,000 from each recording.

A revitalized Carl was booked to return to England in mid-October 1964 for more dates. It was agreed that again a variety of local acts, including the Animals, the Nashville Teens, and the Cosmic Sounds, would pad out the bill, which was christened *The R'n'B Show 64*. Carl would be backed by a group named the Quotations. It was to be another long haul, thirty shows in five weeks, with just one short break. Carl would play 1,000-plus-capacity venues such as the Bradford Gaumont, the Winter Gardens at Bournemouth, Bristol's Colston Hall, the Guildford Odeon, and larger rooms like the Brighton Hippodrome.

Between Carl's two UK tours, his biggest admirers, the Beatles, had undertaken a trip of their own, their first extensive run of US dates, starting on the West Coast on August 19 and winding their way east, for a final show on September 20 at New York's Paramount Theater. They were riding very high—in April, they'd experienced the rarest of feats when they claimed the top five spots on the *Billboard* Hot 100. No one had scaled that lofty peak before (and no one would again until the Bee Gees, during their *Saturday Night Fever* heyday).

During that US tour, while traveling in the Southeast, George Harrison got it into his head that he'd visit Carl at his home in Jackson, as he'd later tell Stan Perkins. "Now here's an Englishman driving an American-made car, probably on the wrong side of the road—I can just picture it—in search of Carl Perkins," Stan said. "He never did get to Jackson. He went a while and then turned around."

Harrison had to be content with performing Carl's "Everybody's Trying to Be My Baby" on the band's return to the UK, for another BBC broadcast. *Rolling Stone* magazine would one day rate that performance as "Harrison's Perkins fixation at its finest." (It was the pick of the five times they played Carl's song on the BBC.) The Beatles released a studio version of "Everybody's Trying to Be My Baby" on the US album *Beatles '65* and on the UK LP *Beatles for Sale*, and played it almost sixty times at live shows during 1965. It generated another $50,000 for Carl in songwriting royalties. As did "Honey, Don't," which also appeared on *Beatles for Sale* (and had also been covered by Canadian firebrand Ronnie Hawkins in 1960). This was more money than Carl had made from "Blue Suede Shoes."

One visitor who did make it to Carl's home in 1964 was Roy Orbison, his former Sun colleague. Like Johnny Cash, Orbison had fared significantly better since leaving Memphis and Sam Phillips, having signed to Monument Records and recorded such stately, epic ballads as "Only the Lonely," "Running Scared," "Crying," and "In Dreams," while—and this said a lot about having a quiet nature and wearing dark glasses—being thought of as a true rock and roll enigma. Orbison was once described as "more a presence than a person." Carl's estimation of Orbison, however, was far simpler: "He's the kind of man you would like to have living next door so you could lay some tomatoes on the fence for him."

Having just cut his latest record in Nashville, Orbison was so eager to play it to Carl that he drove the 130 miles to Jackson, nonstop, in his maroon 1963 Cadillac, with the reel-to-reel tape sitting on the passenger seat. The song was "Oh, Pretty Woman," inspired by his wife, Claudette. By the time Carl left for England in October 1964, it was number 1 on the *Billboard* Hot 100.

Carl, however, was lucky to be in any shape to tour the UK at all, having snagged his left hand in a fan while playing a fundraiser for the governor of Tennessee in Dyersburg, Tennessee, during July 1964. Carl bled so profusely that Valda feared he might die. On his way to the hospital, Carl had what could best be called an out-of-body experience: "I can remember a dark gray tunnel and a peak of light at the very end of it," Carl said in 1984. "I was just floatin' like a feather."

As Carl would relate, when he reached the hospital, the surgeon told him that he might have to amputate some of his fingers: "They're going to be in your way, that little finger is just hanging there." Carl wasn't having that, and he replied, "You leave it right there and we'll see." After several hours of surgery, Carl awoke to find Valda seated on one side of his bed and the surgeon seated on the other. "You are very, very lucky," the surgeon told Carl. "It was very touch and go. But you're going to be all right." Carl kept all his digits. The *Memphis Press-Scimitar* delivered the bad news: "Word is his hand is terribly mutilated . . . He'll keep his hand but the tendons were severed and it's doubtful he'll ever play guitar again. Chin up, Carl! You can still sing."

Carl remained in a cast for eight weeks and admitted that he wasn't sure what remained of his hand. "I didn't know if I still had my fingers," he said in 1997. When it was removed, as Carl told writer Bill Millar, his damaged hand was almost unrecognizable; he said it "looked like a skeleton's paw." He would never regain the feeling in the two smallest fingers of that hand. During his rehabilitation, Carl squeezed a tennis ball night and day to regain some strength and tried playing simple things like "Guitar Rag" while still heavily bandaged. Carl needed to alter his playing technique to allow for his injury—"now I just make do with three fingers"—but wasn't yet capable of lead guitar duties by the time he boarded his flight to Heathrow in October 1964.

Just before his departure, Carl had done time in the RCA Victor studio in Nashville, again with Owen Bradley in the producer's chair. Bradley assembled a team of renowned players, among them guitarists Charlie McCoy and James Burton (who had played with Ricky Nelson and would soon back Elvis). It was telling that it took two guitarists—both top-shelf players, both richly experienced—to make up for Carl's inability to play due to his injury. Drummer Kenny Buttrey sat in, as did Alan Price, the organist for the visiting British band the Animals, on Carl's invitation. (They remained friends: fourteen years later, Price jammed with Carl at a gig at London's Nashville Rooms.)

But the results lacked the fire of the "Big Bad Blues" session with the Nashville Teens a few months back. The song "The Monkeyshine" was fun, a funky hustle—a sort of dance craze in waiting—that wouldn't have been lost on some of Elvis Presley's recent soundtracks, but it was no classic. Carl also recorded two more originals, the mid-tempo "One of These Days," as well as another rocker called "Let My Baby Be," which had just a hint of Merseybeat to it. His time in the UK had been inspiring, clearly. He also covered "Mama of My Song," which was written by fellow rockabilly rebel, Missouri native Ronnie Self. (Self was a boozer like Carl, who was still drinking, despite his career upswing.) The songs were good enough, the playing competent—as you'd expect from the renowned "Nashville cats"—but there was no spark. It was Carl's last session for Decca, and the songs would remain in the can until May 1965, when "Mama of My Song," backed with "One of These Days," was quietly released. It didn't chart.

A problem with money almost killed Carl's second UK tour before it even began, but that was settled when some "upfront" cash was paid. However, without Carl's biting lead guitar, shows on his return trip were hit-and-miss. George Harrison, who'd heard about Carl's accident and had been in touch, was at one of the first concerts. "You're playing as good as ever," he reassured Carl backstage. But Carl's drinking—vodka had now taken the place of Early Times—didn't help. One gig at the Edmonton regal was rated "lousy" by fans, yet Carl was in fine form on November 2 at the Kilburn State, jiggling about the stage, trying his best to play lead guitar.

As the crowd filtered away after the show, many of them angry that the Animals were headlining above Carl, the man himself materialized on Kilburn High Street outside the theater. Dressed in his street clothes—a suede jacket and a pork-pie hat—Carl performed "Dixie Fried" to a group of stunned concertgoers. They looked on wide-eyed, shouting encouragement to Carl as he played. When he finished the song, Carl thanked the gathering, then jumped in a taxi and disappeared into the night.

The angry response toward the Animals at Kilburn State wasn't the first time that Carl had witnessed this in the UK. During one show on the Chuck Berry tour in May, he'd seen so much garbage hurled at a local band while they played that he joked how it was hard to find a clear spot on the stage to perform.

Offstage, Carl was in high demand, appearing on Granada TV's *Scene* show, miming "Blue Suede Shoes"; BBC Radio's *Saturday Club*, for the second time; as well as other BBC shows *Top Gear* and *The Beat Room*. On the latter he shared the bill with the New York singer Dionne Warwick, who'd just had a huge hit with "Walk On By." During downtime on the *Beat Room* set, Carl hung out with the Nashville Teens, drinking vodka and orange and regaling anyone within earshot with juicy stories and jokes. Carl's fan club cofounder Brian Smith was there, and looked on, laughing quietly, as the filmed performance of "Matchbox" had to be stopped, "because a cameraman was stomping his foot so hard [to the music] that he was buggering up his picture."

Carl, ever the family man, missed his daughter Debbie's tenth birthday while he was in the UK—"he was a bit choked up," recalled Smith—so he posed for a photo holding a card that read *Happy Birthday Debbie.* "His family was one subject he never tired of talking about," Smith said. Back home, Valda told a reporter from the *Jackson Sun* that Carl "was well liked in England. And Carl loves the English people."

Yet, strangely, despite the enthusiasm for Carl and his music in the UK, it would be almost two years before he returned. And when he did, he would be keeping very different company.

CHAPTER 11

Johnny Cash is a humanitarian,
a very charitable man—he's a fine dude

Carl kept a low profile during 1965, enjoying the rare financial security provided by regular Beatles paydays. His deal with Decca was over. It turned out to be another unsatisfactory relationship, much like his time with Columbia. "It was a terrible frustration," Carl said. While with Decca, he cut fourteen songs and came nowhere near a *Billboard* chart. It was only his UK session with the Nashville Teens that captured something like the same kind of energy Carl untapped while working with Sam Phillips in Memphis.

Yet at the same time Carl was happy, by his own admission, to stay home and fish and spend time with his family. "My paychecks was comin' in the mailbox. . . . I never thought I'd drive a Cadillac or own a brick home and when it happened to me, I didn't feel a helluva lot in need of me leaving that."

Carl had other distractions in his life; he seemed to be accident prone. One day, while out hunting, he had a mishap with his shotgun. More of a disaster, really. "I almost blew my left foot away," he told writer Peter Stone Brown. His mishap rated a mention in the *Knoxville News Sentinel*, where it was reported he'd been admitted "in fair condition" to the Jackson–Madison County Hospital. Carl spent several weeks in a cast, sitting around his house and feeling "kind of irritable."

The news of Carl's misfortune reached Johnny Cash, and in early 1966—Carl would cite a date of January 12—while he was still convalescing, a large tour bus pulled up outside the Perkins residence in Jackson. Valda peered out the window. "That's Johnny Cash coming up the drive, Carlie." Cash had a proposition in mind for Carl.

Carl was surprised to see his old friend—he hadn't caught up with Cash for some time, although their relationship remained strong. Of all his Sun labelmates, Carl liked Cash the best. "I think I was closer to John than I was Elvis, or Jerry Lee, Charlie Rich and the boys." They were both sharecroppers' sons, and that would never change. But there was more to it than that, as Cash's biographer, Robert Hilburn, would make clear: "They also understood each other's abuse problems."

Like Carl, Cash had addiction issues—he was hooked on a potent cocktail of amphetamines, sleeping pills, and prescription painkillers. Once, while on the road, he'd been busted by a narcotics squad in El Paso, Texas—Cash was gun-shopping at the time—and more than a thousand pills were found inside his guitar case. (He received a suspended sentence.) And, just like Carl, he had become accident prone—in June 1965, while on a fishing trip in California's Los Padres National Forest, Johnny's camper burst into flames, setting alight several hundred acres of forest, torching wildlife, endangering other campers, and almost killing him. As Cash would observe in his autobiography, "I was a walking vision of death—and that's exactly how I felt." Cash was also in the midst of a tug-of-love, torn between his wife, Vivian, and his powerful feelings for June Carter.

Yet somehow Cash continued to work. He'd had hits in recent years with "Understand Your Man," "Orange Blossom Special," and the haunting, World War II–era story song "The Ballad of Ira Hayes," and he'd play some seventy shows in 1965, with another eighty booked for 1966, across North America and Europe. It was while he was on the road that Cash decided to swing by Carl's home in Jackson. Cash had some shows in the area over the next couple of days. "Come with me, Carl," he suggested. "We'll play the shows and then I'll bring you home. I'd love to have you along." It didn't take Carl long to make up his mind, despite his crutches. "All right," he said. "I'll go."

With that, Carl limped onto Cash's tour bus, for what he thought was a brief sojourn. "It was just to get me out of the house, more or less," he said. He'd play a little guitar, sing a few songs with his old buddy, and then come home and work out what to do next. At least that was the plan.

During their first show together, Cash welcomed Carl out to the stage to perform some of his own material, even though Carl had specifically asked him not to. "But that's John," Carl explained. "I was in the company of what I consider one of the greatest men in the music business. Johnny Cash is a humanitarian, a very charitable man. . . . He's a fine dude. . . . I love the man, I really do."

After these few dates, Cash asked Carl if he'd like to join the act on a permanent basis, which was billed as the Fabulous Johnny Cash Show (or sometimes the Johnny Cash Spectacular). Carl's old bandmate, Fluke Holland, was Cash's drummer, while the venerable Carter Family—matriarch, Mother Maybelle, and her daughters, Anita, June, and Helen—were part of the ensemble. The Carters were American music royalty, influential figures whose images probably belonged on Mount Rushmore. Mother Maybelle had been performing since the 1920s, when the original Carter Family—A. P. Carter; his wife, Sara; and Maybelle, who was Sara's first cousin— were recorded by field music archivist/folklorist Ralph Peer. The Statler Brothers, four sharp-dressed gospel singers from Staunton, Virginia, were also part of the roadshow, opening each concert and then singing backup vocals for Cash. Curiously, the "Brothers" were unrelated; they'd taken their name from a box of Statler tissues they once spied in a hotel room. (Their in-joke was that they might have called themselves the Kleenex Brothers.)

Joining the tour appealed to the pragmatic side of Carl's nature, even though he didn't like being away from home for too long. But there were obvious benefits. "With Cash," he explained, "I didn't have no worries about no bands or nothing on my shoulders, and it was good money . . . I just floated along, saw the world, played to the kings and queens and the convicts too. It was real interesting."

The "few dates" that Cash originally suggested Carl play would roll on into the hundreds—he'd be part of the Johnny Cash show for the next ten years. On the road, Carl would room with Fluke, just like the old days of the Perkins Brothers Band. Carl acknowledged that joining the show didn't help his solo career, but it did help provide some creature comforts. "It means a warm bed, a bicycle for my boys, and a good guitar to play. I'm enjoying life. I'm not worried about the top."

Early on, Carl and Cash came to an agreement on one key issue—Cash would never refer to Carl as "my guitarist." "He is, after all, Carl Perkins," Cash wrote knowingly in his autobiography. He admitted that he never got completely comfortable with knowing that Carl was standing behind him onstage, "literally in my shadow." Cash had the sense, with justification, that Carl didn't get the credit he deserved. He was as much an American original as Cash himself. For one thing, Cash was fully aware that it had been Carl's "Matchbox" recording session, back in 1956, that had resulted in Cash, Presley, Jerry Lee Lewis, and Carl being dubbed the "Million Dollar Quartet." But somehow, wrote Cash, "Carl's name always seems to come last" when that flashpoint in Sun history was mentioned. It wasn't right. Maybe coming out on the road with him would remind audiences that Carl was one of the greats.

Given that Carl was to become part of Johnny Cash, Inc., he was joining a sartorially splendid ensemble. The Carter women typically took the stage in their best evening gowns, while the Statler Brothers' suits—designed by their bass man, Harold Reid—glowed so brightly that they could probably be seen from outer space. Cash himself now sported a suit and sometimes a bow tie when he performed. Carl had no problem wearing a tux but he did have some more cosmetic issues to tackle. His hair had been thinning since the 1950s, so he invested in a toupée (that over the years, via some miracle of trichology, managed to slowly gray in sync with his remaining hair). Carl made no effort to hide his hairpiece; one day he'd even appear in print ads plugging toupées for the Memphis salon Apollo Hair Systems. Carl's rug was known as "semi-permanent," meaning he could take it on or off at a whim. He came to laugh about what he called "that ol' fake hair." Carl began growing his sideburns long, a nod to the current trend, and got fitted for a dental plate. Soon enough Carl had a million-dollar smile to go with his new head of hair.

During March 1966, Carl, Cash, and the troupe hit the road and headed north of the border for dates in Canada, playing a run of shows in Ontario. In April they played in Des Moines, Minneapolis, Rockford, Duluth, and Madison, before setting out on a UK tour that would run until the final weeks of May. It had been eighteen months since Carl was last in the country that had helped revitalize his career. With Cash he plugged in for shows at such sites as the Hammersmith Odeon in London and the Portsmouth Guildhall. The format for their live shows gradually took shape—Carl would play "Blue Suede Shoes" and a few other crowd favorites, then, later in the show, along with the rest of the troupe, he'd join Cash and his backing band the Tennessee Three as the show built to a big finale. It was a polished, family-friendly, "Let the Circle Be Unbroken" night of song.

But both Cash and Carl were still battling their personal demons. Pills had reduced Cash to a stick figure of a man weighing barely 100 pounds—he was literally skin and bones—while Carl continued swilling booze to ease the pain. "There always had to be a bottle of whiskey," drummer Fluke Holland said about Carl, "and then there was the drinking in the morning."

Sometimes after a show, Carl and Cash would be so wasted that they'd start crying. "We'd sit there and talk about our dead brothers and get to feeling sorry for ourselves," said Carl. They both knew they had to give up their addictions or, as Carl said, "the way we were going we would wind up dead." Mother Maybelle Carter would prove to be a godsend for the two former Sun stars. Most nights would end with the troupe, including Carl, in the back of the bus singing gospel songs as they drove to the next city. Mother Maybelle usually took the lead. To Carl she was a "sweet, gentle lady," a comforting presence for a man who didn't relish being away from his family for long stretches of time.

"The easiest part of this job," Carl once said, "is when you are on that stage." Getting through the rest of the day, however, was a big challenge. But Carl had a novel way of dealing with his homesickness. He'd call Valda after most shows, and one of the first things he'd ask was, "Can you see the moon?" When Valda said that she could, Carl would say, "It's beautiful, isn't it?" Carl would then tell Valda that he was convinced their love traveled "from each of us, to the moon, and then to the other." The moon was their touchstone, their connection, and just for that moment it erased the distance Carl was from the family home in Jackson and eased his loneliness ever so slightly.

Carl would get some ribbing from the other musicians about his phone conversations with Valda, but Johnny Cash had the last word. "Those," Cash said, "are the tender outpourings of a man's heart."

The year 1967 was busy for Carl, who played another seventy-plus dates as part of the Cash roadshow. In between touring for ten to fifteen days of every month and playing the guitar on Cash and June Carter's smash hit, "Jackson"—a number 2 on the Country chart that would go on to win a Grammy—Carl found the space to record an album called *Country Boy's Dream*. He was now recording for Dollie Records, a Nashville-based label owned by his publisher, Cedarwood Music.

This was Carl's first true studio album; his two previous long-players, 1957's *Dance Album* and 1958's *Whole Lotta Shakin'*, were basically collections of his Sun and Columbia recordings. Carl was now operating at a time when the studio LP had taken over from the 45-rpm single as the most important statement a musician could make. The year 1967 alone produced such classic albums as the Beatles' remarkable *Sgt. Pepper's Lonely Hearts Club Band*, the Beach Boys' *Smiley Smile*, and the Byrds' *Younger Than Yesterday*, among many other greats, including debuts like Jimi Hendrix's *Are You Experienced?* and the Doors' eponymous LP. Another key record of 1967 was *Disraeli Gears* from British supergroup Cream. Their roots music–loving guitarist, Eric Clapton, admired Carl's playing almost as much as George Harrison. One day, a little further down the road, the paths of Clapton and Carl would intersect, and the results would be memorable.

Country Boy's Dream was no *Disraeli Gears*, by any means, but it was way more unified than anything Carl had released before. A vaguely autobiographical theme ran through many of its songs, as Carl reflected on his rural, cotton-picking childhood. "I think the happiest time in my life," he told writer Michael Lydon, "was when I was a little boy in the country in summer," and such originals as "You Can Take the Boy Out of the Country," "Poor Boy Blues," and "Home (That's Where the Heart Is)" captured that sense of time and place, even though Carl's sentimental tendencies sometimes came on a bit strong. The words for the album's title track may have been the work of songwriter Ernie Newton, but there was no doubt that Carl felt deeply connected to them.

Aside from his few originals, Carl cherry-picked material from Music City's best songwriters for the album, most of them published by Cedarwood. These writers included Mel Tillis (the quirky "Unmitigated Gall" and "Stateside," the lament of a homesick soldier), Webb Pierce (the honky-tonk tearjerker "If I Could Come Back," awash in pedal steel guitar), and Jan Crutchfield, who cowrote "Sweet Misery," which might have been better suited to a Vegas lounge act, and the mellow, moody "Dream On Little Dreamer." Yet the most personal of all the songs Carl wrote during this time, "Lake County Cotton Country," didn't appear on the album; instead, it was released as a single in mid-1968. During "Lake County," Carl looked back on his long days picking cotton and his even longer nights working the tonks and how he dreamed of the Opry and stardom.

Country Boy's Dream didn't do any business on the mainstream chart, but two singles—the title track and the gospel-tinged rockabilly of "Shine, Shine, Shine"—managed to breach the US Hot Country Songs Top 40. Carl thought the title track could have been a bigger hit, "if [the record company] knew what to do with it." A lack of distribution on the part of Dollie Records didn't help matters.

As writer Bill Millar observed a few years after the release of the LP, "Carl Perkins made 'Matchbox' in 1957 and 'Country Boy's Dream' in 1967. The differences between them are negligible. A string bass has been traded in for an electric one but little else has changed." He'd stuck tight to his origins and remained unapologetically rootsy, even down to the earnest cover photo of Carl picking a guitar, dressed in a plaid shirt, lost in the music he was playing. It was a study in pure country.

In mid-June 1967, having just played another Cash show, this time at the Seattle Opera House, Carl sat down for a rare interview— nowadays it was his boss who did most of the talking to the media. Carl spoke with "Bashful" Bobby Wooten, a popular DJ at radio station KAYO; their chat was being recorded in order to be shared with American soldiers stationed in Vietnam. While Carl had never served, he'd played for servicemen in Europe and had strong (and unashamedly conservative) feelings about the Vietnam War. "Everybody has done a great job regardless of what the few who protest will say back here," he told Wooten. "These boys are out there fighting for something we all know is right." (Carl would play for American troops in Saigon with the Cash troupe in late 1968.)

It was a wide-ranging discussion, taking in everything from Carl's early days with Sun and Sam Phillips to the 1956 car crash that had short-circuited his rise to the top, something he described as "the saddest, most disappointing thing." Carl expressed deep regret for the driver of the other vehicle in the accident, who'd been killed. Carl also talked about the excitement of being in Abbey Road while the Beatles recorded "Matchbox" and how he felt "blessed" to now be part of the Johnny Cash Spectacular.

In typical Carl fashion, he spoke honestly when asked whether he'd been tempted to give up music. *Had he ever considered quitting?* "Definitely," Carl replied, before going on to explain how just a few years back he'd had enough of the highs and lows of the music biz. "But," as Carl explained, the interview coming to an end, "I had wrapped up so many years and so much time in this that I found out I wouldn't make a good cabdriver."

Johnny Cash had agreed to never refer to Carl as "my guitarist," but they'd also made another pact. They'd agreed to help each other overcome their addictions. Cash was the first to confront his demons, although he almost lost his life in the process. In late 1967, having completed yet another stretch of live shows that took Team Cash to Wheeling, West Virginia, Springfield, Missouri, Norfolk, Virginia, and elsewhere, Cash decided that he'd had enough. He was done with the pills and all the madness. He took a trip to Nickajack Cave, which was on the Tennessee River, not far from Chattanooga, a system of caves that stretched underground for miles. Cash was familiar with Nickajack, having visited there when hunting for Civil War and Indian artifacts. Cash's plan was simple—he was going to crawl into one of the caves until he couldn't crawl any farther. Then he was going to lie there and, as Cash would tell the story, let his God "put me wherever He puts people like me."

But upon reaching what he thought would be his final destination, Cash felt a powerful urge to keep moving. He suddenly needed to get himself out of the caves. When he finally managed to emerge, he was met on the outside, miraculously, by his soon-to-be wife, June Carter, and his mother. June had sensed something was amiss and followed him all the way to Nickajack. Cash saw this as a sign from God and within days began his recovery, and he and the troupe were back onstage by November 17, playing at a high school in Hendersonville, Cash's new hometown. To his surprise, Cash discovered "that the stage without drugs was not the frightening place I'd imagined it to be."

Cash also sought assistance from a psychiatrist, Dr. Nat Winston, and encouraged Carl to do the same to try and end his alcoholism. But Carl wasn't comfortable with that—in much the same way, a few years later, Cash was uncomfortable with Carl's efforts to have him join the Masons. (When Cash met Carl's fellow Masons, he said they looked at him with such disdain, it was as though "they were being asked to kiss a rattlesnake.")

Instead, Carl found solace in a book, Norman Vincent Peale's *The Power of Positive Thinking*, which had been a bestseller since its publication back in 1952. Peale was a minister who had studied theology in his native Ohio and then in Boston and became the pastor of New York's Marble Collegiate Church. Peale wrote more than forty books, but it was *The Power of Positive Thinking* that struck a collective nerve and set cash registers ringing, selling five million copies and being translated into forty languages. (An adolescent Donald Trump was a big fan.) *Positive Thinking* was a self-help bible before the term even existed. Echoing Alcoholics Anonymous's Twelve Steps, Peale spelled out ten key rules for "overcoming inadequacy attitudes and learning to practice faith," such as "picture yourself succeeding" and "develop a strong self-respect." Carl appeared to pledge allegiance to all but one, rule 6, which was to "work with a counselor." But when Cash recommended Dr. Winston, Carl demurred.

Carl approached *Positive Thinking* very seriously, even though Peale copped a lot of criticism from mental health experts (and the occasional book reviewer). "I learned some real wisdom from that book," Carl insisted. He'd carry a copy with him on the road and bury his nose in it as the miles passed by his window. When Michael Lydon, a *Rolling Stone* reporter, spent some time on the Cash tour bus in 1968, Carl spoke like a man who'd been sipping heavily from the Norman Vincent Peale well. "I've been at the top of the bill and I've been at the bottom," he told Lydon, "and there's no comparing them. The top beats the bottom every time."

Johnny Cash's recent efforts to get straight inspired Carl to try to finally stop drinking. Of the entire crew, only Luther Perkins, Cash's guitarist, was now likely to indulge, so it had become a lonely environment for a boozer. The Statler Brothers, the Carters, and two-thirds of the Tennessee Three were all teetotalers. Carl had weened himself off hard liquor and was sticking to beer, at least for the time being, but that meant he blew up physically—at his heftiest, he tipped the scales at about 230 pounds, at least 65 pounds more than his usual weight.

Carl, however, did find some distraction by helping his parents build a new home. Carl had paid $6,500 for sixty-six acres of land and a house in desperate need of repair in Clarksburg, about thirty-five miles from Jackson, and finally moved Buck and Louise out of government housing. Carl's former guitarist and friend Edd Cisco was a neighbor. "I loved every nail I drove," said Carl, who took great satisfaction in being able to give something back to his parents. When the work was done and they were able to move in, Carl made Buck and Louise a promise: "Your next address," he announced, "will be in heaven." They dropped to their knees and thanked God for the house. The work also helped steer Carl away from the bottle, at least while on the property, because he was simply too busy, or too tired, to drink.

But Carl's alcoholism reached a crisis point in the late summer of 1968, not too long after he and the Cash roadshow had returned from another successful UK jaunt. It was a tragic time: Cash's long-time guitarist Luther Perkins had died on August 5, aged just forty, after a house fire in his home in Hendersonville, while two of Roy Orbison's sons, Roy DeWayne and Anthony, had recently perished under similarly awful circumstances, also in Hendersonville, where Orbison owned a house.

Cash asked Carl to take Perkins's place, at least temporarily, until he hired a full-time replacement, and Carl played some shows using Luther's old Fender guitar, a poignant touch. Bob Wootton, an Arkansas guitarist who'd played in a Cash covers band and been a lifelong fan of the man, joined in September. Wootton had come to Cash's attention during a show in Arkansas—he had been in the audience, and when he learned that Carl and Cash's band were stuck in transit, Wootton strode up onstage, borrowed Carl's guitar, and played each song note perfect. Wootton roomed with Carl (and Fluke Holland) on the road and admired him hugely. "Carl Perkins was one of the funniest men I have ever known," Wootton told *Rolling Stone* not long before his death in 2017. "And you talk about owning a stage . . . that guy could do it."

But right now, Carl was in bad shape. He'd been on a lengthy bender with John Swanner, an old drinking buddy from the Golden Nugget in Las Vegas, when he turned up drunk for the next Cash concert, which was in San Diego. They were about to play to a full house of 6,500 fans. This was a new, dark turn for Carl; despite all his drinking, he'd never been drunk at showtime. He pleaded with

Cash to let him sit this one out; he just couldn't face the crowd in the state he was in. He was too wasted, too weak. Surely Cash, of all people, would understand.

"Carl," explained Cash, "this show is sold out. And they really want to see you."

Though he could barely stand, Carl managed to make it onstage, play his four songs, and then all but ran to the tour bus. He was embarrassed, appalled by his own weakness, and drank until he lapsed into unconsciousness. Yet he awoke to a bucolic scene—the tour bus was parked at a beach, and everyone else was outside, soaking up the sunshine. But the bright light was too much for Carl, who retreated to the womblike comfort of the bus. As he'd relate in his memoir, it was then that he made a deal with himself: if he could resist the urge to keep drinking—and he was poised to open another bottle—he just might make it home to Valda and the kids and some kind of safety. With that, he walked out of the bus and up to the water's edge, took the bottle out of his back pocket, and threw it as far as his weak arms could manage. "I thought I was dying," Carl said many years later. "I'd been drunk for three days. And I said, 'God, if you let me get home, let me see my wife and children . . . Please don't let me die here.' I got scared."

When Cash approached him and said that he seemed a little better, Carl looked him in the eyes and said: "John, I'm gonna make it." Cash replied, "You don't take a drink and I won't take another pill." It was agreed.

Given that it was a Carl Perkins story—and he was prone to embellishment—not everyone who was there remembered it playing out exactly the way he described it. The Statler Brothers didn't recall the event at all, although Cash did later state that he saw Carl standing by the water and when he came back, "he looked like he felt better about everything." In another variation, Carl said that he and Cash made a $100 bet, and a few days later, Cash gave him a check for $100, admitting that he'd taken some pills. (Carl said that he tore up the check.) Still, specifics aside, there was no denying that Carl had made himself a deal and was hell-bent on carrying it out. And it's likely that it was the act of throwing away his booze that would, over time, bring Carl closer to the Christian way of life. "It was God that brought me out of the bottle," he declared. "I just made up my mind and God did the rest. My Christian faith was something I could cling to."

"Now every time I walk on stage with a clear head," he told a writer from the UK's *Daily Mirror*, "I thank God for His deliverance."

Of course, sobriety wasn't that easy; both Carl and Cash would be tempted to lapse while out on the road. But more often than not, they came to Mother Maybelle for support. Most nights, after another gig, as they settled onto the bus, she'd remind them how they'd both made it through another day, and that they should take pride in the fact that they'd hung on to their sobriety. And then the whole troupe would start singing.

CHAPTER 12

I don't think "Blue Suede Shoes" touches a song like "Daddy Sang Bass"

Carl's reputation as a songwriter was often overlooked. He was more often praised for his work on the guitar or for being the guy who popularized blue suedes. But that changed in mid-1968, when he approached Cash with a song called "Daddy Sang Bass." The idea came to Carl one night backstage during a Cash concert. Carl had been quietly humming the old standard "Will the Circle Be Unbroken" when his thoughts turned to his roots, much as he'd done with "Lake County Cotton Country."

"I was thinking about my home as a child," he recalled. Carl flashed back to the long, hard days spent knee-deep in cotton, hands stinging, when the only thing that would lift his spirits was singing with his family and all the other pickers.

Carl mixed those memories with slightly reworked lyrics from "Will the Circle Be Unbroken," and the result was a heartfelt snapshot of music and memory, with the additional benefit of a catchy, if ever so corny, chorus. "That's the way it was in my house," Carl explained. "[My] Dad[dy] sang bass, [my] Mama sang tenor, and me and my little brother would join in."

Carl played it to Cash, who asked him, "Whose song is that?"

"Mine," replied Carl.

But Cash had other plans. He liked what he heard and figured it would be ideal for the album he was set to record with producer Bob Johnston. Cash related strongly to the line Carl wrote about singing with his deceased sibling, Jay, which for Cash stirred up memories of his late brother Jack. Carl had wanted to record his own version, which he eventually did, but gave the okay for Cash to have the first shot at "Daddy Sang Bass." Carl knew it was a good song; in fact, he liked it more than his most famous original. "I don't think ['Blue Suede Shoes'] touches a song like 'Daddy Sang Bass,'" admitted Carl.

Don Reid and Lew DeWitt of the Statler Brothers—who'd also had designs on the song—helped on the studio recording, as did Grand Ole Opry member Jan Howard. June Carter would take a vocal when they played the song onstage—and it proved to be such a hugely popular live number that Cash would still be playing it during his final shows, in 2002.

"I guess I came out better by having John record it," Carl said in 1972. "In this business the public decides." As it turned out, the public had no problem with "Daddy Sang Bass." None whatsoever. "Daddy Sang Bass" was released in November 1968—despite some resistance by execs at his label, Columbia—and became Cash's next big hit, reaching number 1 on the *Billboard* Hot Country Songs chart and number 42 on the *Billboard* Hot 100. It charted for five months and was featured on Cash's gospel concept record *The Holy Land.*

"Daddy Sang Bass" was also in the running for CMA Single of the Year in 1969—Cash, Carl, and the troupe performed the song at the awards ceremony at the Ryman Auditorium—but would be pipped by Cash's other contender, "A Boy Named Sue," such was his current hot streak.

When Cash played "Daddy Played Bass" for inmates at San Quentin during 1969, he said this: "Carl Perkins wrote a song that tells about the reason for it all; it takes us back home and tells it like it was when I was a little-biddy kid and we'd gather around the piano and me and little brother would join in and Momma would sing tenor and Daddy sang bass." As simple as that.

The song would prove to be a steady earner for Carl. Over time there were about twenty different covers, including versions by Glen Campbell, Dolly Parton, Kitty Wells, and Leon Russell, while Cash's version would feature on several compilations of his greatest hits. Carl recorded his own version, which featured on a peculiar 1969 release, *Carl Perkins' Greatest Hits*, which was part of a new deal he'd signed with his old label, Columbia, after Dollie Records was shut down. (Its owners found it too hard to juggle a publishing company and a record label.) Even though *Greatest Hits* reached the Top 40 of the *Billboard* Hot Country Songs charts, it was a strange, water-treading compilation, which packaged rerecorded versions of many of Carl's Sun standouts—"Blue Suede Shoes," "Matchbox," "Your True Love"—with "Bass" and Carl's take on Cash's "Folsom Prison Blues." Cash contributed to the liner notes, referring to Carl as "a brother" and encouraging him to "keep on singin' old songs that you know," which made perfect sense, considering the classics on the album.

The success of "Daddy Sang Bass" helped build an even stronger bond between Mr. Blue Suede Shoes and the Man in Black. And it would be a move further into the mainstream by Cash that dictated the next few years of Carl's career.

In the late 1960s, mainstream American TV was dominated by high-rating variety shows, primetime programs hosted by such popular acts as the Smothers Brothers, Andy Williams, Carol Burnett, Lawrence Welk, and Dean Martin. Late night, meanwhile, was the private domain of Johnny Carson, the king of the couch. These shows all featured musical content, some family-friendly performers, others a little more progressive: The Who all but blew up the Smothers Brothers set performing "My Generation," while Janis Joplin's blazing cameos on *The Dick Cavett Show* were legendary. Rowan and Martin's edgy sketch comedy show *Laugh-In*—the home of "sock it to me" and stoner humor—also welcomed a wide range of acts, everyone from Herb Alpert and the Tijuana Brass to Kenny Rogers and the First Edition and the Strawberry Alarm Clock.

In January 1969, CBS had granted country singing star Glen Campbell his own show, *The Glen Campbell Goodtime Hour* (whose writers included comic Steve Martin). When *Goodtime Hour* proved to be immensely popular, ABC—who were a lowly third in the network ratings—approached Johnny Cash about his own, rival program. Carl would become a key player in what would be known simply as *The Johnny Cash Show*.

It wasn't strictly the ratings of Campbell's show that inspired ABC to hire Cash. The success of Cash's two recent live prison recordings, *At San Quentin* and *At Folsom Prison*, both featuring Carl, also helped seal the deal.

A crew from Granada Television in the UK had shot a documentary around Cash's San Quentin performance, with Carl featuring prominently. Carl played a short set about midway through Cash's performance, then joined Cash and June Carter for "Jackson," a favorite of the 1,400 inmates gathered to watch the show. It said something about the respect Cash commanded that there wasn't a stage invasion when his wife flashed a sexy smile for the female-starved audience—or perhaps it was due to the armed guards who kept a wary eye on proceedings. Either way, it was a surprisingly well-behaved gathering—rowdy at times, but not as fearful as the proposition of a prison gig might have seemed. Carl also joined Cash for "A Boy Named Sue," the funny-sad tale of a very complicated father-son relationship. Carl cracked a wry smile when Cash spat out the song's killer punchline, as the crowd erupted in cheers and laughter.

"Sue" was a smash on release in the summer of 1969, topping the *Billboard* Hot Country Songs chart, hitting number 2 on the *Billboard* Hot 100, and selling more than a million copies. Once again Carl was lurking in the shadows of a huge Cash hit. But if Carl had any reservations about taking a back seat to his more charismatic and successful boss, he never aired them publicly. "I make a pretty fair living," he told a writer from *Country World* magazine, "and workin' conditions are good. I'm happy."

In mid-March 1969, just weeks after Carl had been the guest of honor at Carl Perkins Day, staged in Jackson, the first *Johnny Cash Show* was filmed. But rather than use some drab Hollywood soundstage, the program was shot at the Ryman Auditorium in Nashville in front of a live audience. It would be the first network series to be produced in Music City. From the moment he uttered those immortal words, "Hello, I'm Johnny Cash," the Man in Black had the audience under his spell.

Cash and show producer Bill Carruthers led with their aces—the first episode, which would screen on June 7, featured the preeminent singer-songwriters Joni Mitchell and Bob Dylan, who'd rarely been seen in public since his 1966 motorcycle accident and a retreat to Woodstock and family life. While rehearsing for that debut show, the reclusive Dylan dropped by the dressing room and jammed with Carl. A song called "Champaign, Illinois" gradually began to emerge, which Carl would later finish and add to his next album, called, simply, *On Top*.

Carl was very impressed by the man sometimes referred to as the voice of his generation (a tag Dylan disliked). "He's a fine dude," said Carl, "a Shakespeare with words, and one of the finest songwriters to come along."

On that debut Cash episode, an almost unrecognisable Dylan—his once-wild hair combed and styled, a wispy beard outlining his face, dressed conservatively in a black suit—played "Matchbox" with Cash and Carl, who delivered two inspired guitar solos during their performance.

Carl quickly became an integral part of *The Johnny Cash Show*, which ran for fifty-eight episodes over the next two years. (Ever the workaholics, Cash, Carl, and the troupe also somehow managed to squeeze in more than fifty concerts in 1969 and another thirty in 1970.) On the eighth episode of the TV show, which aired on August 2, Carl was given a solo spot. In his introduction, Cash referred to Carl as "a buddy of mine who's got almost as much rhythm as he has goodness in his soul." Carl then played "Restless," reeling off some fleet-fingered picking on his cream-colored Fender guitar, which was duly acknowledged by the supportive Ryman audience. "Restless" had been one of the singles he'd cut while on Columbia—and the only one to chart, reaching number 20 on the Country list. Carl was particularly proud of the song. "I wrote it, arranged it, sang it, played guitar on it, and recorded it," he told a reporter. "It was tricky."

Cash was equally generous in his introduction, early in the second season, when Carl stepped forward to perform "Blue Suede Shoes." "There came from just across the Mississippi River from me in 1955 a man who became one of my best friends," he stated, going on to point out how in 1956 "Blue Suede Shoes" was the first song to top all three *Cashbox* charts—pop, country, and R&B—simultaneously. "Down through the years he's written some of the great country and rock songs you've ever heard. Ladies and gentlemen, the fantastic Carl Perkins." This time playing a wide-bodied Gibson guitar, Carl led the band through a revved-up version of the classic, sounding just as raw as it did back in 1956. Cash then joined Carl and the band for the traditional "The Old Account Was Settled Long Ago." "Tell 'em about it, brother Carl," said Cash, as he stepped forward to take a verse, grinning broadly.

During another episode, Carl sat in with Cash and the Tennessee Three for two numbers, "Outside Looking In" and "Luther Played the Boogie." As the show progressed—and began to rate well—Carl looked more and more assured on-screen, his country good looks presenting well on camera.

Much like Carl himself, *The Johnny Cash Show* wasn't strictly country. Mix and match was the order of the day—during one episode, Cash and Merle Haggard were joined by Louis Armstrong, while such contemporary acts as Dylan, Mitchell, Neil Young, James Taylor, and Creedence Clearwater Revival were welcomed to the show by Cash, along with more traditional Nashville artists. The program was progressive in its own way, with appearances by such African Americans as Stevie Wonder, Ray Charles, the comic Flip Wilson. and Charley Pride.

As the host, Cash would flex some muscle when necessary, standing his ground when the network wanted the word *stoned* excised from Kris Kristofferson's "Sunday Morning Coming Down." He also stood firm and shut down network resistance when the blacklisted folk singer Pete Seeger was booked on the show.

~

Carl sometimes downplayed his solo career, insisting that he was happy with his day job and a regular paycheck. He said that he perhaps lacked the ambition of some of his peers. "I've got all the love I need," he told a reporter from *Music City News*. "I may not be as rich and famous as those other guys [from the 1950s], but I've got everything I could ever hope for. . . . [I have] a good woman and children who are not ashamed to say, 'There goes my Dad.'"

Nonetheless, in between Cash commitments, Carl found the time to record a new album for Columbia in 1969, called *On Top*. It was a steady mixture of country, bluesy rock, and more soulful tracks, in which Carl covered Buddy Holly's "I'm Gonna Set My Foot Down" and Chuck Berry's "Brown Eyed Handsome Man," as well as songs from Jimmy Reed ("Baby, What You Want Me to Do?") and Ronnie Self. Carl finally took the time to commit "Champaign, Illinois," his cowrite with Bob Dylan, to tape, and had a fine old time with it, stomping lustily on his wah-wah pedal while celebrating the delights of the city. The pick of the few Perkins originals on the LP was "Power of My Soul," which proved that Carl had a knack for the type of tender ballads that his former Sun labelmate Charlie Rich would soon be taking to the bank.

Highly regarded Australian writer Bruce Elder rated *On Top* "one of the better records to come out of the early days of the rock and roll revival." Via a combination of good songs, strong performances by Carl, and his heightened presence with Cash, the album reached number 42 on the *Billboard* Top Country Albums chart. Not quite "on top," but still a handy reminder that Carl had a lot of good music left in him and hadn't been completely forgotten by the public.

On Top appeared at an interesting time, when the King himself, Elvis Presley, was about to return to (highly lucrative) live work in Las Vegas during July and August 1969—he'd pocket a handy $100,000 a week for four weeks of work—and such aging "nostalgia" acts as Bill Haley, Chuck Berry, Little Richard, and Gene Vincent were all undergoing late-career revivals. Carl had history with

Vincent; they once staged a drag race after a fairground show back at Cincinnati in the 1950s, only to be hauled off the track by the local sheriff. "He was pretty wild," Carl said of Vincent. "The show started when the music stopped!"

Forty-four-year-old Haley was back in demand, playing more than one hundred gigs in 1969, including a headlining show at New York's Madison Square Garden, while Little Richard, as camp and outrageous as ever, played a staggering two hundred–plus concerts in that one year. And even though the recent Woodstock festival had featured such cutting-edge acts as Jimi Hendrix, the Jefferson Airplane, and Santana, it was the rock revivalists Sha Na Na who just about stole the show with a raucous morning set, while the British bluesman Alvin Lee and his band Ten Years After squeezed snippets of "Blue Suede Shoes" into their lengthy "I'm Going Home" jam. It was another highlight of the festival and the iconic documentary film that followed.

This renaissance was best captured at the Toronto Rock 'n' Roll Revival. It was a twelve-hour outdoor musical free-for-all staged on September 13, 1969, which featured Little Richard, Chuck Berry, Gene Vincent, and Carl's peer, piano player, and sometime nemesis, Jerry Lee Lewis, as well as Bo Diddley and numerous others. (Carl was busy, out on tour with the Cash show in Texas.) Fronting the Plastic Ono Band, which comprised Eric Clapton, bassist Klaus Voormann, and drummer Alan White, was a heavily bearded and very nervy John Lennon. Having just thrown up backstage, he stepped up to the mic and declared, "We're just going to do numbers we know 'cause we've never played together before." (Their only rehearsal had been on the red-eye flight from London to Toronto.) The group launched into a rowdy take on Carl's "Blue Suede Shoes" and when Lennon growled the familiar opening lines, the twenty-thousand-strong crowd, most of whom had been mere kids back in 1956, absolutely erupted. Carl loved Lennon's version. "John nailed the punctuation right on, he sure did," he said.

Another member of the Carl Perkins admiration society was Lennon's Plastic Ono bandmate Eric Clapton. In January 1971, when Clapton appeared with his latest outfit, Derek and the Dominos, on the Cash TV show, the bell-bottomed, long-haired English guitarist looked like a man who couldn't believe his good fortune. Backstage, he'd told Carl, "Man, that lick on 'Matchbox' just hooked me." To Carl, Clapton was "a great rock picker."

On the set, Cash spoke with Clapton between songs, talking about musical influences.

"I think probably one of the most important artists that influenced a lot of the groups from England comes from right here in the States," Cash said.

"I think one of the best is right here on the show right now," Clapton replied.

"Do you think we should bring him on?" asked Cash.

Carl duly entered from stage right, playing the opening notes to "Matchbox," forming a tight line of three at stage front with Clapton and Cash. Carl took the first solo, then a smiling Clapton stepped forward for the next lead break, by which time the song was in overdrive. As Carl played the closing solo, his leg twitching wildly, the smile never left Clapton's face. The audience inside the Ryman lapped it up.

By now, Carl had grown accustomed to meeting prominent and influential figures. In mid-April 1970, during a break in shooting, the Cash troupe had been invited to the White House. As they performed "A Boy Named Sue," Carl shot a glance in the direction of President Richard Nixon, thinking to himself, *I'm going to look him right in the damn eye.* To his surprise, Carl discovered that Nixon was staring at him rather than at Cash. *He ain't supposed to be looking at me,* Carl thought, chuckling, as he got back to work.

Carl's profile on *The Johnny Cash Show* continued to grow. Together with the Carter Family and the Statler Brothers he performed "Greystone Chapel," a song written by Glen Sherley, a Folsom Prison inmate, then a few weeks later he was back with the Carters and the Statlers to sing "Seeing Nelly Home," a song with its roots in American Civil War times. He also joined Cash and the Tennessee Three to perform "Big River," one of Cash's signature songs. On an episode that featured guests José Feliciano, Linda Ronstadt, and Bobby Bare, Carl performed "I'll Fly Away," the gospel hymn that he'd sing so loudly in church as a kid that his mother would shoosh him. "Too loud, Carlie," she'd tell him. "Too loud."

Carl's name was popping up all over the place. In 1970, on the suggestion of an executive at Columbia, he collaborated with label-mates NRBQ, a young bar band. They cut an LP that blended songs from the Louisville, Kentucky, quartet with new takes on such Carl originals as "All Mama's Children," "Turn Around," "Sorry Char-lie," "Allergic to Love," and "Just Coastin'." The album's title track was a remake of Carl's 1956 single, "Boppin' the Blues."

As noted by *Rolling Stone* writer Michael Lydon, who watched them at work in Columbia's New York studio, in theory it was "a brilliant stroke—Columbia teamed up two contracted artists whose sales had been unexciting." The way Lydon read the matchup, "NRBQ got a chance to work with the real thing," and as for the "ever-obliging" Carl, well, he was still searching for a comeback smash and seemed happy to record with anyone who might help make that happen. There was one key difference in approach—Carl always swore allegiance to Sam Phillips's keep-it-simple technique and wanted to record his vocals and guitar at the same time. But this simply wasn't the way records were made any more. "[I've] never recorded any other way," Carl explained. "I get more feeling that way." Carl was eventually talked into adopting the modern method and cut separate tracks, but the lukewarm finished product went to prove that he might have done best to stick with his old-school style.

During downtime, Carl regaled the members of NRBQ and the studio crew with tales of his famous Sun peers. He related the story of how he and Johnny Cash had encouraged a young Jerry Lee Lewis to "make a fuss" when he played the piano and "four nights later he was top of the bill," and how Carl came to write "Blue Suede Shoes." ("You gotta be real poor to care about new shoes like I did," said Carl, laughing.) And Carl never missed an opportunity to mention his British buddies the Beatles. In this telling, while at Abbey Road in 1964, when the band asked Carl if he minded if they recorded

"Matchbox," his reply was: "Why, no, not at all, just make sure those royalty checks get to Carl Perkins, Jackson, Tennessee, USA."

As well intentioned as Carl's NRBQ collaboration no doubt was, the record wasn't a hit. *Village Voice* critic Robert Christgau was less than impressed. "Sorry, folks," he wrote, "Carl just can't wear them shoes no more." And NRBQ? "Competent and utterly unexciting," Christgau declared.

Hits continued to elude Carl. Although such singles as the intriguing story-song "Me Without You," as well as "Cotton Top" and "High on Love," all made it onto the Country chart, none cracked the Top 40. He recorded another Ronnie Self number, "What Every Little Boy Ought to Know," a melodrama about country life, which went nowhere on release in late 1970. Likewise, the widescreen, heartfelt "My Son, My Sun," a Carl original, which came and went quickly in 1970. The B-side, the restless country rocker "State of Confusion," dabbled in social commentary, which was a new twist for Carl.

But others had success with Carl's songs. Tommy Cash, younger brother of Johnny, had a number 9 hit on the *Billboard* Hot Country Songs chart in March 1970 with a Perkins original, the upbeat, twangy "Rise and Shine." (Country great Kitty Wells liked it enough to record her own version a few months later.) In early 1971, twenty-five-year-old Arlene Harden had a Country Top 40 hit with a cover of Carl's syrupy "True Love Is Greater Than Friendship"—given that Harden was a Columbia artist, it may well have been the most success Carl ever had with the label. And the covers of "Blue Suede Shoes" kept on coming, the latest being from "the French Elvis," Johnny Hallyday (who would jam the song onstage with Carl in 1984). In between writing hits, playing live, and appearing on TV, Carl collaborated with the other Cash—Johnny—to write music for the soundtrack of *Little Fauss and Big Halsy*, a 1970 vehicle for Hollywood star Robert Redford. Carl's version of "True Love Is Greater Than Friendship" featured on the soundtrack.

While Carl insisted that he was happy taking a back seat to the Man in Black, it seemed as though he was just about everywhere right now. When he traveled to the UK and Europe in early 1972 as part of the Johnny Cash roadshow, his fifth visit since 1964, Carl was buttonholed by die-hard rockabilly fans, keen for a one-on-one with their hero. He may have been a support act, but Carl was a popular man.

In one unpublished interview from the trip, Carl waxed lyrical on everything, from his earliest days, describing himself as "a confused youngster," to his admiration of fellow pickers James Burton, Merle Travis—whom he'd first heard on the Grand Ole Opry radio program—and Chet Atkins, although he made it clear that his eyes and ears were always open: "I can appreciate any style of guitar playing," Carl explained. He also discussed the demands of relentless touring—he was set to play about one hundred shows with Cash during 1972. (Cash's TV show ended production in March 1971.) "You have to work when you are sick," explained Carl. "The [audience] didn't pay to hear you say you feel bad. You have to make sure your nose is halfway clean." And Carl, despite being well into his fourth decade in "the biz," still understood that there were no guarantees beyond the next show. He remained a humble man. "We don't have anything that says we're going to be around next year," Carl said. "We may be back in the service station—not that I'll ever be too good to do that type of work again."

When Carl and the Cash troupe crossed the Channel in late February and reached Amsterdam for shows at the Concertgebouw, he spoke with two Dutch fans, Hans Langbroek and Adri Sturm. The interview was published in *Rockville* magazine. Again, talk turned to Carl's musical beginnings. "I liked country music," he explained, "but I liked it *with a little beat to it*." And what about Sam Phillips— who, in 1969, had sold 80 percent of the Sun label to Shelby Singleton, producer of the million-selling hit "Harper Valley PTA," for $1 million—how did Carl reflect on his time with the man? With absolutely no regrets, as he made clear. "He got full cooperation from his guys 'cause we were all hungry country boys that wanted to sell some records." And the magic of Sun; how did Carl explain that? Simple, really. "It was a combination of a bright engineer, a small studio . . . and a lot of togetherness."

And what about the Sun Studio recording of 1956's Million

Dollar Quartet session, which was now spoken about in reverential terms—would that ever get a proper release? Carl made it clear that he'd love to see it come out, although he understood that it was a complicated matter that would launch "many lawsuits." But as far as Carl was concerned, the recording had the potential to sell millions. "I don't see how it could miss being probably the biggest record of all time," he declared, "due to the fact of Elvis and John and Jerry . . . I'd like to get my hands on it and release it myself."

So, Carl was asked, was it likely that Sun's new majority owner would release the tapes? "If Shelby could get his hands on it, it would [already] be out." Carl, instead, had another theory: "That tape is no doubt in the hands of Sam Phillips, locked in a vault to keep anybody from getting hold of it. That's a valuable piece of merchandise."

The saga of the Million Dollar Quarter sessions wasn't over yet, not by a long shot.

CHAPTER 13

Every time I had a death in my family,
Elvis knew about it

Carl was set for yet another switch of labels, from Columbia to Mercury Records. It was currently the label of choice for Carl's touring buddies the Statler Brothers—who'd had a long-overdue hit with "Bed of Roses"—as well as Nashville-based crooner Faron Young, who'd also returned to the top of the Country charts with the tearstained "It's Four in the Morning." And Carl's first long-player for his new label was as country as hay bales and John Deere ride-ons—the title, *My Kind of Country*, couldn't have made that any clearer. But just in case it wasn't, Carl "dressed country" on the cover of the 1973 LP. With his Stetson firmly in place, Carl picked at a blade of grass while seated next to some antiquated equipment in the field of the Jackson farm that he'd bought for his parents. That image, Carl wrote in the liner notes, was *his* kind of country. "It's my little corner of the big country that you, the fan, afforded me," he acknowledged. Carl went on to explain that his kind of country was also "the music between the covers of this album." On the photo used for the LP's rear cover, Carl's proud parents stood in the background.

Once again, Carl was backed by the cream of the Nashville crop—the Jordanaires provided silky backing vocals, Charlie McCoy blew some bluesy harmonica, "Sneaky" Pete Drake sat in on pedal steel, and "Pig" Robbins switched seamlessly between piano and organ. Some of the songs were familiar: Carl rerecorded 1956's "Dixie

Fried," which he retitled "(Let's Get) Dixiefried," and he closed the album with a cover of "Ruby, Don't Take Your Love to Town," a Mel Tillis song about a disabled veteran that was a huge hit for Kenny Rogers in 1969. He also covered another Tillis track, "Honky Tonk Song" and Johnny Cash's "Goin' to Memphis." Of Carl's originals, "Love Sweet Love" brought a bit of gospel to proceedings, while "You Tore My Heaven All to Hell," which was released as a single, was yet another bighearted ballad that should have been a hit. It wasn't, and neither was the LP, although Carl could take some solace (and bank some more checks) when, at around the same time as *My Kind of Country*, Johnny Rivers recorded a revved-up version of "Blue Suede Shoes" that returned the song to the Top 40 of the *Billboard* Hot 100. It was a rare feat: The same song had made the business end of the Hot 100 three times—first Carl, then Elvis, now Rivers—over a span of seventeen years.

While out promoting *My Kind of Country*, Carl was in a reflective mood. He admitted that in between Cash commitments and studio sessions, downtime was become increasingly rare: "It's pushin' me a bit. I dunno," he added, "I like to strap on my old blue-jeans and go rub my cows between the ears or go fishin'. I just like to live." He was as excited by the prospect of jamming at home with his boys Greg and Stan, with Valda sitting in on piano, as he was playing to the Cash faithful. Carl laughed about being at home, how he could slip off his toupée, set his false teeth by the sink, and "really enjoy my music." There was no showbiz at Chez Perkins in Jackson.

Still, when Carl stepped out in the summer of 1973 to promote *My Kind of Country* at a Mercury showcase in Nashville before ten thousand die-hard fans, he didn't hold back—Carl played with as much energy and fire as any of the other acts on the bill. "I saw little girls in the aisles kind of shakin'," Carl said after his set at the second annual Country Music Fan Fair, wiping the sweat from his brow. "And y'know, fellas, that pops it to you!"

An idea gradually started to form in Carl's mind—maybe there was a way to keep playing music *and* be a good father at the same time. This notion would grow stronger and stronger over the next couple of years.

~

It seemed that throughout Carl's life, moments of personal and professional satisfaction were regularly undermined by tragedy. It had been ten years since Carl had fired his brother Clayton from the band after that one final blowup in a hotel room with Red Foley. Carl, of course, had moved on considerably since then, finding steady work with Cash and never lacking in supportive record labels, but Clayton hadn't ever really recovered from the shame of being fired by his own sibling. He'd been unemployed since Carl delivered him to his parents' doorstep in Jackson back in 1963 and drove off. His wife, Ruby Sue, had left him, taking their three children, and remarried. Clayton lived the life of a hobo, drinking heavily, sleeping in boxcars, and spending much of his time with fellow drifters in Jackson. Clayton always had a thing for guns, and that would prove to be his undoing.

During Christmas 1973, Johnny Cash was in California, filming a cameo in the TV detective show *Columbo*. There was also a part in the program for his band, including Carl, who were in the process of flying out to join Cash. That's when Cash received a call—Clayton Perkins was dead; he'd shot himself. No one could confirm if it was intentional or accidental. His body had been found by Carl's sons, Greg and Stan, who'd been sent to look for their uncle. Carl was still in transit and hadn't been alerted to the horrible situation. Cash was mortified—he knew he'd have to be the one to tell Carl, but, as he'd later write, "I never did anything with so much regret. But I had to do it."

He called the airport and got Carl on the phone. Cash told Carl that "something bad wrong" had happened. Carl's first concern was his parents—were they okay?

Cash then gave him the terrible news about his brother. "Carl, the report is that he killed himself. He's shot himself in his bed with his pistol." Carl didn't answer; instead, he dropped the phone and started sobbing. Fluke Holland immediately put Carl on a plane back home to Tennessee.

At the service for Clayton, Elvis Presley sent a weeping willow tree with twelve papier-mâché redbirds attached to its trunk. Presley may not have spent much time in recent years with his former Sun labelmates—he was either holed up at Graceland with his "Memphis Mafia" entourage, in the studio, or on the road—but he still respected them and grieved deeply with Carl over the loss of another brother, gone far too young. Clayton was just thirty-eight years old. "Every time I had a death in my family," said Carl, "[Elvis] knew about it." Carl planted the weeping willow in his yard—and clung desperately to a belief that Clayton's death had somehow been an accident.

Clayton's death made Carl think more seriously about working with his sons. Perhaps forming a band with Stan and Greg would help fill the hole left by the deaths of Jay and Clayton. And finally, after another hundred-plus shows with Johnny Cash during 1974 and again in 1975, Carl made the decision to leave and form his own group. Carl had devoted almost a decade to the employ of the Man in Black, traveling the globe while playing for presidents and murderers and just about everyone in between. His decision was made easier when Cash brought his brother Tommy into the band, who'd been going through some personal troubles, and cuts needed to be made to the troupe.

Carl freely admitted that life in the Cash roadshow, particularly in the later years, had many benefits—financial security, for one. "[And it was a] good place for me to sober up." They'd never had a formal contract; it had always been strictly an understanding between two close friends. "We worked with a handshake," Carl told the *Jackson Sun*. "It was a good association."

But now Carl wanted to spend more time at home in Jackson and devote quality time to his family—he'd recently become a first-time grandfather. Carl had also lost his father, Buck, who died in January 1975, at the age of sixty-six, after a long battle with cancer, and was laid to rest in Jackson's Hollywood Cemetery. With what was almost his dying breath, Buck told Carl how proud he was of what he'd achieved with his music. Buck died on the same day as Ezra P. Carter, Cash's father-in-law. Once again, Elvis Presley sent a large wreath, as he'd done when Carl's brothers died.

In the wake of Buck's death, Carl was appointed regional chairman for the American Cancer Society, whose aim was to provide improved treatment and rehab for cancer patients. It was the first of many local community roles that Carl would take on during the ensuing years. "Let us not forget that God, you, and I can move mountains," Carl told the *Jackson Sun*. "Many forms of cancer are curable if detected early and treated properly."

Having made up his mind to leave Cash's employ, Carl admitted, "Now I can rest in my own bed—and my wife's cooking is tasting fine." (He told another reporter that Valda's biscuits tasted good "because the same sweet hands rolled the dough like they've been doing for twenty-three years.") And as for playing in a band with his sons, that would be the perfect combination of family and music. What more could Carl ask for?

For a very long time, Carl had been willing to accept that "your star doesn't shine when you're behind a bright star like Cash." But, as Carl also explained, "As long as I was standing behind someone else, I didn't have a chance to stand alone." Carl was much more than a sideman—now it was time for him to shine more brightly.

Carl showed off his new band during a hometown show—"for the first time in 10 years," as a flyer proudly proclaimed—at the five-thousand-capacity Coliseum in Jackson on January 17, 1976. The original lineup for what became known as the C.P. Express was Carl on guitar and vocals, while his sons Greg and Stan played played bass and rhythm guitar. The C.P. Express would be fleshed out by Lee McAlpin on keyboards, Gary Vailes on drums, and musical all-rounder David Sea, who played harmonica and saxophone. (Over time, Stan would move to drums.) They'd also played a few days earlier to six thousand people in Alexandria, Louisiana, as part of a bill headlined by Willie Nelson (who had featured in Jackson, too). Before they took the stage, Carl pulled his boys into a huddle and said a quick prayer. His sons, understandably, were "scared to death," as Stan later admitted. Until now, they'd played strictly in local rock bands in and around Jackson. "We were just young kids." But both Greg and Stan understood that their father wouldn't put them through this if he didn't believe in their musical ability. "I'm lucky enough to walk in the tracks [of my father]," said Stan, who was a huge admirer of Carl's "talent, his humbleness. He's just a good solid man."

The way Carl had it figured, "I lost two of the best players I ever had in my brothers, and God came along and gave me two sons that are better players than they were. To have those boys on stage with me fueled a brand-new fire." Carl waxed philosophical about this fresh phase of his career. "It just seems that every time something's knocked me down, something's replaced it that's even better than what I had."

They began slowly, playing about twenty gigs in 1976. Carl also took a trip to the International Festival of Country Music, a three-day annual event staged at London's Wembley Stadium during April. Also on the bill were Waylon Jennings, Tammy Wynette, and Dolly Parton, with whom Carl would soon collaborate.

Demand for the C.P. Express grew, but rather than cash in on the "oldies circuit," which Carl could have easily done, they opted to play clubs and venues that were not always on the typical tour itinerary. Traveling in a GMC Motorhome dubbed the Matchbox Express, during a run in June 1977 they'd play such towns as Port Huron, Michigan, Laurel, Mississippi, Poplar Bluff, Missouri, and Poteau, Oklahoma. Things could get tough on the road; sometimes there'd be disputes about getting paid. "We did some bad places," said Stan. Money was tight.

"America's still out there if you'll just get off the interstate highways and look for it," Carl told one of the many writers who spoke with him on the road. He enjoyed the sensation of playing packed clubs, often in towns that didn't see a lot of live music, and really interacting with his fans. "I can get closer to a small audience," he told *Country Style* magazine, "and communicate with them better."

Carl would take any opportunity to talk up the musical talents of his offspring. He told reporters that Stan had "been pounding on buckets since he was this high" and would frequently praise Greg's rock-solid playing. "That little Greg, he's hot," Carl told *Goldmine* magazine. "That little critter picks left-handed, upside-down, and all from watching me play, like in a mirror."

Being in the spotlight was a new sensation for Carl after a decade as sideman to Cash. In the past, Carl often had to reassure a nervous Man in Black before he took the stage, and now he drew on some of those experiences to ease his own nerves. "I'm getting a little taste of that now," he said. "It's very beneficial." But once onstage, freed from the restraints of replicating Cash's music—which he readily admitted didn't stretch him too much as a player—Carl was free to truly cut loose, playing extended guitar solos. He also began moving a lot more onstage. As Carl explained, when his sons urged him on, shouting "Go, Daddy!", he had no option but to react. "It don't leave me much choice but to rear back and do all I can."

One critic, who caught Carl and his band at an Elks Club dance in Missouri during early 1977, noted: "Watching the Carl Perkins revue . . . one can almost see the old Carl Perkins, the Sun Records Carl Perkins. . . . He does a little dance, a 'bebop' step, guitar on hip, as he sings. *He enjoys himself.*"

Playing with his boys was proving to be bit as satisfying as Valda had told Carl that it would be. "My wife always predicted that we'd end up playing together," Carl told the *Music City News*, "but I said no. I just thought that was just too much to expect out of this life. . . . I feel good," said Carl. "It's like starting again in the business."

Backed by his sons and the rest of the C.P. Express, with Judy King (Stan's wife) contributing vocals, Carl released a new album, simply titled *The Carl Perkins Show*, which he released on his own Suede label and sold via mail order. The LP mixed old favorites ("Matchbox," "Let it Shine," "Country Boy's Dream") with such covers as "CC Rider" and "Green, Green Grass of Home." In the liner notes, Carl reflected on how it had been twenty years since his first long-player for Sun, back when his brothers were in his band. Now their places were taken by his sons. "I've been blessed many times in the music business," wrote Carl, "but making this album was no doubt one of my greatest pleasures."

During downtime, a rejuvenated Carl spent as much as three hours a day playing his guitar at home, fine-tuning his chops. "In my line of work," he said, "I'm always tied to a guitar." Carl would also sing at his local Methodist church, where he was president of the men's club. As Carl told yet another journalist, he was just as happy at home "with a catgut guitar, singing 'What a friend we have in Jesus,'" as he was out on tour performing "Blue Suede Shoes." "It's a dream come true for a Daddy," Carl said of his new work-life balance.

Carl was also at work on a book about his spiritual life, which he titled *Disciple in Blue Suede Shoes*. "I wrote every word of it with a pencil, and my daughter, Debbie, typed it and spelled some of the words right," said Carl, who admitted that he did intervene, however, when Debbie changed some of the words he used. "I told her I had said 'tater' for years and that stayed in the published version," he said with a laugh. (*Disciple in Blue Suede Shoes* would be released by the Christian publisher Zondervan Books in 1978.)

While Carl's star was rising once again, the same couldn't be said for some of his peers. Despite a recent resurgence in his recording career with such hits as "Suspicious Minds," "Kentucky Rain," and "Burning Love," Elvis Presley's dependence on prescription drugs and his twilight zone lifestyle had diminished the power of his live shows. His health was also in rapid decline; his weight had ballooned to more than three hundred pounds. Carl hadn't seen Presley for several years but in 1975 he recorded a song that he thought might just work for his old Sun Records buddy. Titled "The EP Express," it was jam-packed with Elvis song titles and references. Carl was uncomfortable about pitching the song "cold" to Elvis, but his son Stan and daughter, Debbie, told him they'd take up the challenge. The only caveat was that Carl would allow them to drive his brand-new Cadillac to Graceland. With that agreed and with song in hand, they set out for Memphis.

The Perkins siblings were greeted by Elvis's uncle, Vester Presley, who was one of the gatemen at Graceland. Stan and Debbie introduced themselves and Vester placed a call to the house. Elvis was home, he was told, but not yet out of bed. He did, however, have a message, which Vester related: "He wants to see you guys." When they returned in a couple of hours, as advised, the King was still in his chamber, so they gave up and drove back to Jackson.

Jerry Lee Lewis, meanwhile, used a far more brazen tactic to gain an audience with the King. Early on the morning of November 22, 1976, he pulled up at Graceland behind the wheel of a Rolls-Royce Silver Shadow. He, too, was told that Elvis was asleep, and drove away. Some twenty-four hours later, after a big night at the Vapors, a Memphis nightspot, a drunken Lewis again arrived at the gates of Graceland, this time driving a new Lincoln Continental. According to the gateman on duty, Harold Lloyd, the man known as "the Killer" was "outta his mind . . . screamin', hollerin', and cussin'."

"Tell him the Killer is here to see him!" he yelled at Lloyd, who instead put in a call to the local police. Soon after arriving, they noticed that Lewis had a .38-caliber derringer pistol wedged between his knee and the car door. In Lewis's version of the story, however, he said that the pistol was a gift from a local sheriff, who'd told him to store it on the dashboard of his car because he didn't have a concealed weapons permit. Lewis also said that when he was asked by the gateman what he intended to do with the gun, he replied sarcastically that he didn't intend to kill Elvis. "Everyone can relax." He was arrested and charged with possessing a firearm and being drunk in a public place.

Whatever the exact truth was, it was the type of drama that Carl had come to expect from Lewis, and that he was very comfortable avoiding. He'd had his fill of Lewis during their time together at Sun. "Wavin' that gun around Presley's gate," Carl said with a mix of concern and frustration in his voice, "that stuff is a little too far out. I'd like to see the man get this out of his system before he hurts somebody."

Carl had talked about Presley with a journalist in March 1977. "I'll bet Elvis would be happy to trade places with me," he said. Carl was referring to his rock-solid marriage with Valda and the pleasure he took from his family—his daughter, Debbie, was about to be married—but his words would soon take on a bigger meaning.

~

In early 1977, Carl decided he'd try to visit Elvis. He'd recently seen him singing on TV and was concerned for his friend; it was clear that he was in bad shape. Yet at the same time Carl was so struck by the power of Presley's performance that he sat in his den and started to cry. "I never heard him sing as good as he sang 'My Way' and 'How Great Thou Art.' . . . He was a sick man, but it seemed that on that show he said, turn on the switch."

Carl drove to Graceland but had the same experience as Stan—Vester greeted him and called the house but was told that Elvis was still asleep. Perhaps he could wait? Carl stayed for a time, signing autographs for the fans gathered at Graceland's gates who recognized him, but then gave up and drove back home. He wasn't offended, though. "I always felt sorry for Presley," Carl told a reporter. "The life he was forced to live, not being able to get out in the daytime and enjoy life anywhere in the world—I wondered about it for many years: 'When will the boy break?'"

Carl, like the rest of the world, learned the answer to that question on August 16, 1977, when news emerged that Elvis had died at the age of forty-two. The official cause was cardiac arrest. When Carl's son Greg told him the news, he felt like he'd been punched in the stomach. Carl tried to describe the feeling; he said it was as though "an emotional drop took place inside my soul." When a reporter from the *Jackson Sun*, Carl's local newspaper, called him soon after Presley's death, he struggled to put his emotions into words. "It just seems so unreal. It just ain't found a landin' place inside me yet."

Soon after the news about Elvis's death went worldwide, Carl got a call from Presley's producer, Felton Jarvis. About six months before Elvis's demise, Carl had met with Jarvis in Nashville and played him several songs he thought Presley might be interested in recording. Among them was a song called "Mama." A little while later, Jarvis called Carl from Charleston, South Carolina, stating that he hadn't forgotten about him or his songs, but was having great trouble getting Presley back into the studio. "He just doesn't want to record. He ain't heard your songs, but he's going to," Jarvis reassured Carl.

Now, just days after Presley's death, Felton said that Elvis had finally listened to "Mama" and had agreed to record the song when he had a break between tours. (Presley had been scheduled to go back on the road the day after he died.) But now that opportunity was gone.

Clearly devastated, Felton admitted to Carl that he didn't know if he'd ever want to make another record. However, as Carl revealed to a writer from *Country Music People*, Jarvis told him that if he did one day return to the studio, "he said he would like to produce me." When Carl related this conversation to Valda, she told him it was a sign, that it was "God who made Felton call you." Carl accepted that, yes, something special had taken place. "I felt that it wasn't just a coincidence that Felton had called. It was something stronger than either one of us."

Jarvis wasn't the only person to reach out to Carl at the time of Presley's death. He was contacted by a record label exec and was pitched the idea of recording some kind of Elvis tribute album. "You had a similar style," they explained, "and you knew the man." Carl thought it was way too soon to even consider something like this; he also felt that the idea of making a few bucks from his friend's death was distasteful. "It could have easily been interpreted that I was trying to jump on a bandwagon." He called Jarvis, who agreed. "I thought somebody out there might feel that Presley's producer and Presley's friend were tryin' to cash in on something," said Carl. The idea went no further.

Valda was currently in the hospital, so Carl couldn't attend Presley's funeral service on August 17. Instead, he watched on TV, "bawling my eyes out" as he saw the long line of mourners assembled outside the gates of Graceland staging a vigil. (Two of the mourners were killed by a drunk driver outside the gates, adding to the chaos.) The gathering in and around Memphis was so sizable, in fact, that President Jimmy Carter despatched three hundred National Guardsmen to the city to maintain order. Roughly thirty thousand people viewed Elvis's casket at the Memphis Funeral Home, where he had been embalmed. (The funeral home's switchboard was jammed by grief-stricken calls from around the world.)

Only a select group, however, were allowed inside Graceland for the private service. Among them were music greats Charley Pride, James Brown, and Chet Atkins; Hollywood stars John Wayne, George Hamilton, Burt Reynolds, and Ann-Margret (who'd costarred with Presley in the movie *Viva Las Vegas*); and such powerful figures as Caroline Kennedy. Elvis's longtime manager Colonel Tom Parker was also there paying his final respects to the superstar whose career he had controlled for twenty years. After the service, a motorcade escorted Presley's body the few miles down Elvis Presley Boulevard to Forest Hills Cemetery, as about eighty thousand people lining the street looked on. Some fans were so distraught that they threw themselves at the hearse containing Presley as it passed—but perhaps no one was quite as distraught as the stonemason who'd misspelled Presley's middle name as Aaron, not Aron, on his tombstone.

"Whether you liked him personally or not," Carl said, "you were touched by Elvis Presley during his forty-two years on this earth. . . . I guess we all thought that maybe somehow Elvis would never die."

Presley's death encouraged Carl to think more about what was now known as "the Million Dollar Quartet," the impromptu jam with Cash, Presley, and Jerry Lee Lewis on the afternoon in December 1956 when Carl was recording "Matchbox." It was around the time of Elvis's passing that Carl got to hear that recording for the first time. Carl felt it was a signal; he even told the writer Peter Guralnick that Elvis had spoken to him one night from the great beyond. "Elvis told me, 'Fight it. Get it. Do something good with it.'"

Carl admitted that if he had the cash, he'd try to buy the tapes and release them himself. "I'd love to get hold of it." As Carl saw it, the problem was that two major labels were involved—Columbia, Cash's label, and RCA, which controlled Presley's music—that were unlikely to grant the other permission to release the sessions. "These two real big companies," said Carl, "I think will never agree to get it released on any label except their own."

Shelby Singleton, who'd bought the Sun label from Sam Phillips, had his own plans for the Million Dollar Quartet recordings. When Singleton made it known that he intended to clean up the tapes by adding some overdubs, Carl and Cash reacted negatively. "It would have been terrible," Carl insisted, "and would ruin the authenticity of it." As far as Carl was concerned, he had a fair claim to the material—after all, it had been recorded during a Carl Perkins session. "I was charged for the session," said Carl, "so my lawyers feel that I am the rightful owner of the tapes."

For the time being, the future of the Million Dollar Quartet remained uncertain. But in August 1978, Carl did have a win. He'd been in a long dispute with Sam Phillips and was finally awarded some royalties earned from various Sun releases featuring his music between 1969 and 1977. When his lawyers threatened another lawsuit, a deal was reached and Carl was granted control of the copyrights of all the songs he'd written while with Sun, which was a significant score. (Over time he'd form two music publishing companies, Carl Perkins Music and Godfather Publishing.)

With the proceeds from the settlement, Carl bought a new property, where he and Valda would spend the rest of their lives. It was by far the biggest home they'd ever owned, a one-story brick residence on Country Club Lane, located in the swankier part of Jackson. Les Paul guitar motifs decorated the front door of the house; a birdbath was a feature of the front yard. Carl would eventually add a home studio.

A very house-proud Carl took particularly good care of the lawn and grounds, sometimes also mowing the lawn of his neighbor, Gary Deaton, if he was out of town. Dressed in work clothes and a baseball cap, Carl would occasionally be mistaken for the gardener when fans drove by his house, hoping to spot him. When asked if Carl was home, he'd usually reply, "I think he's around here somewhere." He'd climb down from his ride-on mower and wander off for a moment. Then he'd return and reveal the truth. Carl liked to describe himself as "just the guy who mows his own lawn."

One day a woman pulled over and complimented Carl on his handiwork, not knowing it was his house or who he was.

"Would you be interested in doing my lawns?" she asked.

Carl, who was wearing his baseball cap and sitting astride his John Deere mower, replied, "Well, ma'am, I don't really know what to charge you."

The woman explained that she'd be happy to match whatever he was being paid for looking after the grounds at the Country Club Lane house.

"Well," Carl said, trying hard to suppress a grin, "all I can say is that the lady that lives here lets me sleep with her every night."

CHAPTER 14

There's no better place in the world for a man to be number one than in his own home

When Elvis Presley died, his producer, Felton Jarvis, had floated the idea of working with Carl, and in 1978 they joined forces for an album titled, appropriately, *Ol' Blue Suede's Back*. Carl had a very simple plan for the record, which he outlined to Jarvis: "I told Felton I just wanted to do an album with my favorite rock and roll songs." Carl had done this before, of course, but not with a producer like Jarvis, someone who really understood his style of music—and whom Carl liked a lot.

Before recording with Jarvis, Carl had laid down twenty-four tracks in a studio in Muscle Shoals with a producer named Johnny Morris. "They're as good as anything I'd ever recorded," said Carl. Morris's plan was to pitch these songs to different labels, but, according to Carl, "he was asking too much money" and despite various offers, the project was stillborn, and the songs gradually popped up on various Carl bootlegs. (In 1993, BMG officially released the material over three albums: *Disciple in Blue Suede Shoes*, *Take Me Back*, and *Carl Perkins and Sons*.)

Carl then signed with a new manager, Mervyn Conn, who promoted the annual Country Music Festival staged in London, where Carl had appeared several times. Conn asked Carl who he was recording for, and he replied, "Well, nobody." Carl explained his problem. "I just haven't had a record label that cared enough to pay the postage from Nashville to New York. It takes promotion in this business." Conn struck up a deal with UK-based Jet Records, a "progressive label," according to Carl, founded by Don Arden, who'd promoted Carl's earliest UK tours. Carl was now an unlikely labelmate of the Electric Light Orchestra and Roy Wood from the rock band Wizzard. In North America, his music would be distributed by CBS.

"I've been through the process many times before," said Carl after signing the deal, "but this is the first time I've ever seen the excitement like what's going on now."

Carl then reconnected with Jarvis, which led to *Ol' Blue Suede's Back*. The album's working title had been *The History of Rock and Roll*, which wasn't as overstated as it appeared, given that the tracks they recorded included "Shake, Rattle and Roll," "Tutti Frutti," "Maybellene," "That's All Right (Mama)," and, of course, "Blue Suede Shoes." They also cut Bill Haley's "Rock Around the Clock," which inspired Carl to go away and write and record a sort of modern-day response to that classic that he called "Rock On Around the World," the only new original on the LP, which closed the album.

In the end, *Ol' Blue Suede's Back* was a collection of old school rock and roll classics played with great heart and soul. It was a fitting tribute to the end of the era that was signified by Presley's death. As a writer from *Country Music People* noted, rather than a straight-up Elvis tribute, Carl and Jarvis took a fresh approach, "tackling songs that contributed to the success of the music." As Carl explained, "It ain't a lot of screaming guitars and electronic inferno." The album resonated strongly with Carl's rock-solid UK fanbase, selling around 100,000 copies.

In early 1979, Carl and the C.P. Express stepped out for a run of shows at New York venue the Bottom Line, as part of a two-month-long US tour. Carl, introduced as "the godfather of rockabilly music," was in fine form, looking sharp as ever and jokingly changing the lyrics of his signature song, singing: "I would dance / but I'm too old." His set list was now heavy with such classics as "Dixie Fried," "Turn Around," and Carl's own take on "That's All Right." As one critic noted, "Feet that can remain still when Perkins and his band play 'Honey, Don't' are feet that are tied down."

Backstage, Carl held court with John Morthland, a writer from *Rolling Stone*, talking about the Sex Pistols, of all bands. While Carl couldn't quite grasp their fashion sense—"I didn't understand what they meant by sticking pins through their noses"—he had a fair grasp of where they were coming from creatively. "Their music was almost like some of the Fifties-style stuff, it was so simple." Carl was right—if you looked beyond the Pistols' anti-everything lyrics, what remained was a band with a rock and roll heart. (As if to prove his point, later in 1979 Carl jammed with the American punk band the Dead Boys in an LA club.)

As John Morthland noted with ample justification, Carl was "arguably the first rock and roll instrumentalist to be a star." Carl certainly looked the part at the Bottom Line, decked out in a full-length pantsuit like those favored by Elvis in his Las Vegas prime. Carl was asked about his late friend—was there ever a chance he could have outranked the King? "No way," insisted Carl. "Any person playing this music," explained Carl, "was so fortunate that we had a guy to open the door like Elvis."

Carl then proudly posed for photos with his sons Stan and Greg, who were now twenty-four and twenty and had become part of a well-oiled machine onstage backing their Dad. Despite all the twists and turns of his life and his career, Carl still considered himself a very fortunate man. His marriage remained strong and his bond with his sons couldn't be tighter. "There's no better place in the world for a man to be number one," Carl said with a smile, "than in his own home." With that, Carl and his team boarded the Matchbox Express and headed for their next gig.

One morning at home in Jackson, Carl read a story in the *Jackson Sun* that truly spooked him. The report was about a young man from west Tennessee, roughly the same age as his boy Stan, who had been killed by his parents. A local musician named Wes Henley was sitting with Carl at the time, and as he told the *Jackson Sun*, the story's impact on Carl was immediate. "He just shook his head," said Henley, "and he looked at me and said, 'We've got to do something.'" Carl also felt that the boy in the story bore a strong resemblance to his own son, Stan, something Valda confirmed.

Carl did some research and was shocked to learn that only three centers for the prevention of child abuse existed in the entire country. He was put in touch with the Jackson Exchange Club, which was part of a nationwide alliance of community groups, much like Rotary Clubs, and the idea grew for what would become the Exchange Club–Carl Perkins Center for the Prevention of Child Abuse. A fundraising drive was initiated in 1979; the goal was $6,000, but Carl raised more than $30,000 when he staged a concert with his old Cash roadshow buddies the Statler Brothers.

A typically modest Carl had at first been unsure about putting his name to the center. "What good would that do?" he asked. There was also some resistance from the Exchange Club themselves. According to Henry Harrison, a founding member of the center, and later the founder of Jackson's Rock-A-Billy Hall of Fame, it took months of work to convince Exchange Club members that Carl was going to be "actively involved in the work of the center, not just a celebrity name."

Once that was sorted out, establishing the center became "very dear to my heart," Carl told the *Jackson Sun*. "This is an effort to do something about a problem more wide than I ever thought about in our community. It's just [an effort] to make a little better place out of one of the greatest places in the world."

In July 1980, when Carl played another fundraiser for the center, this time sharing the bill with Stella Parton, he was given the keys to the city and made an honorary sheriff's deputy. "We are envisioning this as an annual affair," said Carl, who'd also begun hosting the Carl Perkins Fishing Tournament and Family Weekend Bonanza. Carl typically closed that event, which ran for much of the 1980s, with an afternoon outdoors show on the shore of Reelfoot Lake in Tiptonville. Proceeds from these shows went to the nonprofit Easterseals Society. Carl was on its board in the role of special events chairman. "Carl could probably win the bass [fishing] tournament," noted the *Memphis Press-Scimitar*, "but the country music star will stick to picking and singing."

The purpose of the abuse center was simple. Through the work of trained professionals and volunteers, it would provide support for families in the hope that it would prevent child abuse. A caseworker could be involved with a family for anywhere between six and eighteen months. "Our focus is on the parent," said Deana Claiborne, the director of the center. Carl believed that the work done at the center would "teach the parents that there's another way." Valda, too, would become involved with the center, attending events with Carl, including the annual Blue Suede Dinner & Auction, which became a feature on the Jackson social calendar.

Carl would often tell his son-in-law, Bart Swift, that he never wanted to forget how it felt to struggle, regardless of how comfortable his life had become. As Swift saw it, Carl's involvement with the development of the center reflected that. "He always said that he never knew . . . when we can be a great help to someone when they're on the bottom in their life," said Swift. "That's why he was so nice and generous with his time."

The Exchange Club–Carl Perkins Center for the Prevention of Child Abuse was officially opened in October 1981. It was the first of its kind in the state of Tennessee and was initially housed in an old dorm room of the local university, moving to a larger downtown facility four years later. The Circle of Hope telethon, originally staged in 1983 at WBBJ-TV in Jackson, would become a reliable fundraiser for the Center, raising some $33,000 in its inaugural year. (Carl regularly hosted the telethon; in 1985 it raised more than $40,000 and he would always make an on-screen appearance.) Over time, Carl would see tangible results of their work when the first group of children helped by case managers grew older and got married. "Now we're looking at second generation," said Carl, "those that were rescued when they were little."

The establishment of the child abuse center was the starting point of what would be a hugely successful decade for Carl. During the

1980s Carl would reconnect with no less than three Beatles and two old buddies from Sun, make his proper big-screen acting debut, and receive various accolades, while continuing to blow away audiences with the C.P. Express, whose nightly fee would rise to $10,000 per show. He also got to look on proudly as rockabilly underwent a revival, thanks to such new outfits as the Blasters and the Stray Cats, who cited Carl as a major influence. Retro rockers Ray Campi & His Rockabilly Rebels covered Carl's "Gone, Gone, Gone," while an English quartet actually called themselves Match-box. Queen's huge hit "Crazy Little Thing Called Love" packed an unmistakable rockabilly swing, as would George Michael's 1987 smash "Faith." "I like today's rockabilly cats," Carl noticed, "mostly because they're simplifying the music back to where young kids can get interested. . . . Four guys can get together, learn to make mistakes at the same time, and they've got a shot at it."

One night in February 1981, Carl was at home when the phone rang. Valda answered and spoke briefly before turning to Carl. She covered the mouthpiece of the phone as she spoke: "Carl," she said, "he says he's Paul McCartney." Carl hadn't spent much time with McCartney in his post-Beatles life, but he'd been on his mind recently after the tragic assassination of John Lennon in New York City three months earlier. "It was so, so terribly sad," Carl said of Lennon's death, "that this boy had to be taken out at a time when he was touchin' reality."

It turned out to be the real Paul McCartney on the line. He had a simple question for Carl: "What are you doing? Would you like to come down to Montserrat?"

Carl was excited by the prospect of reuniting with the former Beatle but had one small problem, as he told McCartney: "If I knew where it was, it would help."

McCartney explained that in 1979, George Martin, the Beatles' producer, had established the AIR Studios at Montserrat, which was part of the Leeward Islands in the Caribbean. Paul was currently there recording what would become the *Tug of War* album. McCartney sent Carl an air ticket and asked him to set aside a week or so to work on a song he had in mind for him called "Get It."

Carl, having flown from Antigua in a small plane, was met on arrival at the airfield by McCartney and his wife, Linda, in a jeep. "They took me across the mountains [to the studio]," said Carl, who was dazzled by the scenery. "We were like kids again; it was a wonderful time." Carl wasn't the only guest; Motown superstar Stevie Wonder had also been invited to Montserrat, and together he and McCartney recorded the song "Ebony and Ivory." It was a feature of the finished album, easily McCartney's best since *Band on the Run*. (The album hit number 1 in both the United States and the UK.) Jazz great Stanley Clarke sat in on two tracks, while Ringo Starr also played on the album.

Carl's recording with McCartney, however, was something of a throwaway, a likable but easily forgettable country-pop strum. "Strangely," wrote McCartney biographer Philip Norman, "Paul chose to waste [Perkins] on an underpowered oddment called 'Get It,' which, judging by strained laughter at the end, Perkins didn't."

But this didn't prevent Carl from experiencing what he described as "eight wonderful days" with McCartney and his family and guests. On the night before he was due to fly home, Carl sat out on the deck, looking out at a postcard-worthy vista, thinking of a way to accurately describe Montserrat to his wife and kids, "how much of God you can see in that sky at night." Carl also wanted to capture in song the experience of reuniting with McCartney after more than a decade. That night he wrote the bighearted country ballad "My Old Friend."

Early the next morning, Carl played the song to McCartney, who was clearly moved. "Carl, it's beautiful," said McCartney. He asked Carl to play it again but told him to wait just a minute while he brought Linda into the room. They sat together on the floor in front of Carl as he played "My Old Friend" for a second time. By the time he sang the final line, Carl noticed that McCartney had tears rolling down his cheeks. He left the room and stood by the studio pool, wiping at his eyes. Carl apologized to Linda; he had no idea that his sweet, simple song would create such a strong response. "I'm sorry," Carl said. "I'm really sorry."

It was perfectly okay, Linda explained, as she put her arm

around Carl. "He hasn't been able to really break down since what happened to John." But then she asked Carl, *"How did you know?"*

"Know what, Linda?" asked Carl, who was now totally confused.

She explained that only two people on the planet knew the last words John Lennon had said to McCartney, when they met in New York not long before he was murdered. "Now there's three," she said cryptically, "and one of them is you."

Carl was still flummoxed. "You're freaking me out," he admitted. "I really don't know what you're talking about."

Linda explained that during that final get-together, John and Paul were standing in the hallway of the Dakota building when John patted his fellow Beatle on the shoulder and said, "Think about me now and then, old friend." These were the words Carl used in his song.

"Thank you," Linda said to Carl as he gathered his things to leave, still stunned by the moment. "He needed that."

Carl's time in Montserrat with the McCartneys wasn't his only recent reunion. In February 1980, Carl, along with the Statler Brothers, Kris Kristofferson, Waylon Jennings, June Carter Cash, among many others, had been in the house at the Grand Ole Opry to help celebrate Johnny Cash's twenty-five years in music, his silver anniversary, which was filmed for a TV special. "It's great seeing Carl Perkins again," said Cash backstage. "We've talked all about the early days at Sun Records, about Memphis." In late April 1981, Carl had been booked to perform at a festival in Frankfurt, Germany, and discovered that he was on the same bill as Jerry Lee Lewis and Johnny Cash.

The last few years had been an interesting ride for Carl's old labelmates and friends. Since Carl had left Cash's employ, the Man in Black's career had seemed to be in a slow decline. When the hits started to dry up, he resorted to doing commercials for the model rail company Lionel Trains, as well as fuel companies Amoco and STP, perhaps not the most popular options due to the global energy crisis. But his first autobiography, *Man in Black*, was published in

1975 and sold a whopping 1.3 million copies, proof that he hadn't fallen out of favor with the American public.

As for Lewis, despite such random acts of madness as his gunplay at the gates of Graceland, his career had taken a significant upswing with a run of charting country singles—seventeen, all up, in a hot streak between 1968 and 1977. And his latest marriage, his fourth, to Jaren Pate, was by far his most enduring; they'd been together since 1971. (They'd duly split in June 1982 and Pate would drown before divorce proceedings could be finalized.)

After playing the Frankfurt festival, Cash had a gig booked in Stuttgart, and Carl and Lewis joined him onstage. With nothing in the way of rehearsals, the erstwhile Sun trio stuck with the hits: Cash played "Get Rhythm," Lewis rocked "Whole Lotta Shakin' Goin' On," while Carl delivered "Matchbox" and "Blue Suede Shoes." And just as Carl had done back in his days with Cash and the Carter Family, they brought it home with the gospel numbers "Peace in the Valley" and "Will the Circle Be Unbroken." Cash's children John Carter and Cindy joined in on the finale, Hank Williams's "I Saw the Light."

The impromptu gig was recorded, and the results were produced by Rodney Crowell, a highly regarded country singer-songwriter, who also happened to be Cash's son-in-law. The ensuing LP was called *The Survivors*, and in a favorable review, *Rolling Stone* noted how Carl "huffs though his vocal turns, shaky but somehow compelling," while acknowledging that things really heated up when Lewis began pounding the keys. "His self-involved hollering," wrote Fred Schruers, "makes for some real excitement." And Carl's take on the record? "I was never really knocked out with that album," he told the *Gavin Report*. "I think the sound could have been better." Still, *The Survivors* made a reasonable showing on *Billboard*'s Top Country Albums charts on release in April 1982, peaking at number 21. (In what was the season of in-concert recordings, Carl released *Live at Austin City Limits*, on his own Suede Record Company, around the same time.)

It now seemed inevitable that whenever Carl spent time with his former Sun labelmates, talk turned to the Million Dollar Quartet:

Exactly when could the public finally hear this much-talked-about slice of musical history? After all, twenty-five years had now passed since that afternoon in Memphis; bootlegs of the session had since begun circulating. A release in Sweden in 1980 had quickly been stopped by RCA, Presley's label, and the few copies were pulled from the shelves. However, that didn't prevent future Presley biographer, Peter Guralnick, from writing an extensive article for the *New York Times* magazine about the Million Dollar Quartet, which included interviews with Sam Phillips and Carl, who remembered Sun fondly. "There was no rush," Carl said of his time at Sun. "You didn't worry about making a mistake; it was just an easy, carefree feeling we had, and it was the greatest way in the world, really, to cut raw music." But still a formal release was some way off—Shelby Singleton had been wearing a path in and out of court, defending his rights to the tape.

Carl, when asked about the Million Dollar Quartet—as he was repeatedly—had to chuckle. Upon hearing the tapes, he noticed that not one cussword was uttered. He was genuinely surprised. "You take four ol' roughneck boys back in those days and record them without knowing it," Carl explained. "I'm really surprised it turned out to be so clean."

The decade that was shaping up so favorably for Carl took a downward spiral in December 1982. A car crash had short-circuited his career—and almost ended his life—back in 1956 and now Carl's twenty-four-year-old son Greg was embroiled in the aftermath of a wreck. While playing a gig with Carl and the C.P. Express at Dyersburg on December 18, Greg drank several beers over the course of about seven hours. The band finished playing just before one, and that morning, at about five thirty, Greg was involved in a car crash at Tennessee 20 and Country Club Lane, not far from the Perkins family home. It was a stretch of road that locals considered dangerous. Two people died at the crash, Elmer and Emma McLemore; both were burned to death.

Greg, who was injured and required several days of hospitalization, was given a blood alcohol test at the site and blew .11—under Tennessee law, a .10 reading was considered legally intoxicated. Greg took the test willingly and made it known that he hadn't drunk any alcohol since the show. He also didn't request a lawyer, thinking that it wasn't necessary. "At that point," he later stated, "I knew things were serious, but I didn't know anyone had been killed." Greg was charged with two felony counts of vehicular homicide—the maximum sentence was eleven years in prison on each count.

Greg fronted a jury and Circle Court Judge James Todd over four days in December 1983, with Carl, now sporting a salt-and-pepper beard, and Valda, both looking on anxiously in the courtroom. Seven character witnesses, including Jackson mayor Bob Conger and county executive, Alex Leech, spoke on his behalf, testifying that Greg was an "honest, law-abiding young man" with an "excellent reputation." Greg took the stand in his own defense; in a shaky voice he said that he was willing to "put my hand on the Bible" in order to affirm that booze had nothing to do with the crash. He spoke directly to the jury: "I don't know what I could have done differently to avoid hitting that vehicle."

After four hours of deliberation, Greg was found not guilty of the felony but guilty of driving under the influence, a misdemeanor charge. While Greg's verdict was being read to those in the courtroom, Carl sat quietly, holding Valda's hand. The stress of the day caused Valda to faint, although she recovered sufficiently to leave the courtroom alongside Greg and Carl. When asked about his ordeal, Greg shook his head and said, "I just thank God. I just thank God." Carl was a little more forthcoming. "I would've liked for my boy to be totally free," he admitted, "but I'm glad it's over. I guess I'm happy about it." Jail time averted, Greg, Carl, and the C.P. Express were back on the road within weeks, playing their first gig of 1984 at Chicago on January 21.

A few years earlier, Carl had been asked about things he had yet to accomplish. "I'd like to take a pop at some little ol' movie," said Carl, who—quite understandably—didn't rate his cameos in the 1950s' flicks *Jamboree* or *Hawaiian Boy* as career high points. He'd been left behind by many of his contemporaries: Willie Nelson had starred in such Hollywood-goes-country films as *The Electric Horseman* and *Honeysuckle Rose*; Johnny Cash had made a series of TV movies, while Dolly Parton had made a star turn in the box office smash *9 to 5*. Elvis Presley, of course, had made so many mainstream Hollywood films during his life that he'd become a virtual cottage industry. (There had already been a made-for-TV Elvis biopic in 1979, starring Kurt Russell.) Even Roy Orbison, who could never make claim to being much of an actor, had made a guest appearance in the screwball 1980 flick *Roadie*, which starred Meat Loaf. He sang "The Eyes of Texas" in a roadhouse scene alongside Hank Williams, Jr., stopping a wild brawl in the process, before disappearing into the night. As for Jerry Lee Lewis, he was set to get the full biopic treatment with a story of his fast life and times, starring Dennis Quaid as the Killer.

By the mid-1980s, Carl finally had his chance to make his mark on screen, although purely by chance. Filmmaker John Landis had built a bankable reputation with the hit comedies *Animal House*, *The Blues Brothers*, and *Trading Places*, and in 1985 he was casting for a new film, a dark, surreal comedy named *Into the Night*. He caught Carl performing on British TV and had a brainwave— Landis figured he would be perfect in the (admittedly small) role of an underworld heavy named Mr. Williams. He sent the script to Carl.

When Carl told Valda about the movie, she was a little concerned about the abundance of violence and profanity in the script. She told Carl they might be exiled from their church if he took on the part. But Carl was highly motivated—in 1984, he'd passed on a Schlitz beer TV commercial, which he regretted, despite his bad track record with alcohol. "I was a big dummy," Carl admitted. (The Marshall Tucker Band and .38 Special got the gig instead.) "I don't care what the preachers say," he told Valda, "they don't have to go see it." Carl was in.

In his role as tough guy Mr. Williams, Carl had two key moments in the film. He featured in a casino scene with a youthful

Jeff Goldblum, in one of his first leading roles. "You talk to me straight or get your ass out of here," he advised Goldblum, delivering his lines with a convincing swagger. Carl's character eventually ended up in a knife fight with another moonlighting musician, David Bowie, who was playing a hit man named Colin Morris. "Let's not do anything rash," Bowie told him, as he held a knife to the throat of Diana, played by Michelle Pfeiffer. Carl, who'd already been stabbed, plucked the knife from his chest and got into a scrap with Bowie, as all four of them—Goldblum and Pfeiffer included—thrashed around a hotel room, while the old black-and-white movie *Abbott and Costello Meet Frankenstein* flickered on a TV screen behind them. Eventually Carl and Bowie crashed through the room's window and fell to their deaths. Carl and Bowie were two of the many cameos in the film. Also in the cast was the Muppets creator Jim Henson and numerous film director buddies of John Landis, including Lawrence Kasdan, David Cronenberg, Paul Mazursky, Jonathan Demme, and Jack Arnold, who directed the low-budget "classic" *It Came from Outer Space*.

Despite Carl's best efforts, *Into the Night* didn't quite earn back its $8 million budget and received mixed reviews on its release in February 1985. Perhaps director Landis was distracted by an involuntary manslaughter charge against him arising from an accident on the set of the recent *Twilight Zone* movie, which resulted in the deaths of actor Vic Morrow and two children. Writing about *Into the Night*, the *New York Times*' Vincent Canby made the observation that "Carl Perkins, the country music composer-performer . . . may have had more fun playing in the movie than [the audience does] playing in a trivial recognition game."

CHAPTER 15

You're great—you're George Harrison of the Beatles

The thirtieth anniversary of the recording of "Blue Suede Shoes" was set to occur in December 1985, and Carl had been thinking about the best way to mark the event that had changed the course of his life. At first Carl had considered making an album on which he was to be joined by as many as twenty-five guests, but figured there'd be too many labels involved, likely too much business interference, as his experience with the Million Dollar Quartet recording had proved. Instead, Carl came up with the idea of a performance that would feature, hopefully, the pick of his A-list friends and admirers. But rather than cold-call his possible guests, which was not his style, Carl recorded individual video invitations and posted them, along with an accompanying note. His recipients were such buddies as George Harrison, Ringo Starr, and Eric Clapton, as well as Dave Edmunds, another Carl Perkins devotee, whom Carl said was like a living encyclopedia of "old Sun records."

George Harrison had been out of the spotlight for several years, not having released an album since 1982's *Gone Troppo*. He'd also withdrawn considerably from public life since the murder of his Beatles bandmate John Lennon. But he was the first to agree, after a little cajoling from his wife, Olivia. "He's been my hero since I was a kid," said Harrison. "How could I refuse him anything?" Rosanne Cash was another who agreed to participate. Carl also reached out to the members of the Stray Cats, rockabilly true believers with whom he had rerecorded "Blue Suede Shoes" for the soundtrack of *Porky's Revenge*. They were in, too.

In fact, the only invitee not available was Paul McCartney, who was busy in the studio. McCartney offered to tape a segment, and although Carl was hugely tempted—who wouldn't want bragging rights on bringing together the three surviving Beatles?—he decided against it. "The world has waited for you guys to get together," Carl told him, "and I don't want the world thinking I tried to fool them." It was classic Carl: humble and honest.

A deal was set in place with pay TV network Cinemax to film the event that would be known as *Blue Suede Shoes: A Rockabilly Session*. Many of the performers were UK-based, so London's Limehouse Studios was chosen as the site for the shoot in October 1985. A studio audience would help bring the show to life. It would be a historic session on various levels—not only would it mark the anniversary of "Blue Suede Shoes" but it would be the first time Starr and Harrison had shared a stage since the Concert for Bangladesh at Madison Square Garden in 1971. Harrison hadn't played in public since a *Saturday Night Live* spot in 1976.

Carl understood the significance of the event—while filming, Harrison offered him a cigarette, which he chose to keep as a memento, rather than smoke it. "You're kidding," said Harrison. "Why not, man," Carl replied, "you're great. You're George Harrison of the Beatles." Carl also pocketed one of Harrison's guitar picks. (The custom-made Peavey guitar Carl used in the show would find a home in the Rock and Roll Hall of Fame, while the shirt he wore would become part of the Carl Perkins exhibit at the Legends of Tennessee Music Museum in Jackson.)

Prior to the shoot, Carl clashed with the producers from Cinemax. They wanted Beatles songs to be featured on the show, for one thing, which was not something Carl had envisaged. "I was just shooting for simple rockabilly," Carl told *Goldmine* magazine. "I wanted people to feel like they were peeping through a window, watching us have a good time." Playing Beatles songs, Carl figured quite rightly, would make the event more about Harrison and Starr and less about the session itself.

When he arrived at the rehearsal studio to begin a week of preparation, the players, including Harrison and Starr, were already busy at work, rocking "Honey, Don't." Carl was thrilled by their enthusiasm. "It just sent chills through my body," he said. "Harrison looked so great—healthy, radiant, smiling."

The Cinemax execs, however, appeared concerned; they pulled Carl aside and asked about a formal rehearsal, but he shot back: "Don't you think you're looking at a pretty damn good show here?" This band didn't need rehearsing, as far as Carl was concerned. Still, the arguments continued. Cinemax wanted the musicians in formal wear, tuxedos. "No way," Carl replied. "I ain't gonna tell my friends what to wear." They also asked about the possibility of a set heavy with Beatles songs.

In the end, Carl got his way. All the players dressed as they chose. The only Beatles numbers the ensemble played were the three songs of Carl's that they'd covered back in the early 1960s. And, as Carl reported, "nothing was rehearsed." Even the onstage dialogue was improvised—during an unplugged segment, Carl turned to the ensemble and chuckled, "My, my, you look like a bunch of little schoolchildren with your new shoes on!" It was all very off-the-cuff, loose, and freewheeling, just as Carl had hoped.

The hour-long program opened with testimonials. Johnny Cash was up first, talking straight to camera, recalling how they first met at Carl's debut recording session at Sun. "I felt a kindred spirit from day one, you know," said Cash. "He's like someone you meet and you feel like you've known him all your life." Next on screen was Roy Orbison, the Big O, sporting his trademark dark shades. "He's a wonderful, sincere man," he said of Carl. "I love him. Always have and always will."

Then it was Jerry Lee Lewis's turn, that wild look still in his eyes even in his fifties. He wore a white headband that gave the impression he'd come straight from the gym. He made it known that, to his mind, Carl could still be one of the biggest artists in the world. Enough said.

It was now time for some music, as the studio audience—many wearing vintage rockabilly gear—found their seats and the band got ready. Among the audience was Hollywood star Faye Dunaway, who was currently filming in London. And it was quite the band, made up of the Beatles Ringo Starr and George Harrison, as well as Eric Clapton, Rosanne Cash, and Dave Edmunds, all huge fans of Perkins. Edmunds, sporting two-tone shoes, led the band. Welsh guitarist Mickey Gee helped out, as did keyboardist Geraint Watkins. A pair of Stray Cats—Lee Rocker, who didn't so much play his upright bass as wrestle the damn thing into submission, and drummer Slim Jim Phantom—were also in the house. Carl's son Greg sat in on bass.

"They're gonna see this all over the world," Carl, looking sharp in a blue fringed shirt, tinted Carrera glasses in place, told the audience, as he and the band—featuring the two Stray Cats and Edmunds on lead guitar—tore into "Boppin' the Blues." The crowd, of course, lapped it up; they knew they were witnessing something special, music history in action.

A couple of songs in, Perkins told the gathering, "This is the greatest thing could ever happen to me. This is my night with my friends." As he introduced the different players, Carl described them collectively as "the rockingest cats you're ever going to be around." With that, Ringo Starr, his hair slicked back and wearing a full beard, strode up to the drum kit and kicked into "Honey, Don't." Carl and Edmunds traded guitar licks, wide grins on their faces. It was very clear that the party was officially in full swing.

"Oh, my buddy Ringo Starr!" declared Carl, as the audience burst into applause at the end of the song. "Ringo," Carl continued, "in 1964, you recorded an old Sun record that I had—I was in the studio that night—"

"That's what they all say!" interjected Ringo with a grin, flashing his trademark peace sign. Carl laughed along and then introduced "a great, great guitar player." Eric Clapton ambled onstage and plugged in his black Fender as the band ripped into "Matchbox," the song he'd played with Carl on *The Johnny Cash Show* more than a decade earlier. Carl and Starr traded verses before Clapton tore into an extended solo, Carl at his side urging him along. Then Clapton and Carl engaged in a red-hot guitar duel and the song roared into overdrive.

Song over, a smiling Carl spoke with Clapton. "Eric, I'd be

ashamed to play that guitar in front of an old broken-down rocka-billy like me like you do," he said, as the crowd clapped until their hands hurt. "That's not right!"

"Mean Woman Blues," a 1957 hit for Elvis Presley, followed, Carl and Clapton sharing vocals, the song really bursting into life when they both wailed on their guitars, "Slowhand" Clapton play-ing like a man inspired. "Play it again, Eric, I love it!" exclaimed Carl, as Clapton tore off another fiery solo.

"I'd like to do for you kind people tonight the first song I recorded at the great Sun Studio in Memphis, Tennessee," announced Carl, as he and the band turned down the lights for the aching ballad "Turn Around," which wound time all the way back to 1954. Okay, so that wasn't quite the case—"Movie Magg" was probably the first—but the sentiment was clear.

Carl then welcomed Rosanne Cash—"a beautiful young lady"— onto the stage. "I literally rocked this girl when she was a baby and now I'd like to rock with her." Cash, with her short, punky hair and wearing a blue jacket that stretched down to her knees, played June Carter to Carl's Johnny Cash as they duetted on "Jackson," the Cashes' huge hit from 1967.

"She's a doll and does she ever sing a song," said Carl as he gave Cash the stage so that she could sing "What Kind of Girl."

Carl's next guest came with an explanation. "Some said he's retired and that ain't true. He will come out and he'll shake again . . . my dear friend, George Harrison." Clearly not the type of man to mess about with speeches, Harrison shook Carl's hand, strapped on his guitar, and started singing as he and the band ripped into "Everybody's Trying to Be My Baby." A huge smile lit up Carl's face as he and the reclusive Beatle, his number one fan, traded riffs and licks.

"You believe that?" Carl asked the audience at the end of the song, as their applause continued loud and long. "Don't he look good!"

"Your True Love" followed, included at Harrison's insistence. ("George," Carl told him, "that ol' song ain't no good," but Harri-son thought otherwise.) Harrison and Dave Edmunds shared a mic, harmonizing sweetly while Carl sang lead, as the band kept a steady rocking beat behind them.

"Carl Perkins, everybody," Harrison said at the end of the song, as yet another huge round of applause reverberated around the studio.

Harrison and Carl then took seats at the front of the stage, George relating a discussion he'd had with Edmunds "when we were hanging about playing Carl's tunes." It turned out that Carl had a particular guitar technique that he admired. "Maybe Carl would like to tell us about this thing here," Harrison said, throwing to his host. Humble as ever, Carl described it as nothing more than "a bunch of mistakes," inspired by legendary guitarist Les Paul. Carl then began to play some fast, smart licks, simple yet effective, while Harrison tapped out a rhythm on his guitar. Clearly impressed, Harrison stood up from his stool when Carl finished playing and hugged him tightly. It was a love-in.

Stage front soon grew very crowded as Carl and eight of his guests assembled in a semicircle for the obligatory all-star jam finale. They first played "That's All Right," with the onstage setup, and the performance echoed the remarkable *Elvis* comeback special of 1968. "I hear you, George," shouted Carl, "play that thing," and Harrison launched into a stellar solo that would have done Scotty Moore proud. The ensemble segued into "Blue Moon of Kentucky," the song covered by Elvis that in its own way kick-started Carl's career more than thirty years back. Rosanne Cash found it hard to stay seated, rocking to and fro to the driving beat, occasionally harmonizing with Clapton, seated to her right, as they powered through "Night Train to Memphis" and the traditional "Amen."

"Did my class graduate or not? Do they pass?" Carl asked the crowd, his smile a mile wide. Harrison now took the lead for "Glad All Over" after Carl admitted that he didn't know all the words. That didn't matter, because Harrison, with Edmunds at his side, knew the song inside out. "Do it, George!" instructed Carl as Harrison took yet another solo.

"You cannot let a gathering like this go by," declared Carl, "and not remember the Killer, Jerry Lee Lewis," as the troupe ripped into

"Whole Lotta Shakin' Goin' On." It had now become a full-blown jam session, with Edmunds and Harrison sharing a mic, Cash and Clapton another, while Ringo and Slim Jim Phantom thumped out a gutsy rhythm on a snare drum and a tambourine. Behind them, Lee Rocker slapped his upright bass as if it had done him wrong. By now, as they began "Gone, Gone, Gone," the crowd was on their feet, with one particularly keen rocker taking to stage front and busting some serious moves. Soon enough the floor was full, and the band was truly cooking—they'd transformed a chilly London TV studio into something like the roaring "tonks" from Carl's past.

Of course, the show wouldn't be complete without "Blue Suede Shoes," now thirty years old, and Carl and the band played it at full tilt, more like the Elvis cover than his original. But no one seemed to mind; it was the perfect closer to a remarkable night of music. When the song ended, members of the audience invaded the stage, pumping Carl's hand and hugging him joyously. Clearly moved by the experience, Carl spoke haltingly with the gathering after the cameras stopped rolling.

"I have never in my life enjoyed singing that song like I did tonight with my friends, my rockabilly buddies. God bless you. Thank you."

"They all played their hearts out," Carl said afterward. "And I'm proud I was man enough to tell the cats at Cinemax to get out of my way." Carl said that perhaps his favorite moment of what was an immensely satisfying experience came right at the end of the show. "I really liked the smiles they gave each other, the hugs. . . . How can you rehearse that?"

A Rockabilly Session was scheduled to air on BBC Four on New Year's Day 1986 and on US pay TV during January, but even before it screened, Carl was talking about a possible sequel. He hinted at people such as B.B. King, Phil Collins, and Huey Lewis being involved—in a different conversation, he mentioned Linda Ronstadt, Stevie Wonder, Fats Domino, and Paul McCartney. (Nothing materialized, as intriguing as all that sounded.)

Carl was so energized by the event that he set himself a goal of being the man responsible for bringing together the three remaining Beatles—after all, he'd come close to it during *A Rockabilly Session*. When Carl returned home from London, he told a reporter from the *Fort Worth Star-Telegram* that he thought it was possible, despite what he described as "business reasons and some reasons I don't know. [But] it's never too late."

Carl had reconnected with producer Chips Moman in November 1985. Moman was involved in a campaign to promote Memphis's remarkable musical heritage and in an attempt to resurrect the spirit of the Million Dollar Quartet, Moman reached out to Carl, Johnny Cash, and Jerry Lee Lewis and brought them together for a project called *Class of '55: Memphis Rock & Roll Homecoming*. Roy Orbison would stand in for Elvis Presley. Together, they'd return to Sun Studio to record an album, which Moman would produce. It wasn't the first time the four had worked together—they'd performed "This Train" as a quartet on a 1977 *Johnny Cash Christmas Special*, shot at the Grand Ole Opry House—but it was a momentous occasion, nonetheless.

At the beginning of what Carl would describe as a "very emotion-packed week," he and the others met with Moman at the Peabody in Memphis. Moman advised them that it was time to head downstairs to the foyer and meet the press. "I thought that there might be someone down there with a Brownie Hawkeye [camera] and a lead pencil asking some questions," said Carl, but when he stepped out of the lift, he was shocked by the sight of a lobby jam-packed with media. "The place exploded," said the musician Marty Stuart, who was in the Peabody, looking on. "There was five minutes of applause, hollering and tears." *American Bandstand* host Dick Clark was there, too, fronting a film crew from Dick Clark Productions that would document the reunion for a TV special. "I think we realized that we were fooling with much more than making a record," said Carl. They were making—perhaps remaking—music history.

When the Sun quartet first met in the 1950s, they were all, as Carl admitted, "hungry country boys." In the subsequent thirty years, things had changed. Roy Orbison had jetted in from Malibu and traveled in a chauffeured limo; Cash had arrived at the Peabody on his tour bus, his initials emblazoned on the side of the vehicle. Jerry Lee Lewis pulled up in what was described as a "flashy red-and-white sedan," which Lewis explained belonged to his manager. (The IRS had impounded the Killer's own fleet of cars long before.) As for Carl—whom one writer present described as "resembling James Brolin playing Clark Gable"—he turned up in a new white Mercedes, his golf clubs in the trunk. It was a far cry from the rust bucket of a Plymouth he and his brothers had driven from Jackson for their first recording session with Sam Phillips.

But some things hadn't changed a great deal—Jerry Lee Lewis remained as ornery as ever. He attended the first recording session at Sun with a gun tucked into his jeans; his pockets were stuffed with pills, which spilled out onto the floor. "You write about these pills," he told Elizabeth Kaye, a reporter from *Rolling Stone* who was documenting *Class of '55*, "and I'll dance at your wedding, and kill your husband, too." As always, scandal was trailing Lewis like a shadow—there was a rumor that he might have played a role in the August 1983 overdose death of his fifth wife, a twenty-five-year-old waitress named Shawn Stephens. They'd been married for only seventy-seven days. While standing outside Sun, watching a member of the crew walk past carrying a large box, Lewis looked it up and down and asked, "You got my wife in there?"

"This is a case of something," Carl said later of Lewis's wildness, "that I'm not an authority to say. I don't know much about medicine or brain damage . . . but there's a switch in there that violently flies off. It's frightening and it's pitiful."

Carl felt much more comfortable getting down to work with producer Moman. He'd brought a good song into the sessions, inspired by the anniversary, called "Birth of Rock and Roll," that he'd cowritten with his son Greg. He'd also sing lead vocal on "Class of '55," a collaboration between Moman and the Memphis songwriter Bobby Emmons.

With a smoldering Winston Light cigarette wedged between his guitar strings, Carl was a study in concentration as he worked on his parts inside Sun. When the music faded, Carl drummed his fingers on his thigh, waiting for Moman's comments.

"I liked that take a whole bunch," said the producer.

"Sure did feel good," replied Carl.

Various players would be brought in to help during the week. Among them were Dave Edmunds (a big contributor to *A Rockabilly Session*) and John Fogerty, who played on a song of his own called "Big Train (from Memphis)," which he'd previously recorded on his 1985 comeback LP *Centerfield*. Sun founder Sam Phillips joined in on background vocals for the track, which would close the album, alongside June Carter Cash and the Judds, mother and daughter Naomi and Wynonna, who'd grown close to Carl. (Carl called Naomi "Mama," Wynonna called him "Uncle Carl.") Ricky Nelson chimed in, too. He'd once been seen as the rockabilly successor to Carl, having covered "Boppin' the Blues" way back in 1957—Carl's original was the first record Nelson ever owned. During the session, he told Carl that meeting him was a dream fulfilled. It was the first (and only) time Nelson would share a studio with Carl.

"Big Train" was recorded in American Recording Studio, which Moman had founded in 1967. This was where Elvis had recorded "Suspicious Minds" and "Kentucky Rain." During the session, a life-size cutout of Presley, a fixture of an Elvis museum housed inside the studio, had been positioned to face the musicians as they worked on the song. "It seemed as if Elvis himself were watching," noted *Rolling Stone*'s Elizabeth Kaye.

Also helping on the album was Marty Stuart, playing rhythm guitar. Stuart was a big fan of Carl's playing. He was currently Cash's touring guitarist, so he was following in Carl's footsteps, quite literally. He fondly referred to Carl as "Daddy Cat." Sometimes, between takes, he'd say, "Burn one for me, Perkins!" and Carl would oblige with some fleet-fingered picking. On the second day of recording, Carl learned that Stuart had just signed a six-album deal with CBS, and he figured that a gift was in order. He gave Stuart one of his Fender Stratocasters, which he signed: *There's a hit song in here, Marty, find it. Love, Carl Perkins.*

"He's a good dude," surmised Carl. "I like him very much."

Stuart and Carl shaped up like a couple of gunslingers during "Birth of Rock and Roll," swapping guitar licks, as Carl sang about how it felt to be inside Sun creating history. Carl may have been sitting down, but he was kicking up quite the storm. It would be the opening—and the best—song on the finished album. (Rolling Stone Ron Wood make a cameo in the video for the track, along with Carl and Jerry Lee Lewis.)

In between takes, Dick Clark's film crew documented proceedings. "For Carl Perkins," said Clark, as he walked the halls of Sun, "this studio has very special meaning. Carl recorded 'Blue Suede Shoes' right here ... with that song Carl Perkins became one of the founding fathers of rock and roll." Carl discussed "Blue Suede Shoes" with Gene Weed, the producer/director of the TV special, once again laying out the familiar storyline of the sharp-dressed man who didn't appreciate his date stepping on his "suedes." "It tore me up," Carl admitted. "I had not owned a pair by that time—I wanted them but that was a little out of my class to be able to afford that. I couldn't get it out of my mind."

Carl, Cash, Orbison, and Lewis paid their respects during a heartfelt ballad called "We Remember the King." The famous four shared one microphone as they sang about Elvis, their old friend and erstwhile Sun labelmate. "Elvis is with us in spirit," said Orbison. "I wish he was here with us. Wonderful fella." As they listened to the playback, Carl turned to the others and said, "God, I love you all." All four embraced, tears clouding their eyes. Carl summed up his feelings when he spoke with the TV crew: "I feel, without a doubt in my mind, that I'm one of the luckiest men alive walking this earth to be part of what's happening here in Memphis."

Of course, no project of this scope could be hassle-free. Aside from dealing with the pill-popping, gun-toting Jerry Lee Lewis, there were other problems for producer Moman. Johnny Cash was still under contract to Columbia, and the necessary permissions hadn't been granted for his involvement with the album (which was to be released by PolyGram) when the recordings began. In order to keep Cash's gravelly tones on the record, Moman had to cough up

$100,000, much of which he'd raised for the project from Federal Express, which was based in Memphis.

In an ironic twist, Cash soon signed to Mercury, which was owned by PolyGram, but not in time for *Class of '55*, which was only a moderate hit upon its release in May 1986, reaching number 15 on *Billboard*'s Top Country Albums chart, hampered by a lack of promotional support. But the Fab Four were received like homecoming heroes—quite deservedly—when they made a guest appearance at Fan Fair in Nashville on June 10, as part of a Mercury/PolyGram showcase.

CHAPTER 16

I am really so humbled when Eric Clapton and George Harrison say, "Carl, we like what you did"

The biggest tragedy of *Class of '55*, however, was that neither Ricky Nelson nor Roy Orbison would live to see the TBS television broadcast, which didn't air until 1989. Nelson didn't even live to see the record released; he died in a plane crash on New Year's Eve 1985. *Class of '55* was his final recording session. Orbison passed away from a heart attack on December 6, 1988, at the age of fifty-two, just as *The Traveling Wilburys Volume One*, his all-star collaboration LP with Bob Dylan, George Harrison, Tom Petty, and Jeff Lynne, began climbing charts across the globe. The album would eventually sell almost five million copies worldwide and make the late, great Big O a star all over again.

Carl had shared some two dozen live dates with Orbison in 1988, and their friendship, forged back in the 1950s, had grown tighter than ever. "We got very close again," said Carl. "Of course, that was very easy to do with Orbison—he was one of the nicest guys I ever knew."

Carl was inducted into the Rock and Roll Hall of Fame on January 21, 1987, having been made a member of the Nashville Songwriters Hall of Fame two years earlier. Also being inducted was the Atlantic Records cofounder, Ahmet Ertegun, who rated "Blue Suede Shoes" "a rockabilly masterpiece." Among Carl's other fellow inductees on the night were the Coasters, Eddie Cochran, Aretha Franklin, Marvin Gaye, Ricky Nelson, Bill Haley—and Roy Orbison.

Inducting Carl at the ceremony at the Waldorf-Astoria in New York City was Sam Phillips, who, despite their business problems, had been his first and biggest booster. "Ladies and gentlemen," announced Phillips, "it's a real pleasure for me to be here tonight and to introduce Carl Perkins into the Rock and Roll Hall of Fame." Carl, looking cool as ever in a sharp suit, his tinted glasses firmly in place, and wearing blue suede shoes (of course), took the stage. He spoke about how big a thrill it was to be honored in this way, "and what a night it is for a sharecropper's son to stand here in this beautiful building." Carl's voice started faltering with emotion as he promised that from this night onward, "I hope that my life . . . will be lived in such a way that you here and the wonderful fans across America—and especially the people of the Rock and Roll Hall of Fame foundation—will never be ashamed that they placed Carl Perkins among the elite." With a simple thank-you and God bless, Carl returned to his table, which he shared with Roy Orbison. The Big O leaned over and said, "I'm proud of you, Carl. I wish Elvis had lived to experience this."

Heartfelt speeches and tearstained thank-yous were just one part of the evening. Induction ceremonies always ended with an all-star jam, and tonight's was a doozy. A pair of Wilburys—George Harrison and Bob Dylan—got things rolling with "All Along the Watchtower," while at their back, Sting and Daryl Hall squeezed together on a piano bench and Carl and fellow guitarists Bo Diddley, Keith Richards, and former Sex Pistol Steve Jones formed a powerful onstage arsenal. The Coasters shared a mic with Brill Building greats Leiber and Stoller, as Paul Butterfield wailed on harmonica. After the Beach Boys sang "Barbara Ann," Carl, with Richards and B.B. King at his side, powered through "Blue Suede Shoes." Smokey Robinson then sang "Going to a Go-Go" before Chuck Berry jammed "Roll Over Beethoven." The all-star lineup hit the home stretch with "In the Midnight Hour," with John Fogerty taking the lead, and eventually wound up the night with Elton John doing his best Jerry Lee Lewis on "Whole Lotta Shakin' Goin' On."

Afterward, while speaking with reporters, Carl admitted that to finally be officially recognized as a bona fide legend was a lot for him to take in. "I keep waitin' for someone to put a broom in my hand and say, 'Clean up the place. That's what you're here for.'"

It was passing strange, however, given Carl's relationship with George Harrison, and the high regard in which he was held by pretty much everyone whose path he crossed, that he hadn't become a Wilbury. In January 1988, Harrison had invited Carl to the UK to attend the tenth anniversary of his production company, Handmade Films, and the screening of the documentary *The Movie Life of George*. Before the film was shown, George addressed the gathering, joking about "the cartoon world" that was filmmaking, and then specifically acknowledging Carl for "coming all the way from Nashville to entertain me, and you lot, whether you like it or not." He also thanked Carl because he reminded him that while producing movies was interesting, "it's still much better being a guitar player." Carl jammed "Honey, Don't" and "That's All Right" with Harrison, Joe Brown, and his sons Greg and Stan at the event, with many in attendance hitting the dance floor as they played.

While in the UK—staying as Harrison's guest at London's very upscale Mayflower Hotel—Carl visited the former Beatle at Friar Park, his neo-Gothic estate in Henley-on-Thames. The estate was set amid sixty-two acres of sprawling countryside and eccentric curiosities—gnomes, grottoes, and assorted weirdness dotted the landscape. (Harrison wrote a hit song, "Crackerbox Palace," in honor of Friar Park and filmed the video at the site.) Carl had also visited Friar Park in 1985, during downtime while shooting *A Rockabilly Session*, and was stunned by its sheer size.

"I don't know why the queen lives where she does," Carl told a reporter back in the States, "because her castle is second rate."

It was during his 1988 visit that Harrison said that if there was to be a second Wilburys album, he wanted to record "Your True Love" with Carl. Carl reminded him that he had his phone number; all he had to do was call. "That would have meant the world to him," said Stan Perkins, who was with father on the trip, "but it never happened." Carl, however, had no antipathy toward his old friend Roy Orbison; he was thrilled for his success. "I was so proud for Roy ... that the record did so well. I loved him so dearly," Carl told a reporter from *Guitar Player* magazine.

While at Friar Park, Carl and Harrison didn't just talk music— they also discussed religion. Despite their very different perspectives on God—Carl being a regular at his local United Methodist Church, Harrison being a loud and proud devotee of Eastern spirituality, particularly Krishna Consciousness—they found common ground, agreeing that belief in God was at the heart of all faiths. "It's all to do with consciousness," George said in his final public interview, while sitting alongside another musical buddy, Ravi Shankar. "Raise the level of consciousness and everything becomes better," he explained. "We all go through our lives and through our days and we don't experience bliss. . . . To be able to know how to do that is something you don't just stumble across— you've got to search for it."

Carl had visited Friar Park before, but not so Stan, and he struggled to come to grips with the sheer expanse of the estate. "It looked like something from Disney World," Stan said, "it was huge." Harrison proudly showed the Perkinses around his ornamental gardens and then led them into his recording studio, where dozens of guitars hung on the wall. In the corner was a jukebox, which contained nothing but Sun vinyl. Harrison's love for Carl's music had never faded. "If it hadn't have been for your daddy," Harrison told Stan, "I would never have picked up the guitar."

During 1989, Carl and the C.P. Express played about one hundred shows, including dates in Germany, France, and the UK. With Carl's iconic status now well and truly set in stone—he was, after all, a Rock and Roll Hall of Famer—it seemed that every time he played a big show it came with the requisite interview. On May 6, when Carl agreed to perform at *This Country's Rockin'*, a massive all-day (and -night) affair at the Pontiac Silverdome in Detroit, which also featured Gregg Allman, Ted Nugent, the Marshall Tucker Band, Etta James, Stephen Stills, and the Stray Cats, he was interviewed on camera as part of the pay-per-view broadcast of the concert.

A reflective Carl talked about growing up poor, picking cotton, and hearing country music on the radio, but admitted that he occasionally twisted the dial in search of something different. "I heard me some John Lee Hooker. I loved the blues that I would hear." He also admitted that as a kid he had no idea that you weren't supposed to be a lead guitarist and singer and talked about his early playing, what he called "picking out" on one string. Carl also described the method that he and his brother Jay used to learn the songs they heard on the Opry. "Jay would take the first line and he would write it down; when the singer was singing the second line, that was mine to write. . . . That's really how I learned my first songs."

As for his lyrics, well, Carl had a confession to make. He didn't fuss too much about that, especially in the early days—the playing was more important to him. "We wanted that beat that kids could dance to." As for current acts, Carl name-checked the Stray Cats—"as an old picker, I heard original playing; these three guys are strong"—and a new band called Highway 101, who'd toured with the C.P. Express. "It is pure rockabilly," said Carl, who was suitably impressed.

Onstage at the Silverdome, it was very clear that after more than a decade of touring, the C.P. Express had become a slick musical machine. Stan set things up from behind his drum kit, with a simple intro: "The legend, Carl Perkins." Then Carl took the stage, looking dapper in a dark jacket with a little rhinestone embellishment, his sleeves rolled up to the elbows, ready for rocking business. After smiling and waving at some familiar faces in the crowd, he launched into "Boppin' the Blues" at full tilt.

"Howdy, my friends, it's good to see you—and hasn't this been some kind of show?" Carl announced before playing "Matchbox," he and his rock-steady band keeping things nice and tight. "I'm a Tennessee boy, but it feels like I'm home," sang Carl, before unleashing one of many blazing guitar solos, his right leg constantly in motion. "Honey, Don't" was next, Carl singing strongly. "Well, all right, let's rock," he declared before delivering yet another short, sharp guitar solo.

"Birth of Rock and Roll" followed, with Carl explaining that the song was his attempt to capture how it felt to be part of the magic that was happening in Sun Studio in the mid-1950s. (In typically understated Carl style, he neglected to mention the crucial role he played in those early days.) Carl followed with a rockabilly medley, featuring "Long Tall Sally," "Hound Dog," "Tutti Frutti," "Walkin'," and "Whole Lotta Shakin'," slowing down briefly to talk about his first meeting Jerry Lee Lewis, the Killer. "He said all you gotta do is stay in one spot and wiggle around," said Carl, laughing at the memory.

Before his closing number, Carl spoke to the crowd. When he was invited to play the show, he explained, he thought it was a mistake. But then he saw the name of the event, *This Country's Rockin'*, and realized, "That has got to be *the* greatest name for a television show." Carl said that while looking on from the wings today, as the other acts delivered their sets, he came to a realization: "This could be the greatest show I've ever been on. I ain't seen nothing like it." Carl then thanked the audience, acknowledged that it had been "a long day," and broke into "Blue Suede Shoes," encouraging the crowd to sing the chorus at the top of their voices. They obliged.

Carl may have been slightly overstating the case, because the event itself was a flop, drawing only a small crowd, having been overshadowed by the Downtown Hoedown, which was staged the same day at the nearby Hart Plaza. And *This Country's Rockin'* ran way overtime. The *Detroit Free Press* summarized the day neatly with a headline that read, "Acts Keep Rockin' When They Should Be Sleepin'."

Not that this had any impact on Carl's momentum—barely a week later he was playing at Baltimore's Liberty Mall Fishmarket Club, again with the cameras rolling (for a Nashville Network special). Carl, sharp as always in a dark blue suit and jet-black shirt and tie—with a black Fender Telecaster to match—launched straight into "Blue Suede Shoes," reveling in an attentive audience who'd been suitably revved up by Wolfman Jack as Carl hit the stage. ("One of rock and roll's greatest, here he is, Mr. Carl Perkins—yeah!") The band was tight as a nut, in perfect step with their leader, giving Carl plenty of room to let rip on his Fender. When, on the urging of Wolfman Jack, Carl and the band powered into "Matchbox," the crowd loved every minute of it. "Let's rock," declared Carl, unleashing yet another blazing solo. Carl was having fun, no doubt about it, rolling his eyes playfully as he sang his heart out.

"Well, it's a pleasure for me to be here tonight," Carl said between songs, catching his breath, "and I want to thank our great friend Wolfman Jack for all the nice things he said about this old rockabilly." With that, Carl played "Honey, Don't," a song, as Carl reminded the crowd, that was "recorded in 1964 by Ringo Starr and three other cats—they called themselves the Beatles."

Wolfman Jack, a big man all in black, joined Carl onstage, wrapping a bearlike hand around his shoulders. He asked Carl if he was playing the same guitar from back in the glory days of Sun and "Blue Suede Shoes." Carl explained that while it was a newer model, it was "really the old style." Wolfman also pointed out the classic Fender amp that Carl was using—how crucial was it in getting his unique sound? "Well, that," Carl agreed, "and not knowing what you're gonna do." Wolfman Jack laughed so hard he almost fell off the stage.

Soon enough, some of those in the crowd were on their feet, as Carl tried out a new song, "Born to Rock," which he'd written with Greg and Stan. Carl's lyrics wound back time to his youth on the farm in Tiptonville, and how he'd bonded so closely with his guitar that his father wondered if it had somehow "grown onto my arm." The crowd loved it.

"You've come a long way since 1956," said Wolfman Jack as Carl prepared to play the last song of his short but stellar set. "How do you feel about that?"

"About that tall," joked Carl, holding his hand at hip height. Then he took a more serious turn: "I am really so humbled when the great guitar players like Eric Clapton and George Harrison say, 'Carl, we like what you did.'"

As Carl and the band delivered "Gone, Gone, Gone," the

audience were now standing, clapping along, encouraging him to peel off one more solo. He gladly obliged. It had been a huge night, yet another Carl Perkins love-in.

The Wolfman had little left to do, except to growl: "He is the greatest, absolutely!"

CHAPTER 17

Not knowing about radiation, I didn't know what I was in for

During the final few years of his life, Carl's enigmatic friend Roy Orbison had undergone a stunning career upswing. His song "In Dreams" had featured prominently in David Lynch's 1986 movie *Blue Velvet*—creepily lip-synched by Dean Stockwell, no less— and the first Traveling Wilburys' album had been a massive success, spending a year on the US charts. Orbison had been inducted into the Rock and Roll Hall of Fame on the same night as Carl. ("I wanted to sing like Roy Orbison," Bruce Springsteen told the gathering.) And the Boss was again by the Big O's side in September 1987 at the Cocoanut Grove nightclub in LA, along with guests Jackson Browne, Elvis Costello, Tom Waits, Bonnie Raitt, and James Burton, all playing Orbison's best-known songs. Clearly inspired by the positive reaction to Carl's *A Rockabilly Session* (despite the conflict), Cinemax filmed the show and released it on video as *Roy Orbison and Friends: A Black and White Night*. It sold some fifty thousand copies in America, big numbers for a music video.

And Orbison's final album, *Mystery Girl*, released soon after his death in December 1988, contained the song "You Got It," cowritten by his fellow Wilburys Tom Petty and Jeff Lynne. Orbison delivered one final soaring vocal, and the song became a Top 10 hit in the UK and the United States. "The album encapsulates everything that made Orbison great," declared *Rolling Stone*. "For that reason it makes a fitting valedictory." In April 1989, Orbison became the first musician since Elvis Presley to have two albums, posthumously, in the US Top 5 at the same time. Johnny Cash, too, would come to make the defining music of his career late in his life, finding an unlikely collaborator in the bearded guru Rick Rubin, better known for his work in the world of hard rock and hip-hop.

Throughout the last decade, via his numerous awards and big events such as *A Rockabilly Session*, Carl's important contribution to rock and roll had been acknowledged. He was establishing a very healthy legacy. But one thing that had eluded him—not just in the 1980s but throughout his career—was an album that was both a commercial and critical success. Inspired by the response to Orbison's *Mystery Girl*, Carl set to work on a new record, which he titled, simply, *Born to Rock*. In what came as no surprise at all, given his bumpy track record, Carl was recording for yet another label. This time around it was Universal, as part of a deal set up by the label's founder Jimmy Bowen. A former rockabilly "cat" himself, Bowen had produced such big names as Frank Sinatra ("Strangers in the Night") before establishing himself as a music industry executive and kingmaker.

Carl, working with the Judds' collaborators Brent Maher and Don Potter at Nashville's Creative Workshop recording studio, tried to make a record in the Sun style, as simple as possible, pretty much live. Only his guitar solos were overdubbed. "There wasn't any isolation," reported Carl. "It really had a good, clickin' feel. . . . That's the way I play and sound on stage." The Jordanaires, who'd worked with Carl in the past, added some silky background vocals to the ballad "A Lifetime Last Night," while such classy players as drummer Eddie Bayers and pianist Bobby Ogdin also helped.

Of the four cowrites on the LP with his son Greg, the pick was "Charlene," a good-natured rockabilly rave-up in which Carl told the story of a heartbreaker of a woman from the type of traveling carnival that he might have checked out back when he was a wide-eyed country boy, as the band kicked up some dust behind him. Charlene was a free spirit, but by the sound of things, Carl enjoyed the ride. As for the album's closer, "Love Makes Dreams Come

True," yet another cowrite with Greg, it was a bighearted tribute to Valda, who'd been with him now for some forty years.

The record didn't prove to be Carl's *Mystery Girl*, but as *Rolling Stone*'s Jimmy Guterman observed in his three-star review, Carl, unlike many of his peers, was fully invested in the album's ten tracks. He wasn't coasting on his reputation. "[*Born to Rock*] shows the master willing to get his hands dirty," he wrote. "[It's] an album for both the faithful and those just discovering him."

Carl may have been the definition of humility itself when he thanked his supporters "for one more shot," during the LP's sturdy title track, but when he next appeared on *Late Night*, David Letterman made it clear that he and his audience were in the presence of greatness. He introduced Carl as "the man who wrote the national anthem of rock and roll." Carl smiled broadly and proceeded to rock "Honey, Don't" like a man half his age.

A section of Main Street in Tiptonville had been renamed Carl Perkins Square and opened to the public in April 1988. What was until recently a strip of burned-out buildings was now a tourist attraction. Carl's boyhood home on the cotton plantation was uprooted and moved to a spot in the square, where it was opened to visitors. The interior of the house was restored to resemble how it appeared when Carl lived there as a child: sparsely furnished and still without electricity, no more than a wooden shack. The nearby Carl Perkins Visitor Center contained such memorabilia as the potato bag upon which Carl scrawled the lyrics of "Blue Swade [*sic*] Shoes," as well as a jacket given to Carl by Elvis Presley and, of course, a pair of his blue suede shoes. "Carl comes by here pretty regular," said Jerry Jones, an investor in the venture. "Somebody stopping in stands a good chance of running into him." As Joanna Coyne, co-owner of the museum, recalled, Carl couldn't believe his eyes when he first visited the site. "He said it was so much like home."

Throughout 1989 and 1990, Carl had been as busy as ever, playing almost one hundred gigs each year, including dates at Circus Maximus at Caesar's Palace in Las Vegas and a handful of shows in the UK. A song Carl had written way back in 1965, "When You're a Man on Your Own," had been recorded by George Strait for his 1990 album *Livin' It Up*, which sold one million copies. Another country great, Dolly Parton, had visited Carl at home in Jackson and written "Silver and Gold" with Carl and his sons, which reached number 15 on the Country charts. (Valda served houseguest Parton her favorite food—corn bread and great northern beans.) Carl had also cowritten a number 1 Country hit for the Judds, "Let Me Tell You About Love," proving that he was very much in demand as a writer and performer. Valda generously hosted the Judds at Jackson, too.

Sadly, Carl couldn't hang on to a record deal, though: Jimmy Bowen's Universal was dissolved in December 1989, and Carl's proposed three-album arrangement faded away. He moved on to Platinum Records, a label based in Oak Park, Michigan.

The much-talked-about but rarely heard Million Dollar Quartet tapes finally received an official release in the United States during 1990, through Presley's label RCA, which gave it the questionable title of *Elvis Presley: The Million Dollar Quartet*. Although the label's move was understandable, given how beneficial a cash cow Presley had been since his death thirteen years earlier—and how prominent a role he did play in the session—it gave short shrift to the others involved, especially Carl. After all, it had been at a Carl Perkins session that the A-list jam had been initiated. Still, its official release was received like the discovery of some ancient, holy script, particularly by the music press.

"This is fascinating stuff," *Creem*'s Bill Holdship wrote of the two-CD set, which included fragments of more than forty songs and assorted chatter from that fabled Memphis afternoon. Although *The Million Dollar Quartet* didn't become the hit record Carl had predicted, it served as a handy reminder of the musical magic that he had helped create in that tiny studio in Memphis. Holdship agreed. "Sometimes, when they get 'real gone' and start cooking, you realize that this is the greatest garage band ever. . . . Yep, this is history in the making—but the most refreshing part is that these guys sound like they didn't care if the tape was running."

"This isn't a phonograph record," observed *Village Voice* critic

Robert Christgau, "it's a documentary, audio verité proof ... that they knew and loved all kinds of music, which always bears repeating."

Rolling Stone's David Fricke, when reviewing the collection, declared that December 4, 1956, was a "holy day on the rock and roll calendar," noting how what began as a "casual singalong" had over the ensuing years been transformed into "legend incarnate ... worth its weight in rock and roll gold." As for Carl's role in the proceedings, while he didn't take the lead in quite the same manner as Presley, he did, as Fricke mentioned, "keep the rhythm backfield in motion." It was also acknowledged that despite the collection's official title, Carl was top dog, at least when the get-together took place. "He was Sun's biggest star at the time," wrote Fricke.

Carl, however, had more pressing matters to consider when he hit a serious bump in the road during April 1991. Valda had noticed that he'd been wheezing in his sleep and made an appointment for Carl with a Jackson doctor named Dr. Larry Carruth—his son Greg had also noticed that in the studio Carl had been getting hoarse, which was unusual. Carl, whose mother had recently died at the age of seventy-nine, was wary about what the doctor might tell him. Being a smoker, he feared that he might have emphysema. Although Dr. Carruth assured Carl that wasn't the case, he asked to check his vocal cords. "You've been singing for so long," the specialist told him, "I figured they'd be as big as a mule's." But what he noticed was a small spot on Carl's neck—and he quickly referred him to an eye, ear, nose, and throat specialist.

After a thorough examination, the second doctor sat down and spoke with Carl. The news wasn't good. "I hate to say this," he told him, "but I think we're looking at cancer." Carl couldn't believe it—he'd just been back in the studio, in Nashville and New York, cutting a new record called *Friends, Family & Legends*, which featured cameos from Chet Atkins, Joan Jett, Travis Tritt, and Charlie Daniels—as well as Will Lee and Paul Shaffer from Letterman's house band—and was keen to get out and promote the album. Three days later, Carl was in Nashville's Vanderbilt University Hospital, where his throat cancer was confirmed. Carl consulted with two

specialists, Dr. William Permenter—whose grandfather had sometimes driven Carl and his brothers to school—and Dr. James Net-
terville, who recommended a course of radiation. Carl was assured
that if there was to be any surgery, it would be minor. "Not knowing
about radiation," Carl told *Musician* magazine, "I didn't know what
I was in for."

Carl's recovery, as he admitted to fellow musician Ricky Skaggs,
was tough. He was stuck at home, unable to talk, let alone sing,
thinking that "my whole world had caved in on me." Carl had been
in motion since the late 1940s; not working was as big a shock to
his system as the cancer. "It almost got me," he said in 1997. "It was
an awfully sad time for me. I knew I was in bad shape. I totally surrendered." Carl prayed, asking God that if he could be healed, he'd
never leave a stage for "as long as people wanted to hear me."

One day he was idly listening to the radio when the DJ
announced: "Here's an old Carl Perkins song by Ricky Skaggs, Vince
Gill, Steve Wariner, and Mark O'Connor." Carl couldn't believe his
ears—assembled under the banner of the New Nashville Cats, the
four players had recorded "Restless," one of Carl's best songs from
back in his Columbia years. Carl was thrilled; it was just the tonic
he needed. "When I heard these four cats turned loose on my song
'Restless,' it really did as much for me as the radiation had been
doing for my throat. I cried. It was a very emotional thing. I thought,
'My goodness, I didn't know that song was that good.'" Their version
was so good, in fact, that it won Carl his first and only Grammy, for
Best Country Collaboration with Vocals, and reached number 25 on
the Country charts.

If there was an upside for Carl's cancer, it was that he wasn't
hospitalized—he was able to recover from his radiation treatment
at home. Carl was scheduled for thirty radiation treatments over
the course of two months but ultimately received thirty-seven, each
lasting about twenty minutes, and during the last rounds, as he
painfully revealed, "they turned the rads up—and I knew it." He lost
his taste buds, his salivary glands, his tonsils, and forty pounds in
weight; it was as though he were fading away. (He didn't lose his taste
for cigarettes, unfortunately.) When Carl met with his specialist at

Vanderbilt, he was told surgery wasn't required. "[It] was wonderful news," he told *Musician*.

Carl spent much of 1991 at home in Jackson, surrounded by family, with many of his fans sending him get-well cards and notes. Naomi Judd was a rock; she'd send Carl gifts, such as the book *Releasing the Ability of God Through Prayer*, doing her best to keep him in a positive frame of mind. Having suffered from chronic active hepatitis, Judd saw Carl as a fellow member of what she called the End of the Plank Club. They were survivors.

His voice was little more than a rasp, and he felt constantly weak, but Carl knew somewhere deep inside that he was going to pull through. "I had exactly what we must have to survive some-thing," said Carl, "and that is love everywhere I turned." Valda was, as ever, always by Carl's side—when he was forced onto a liquid diet, she prepared him homemade juice, which he said tasted "like hay." Carl drank them, regardless.

Carl recovered to the point where, later in 1991, he was able to share a stage alongside the New Nashville Cats—with Alison Krauss, Marty Stuart, Bill Monroe, and Vince Gill also sitting in— for a live performance of "Restless" at the CMA Awards ceremony. Thinner than his doctor would have liked, and not yet able to sing, the tuxedo-clad Carl still managed to pull off a roaring solo as the all-star jam reached its climax. Carl didn't need to utter a word, because the blissful look on his face said everything. It was good to be back.

CHAPTER 18

There is a deep love with this little group

Carl may not have been ready to resume heavy touring during his recovery in the early 1990s, but he was anything but silent. He began popping up in unexpected places, appearing in an infomercial with Elvis's guitarist, Scotty Moore, plugging a planned documentary about Presley's early years that was never released. (Moore, fully aware of the historical merit of their exchange, posted the video shot with Carl on his website and his MySpace page.) The pair also recorded an album, *706 Reunion: A Sentimental Journey*, which was released in 1992. Soon after, Carl's doctor told him he was officially cancer-free. In 1993, Carl shared the limelight with Southern rockers the Kentucky Headhunters in a rowdy video for their version of Carl's "Dixie Fried," looking every inch like the coolest patron a young band like the Headhunters could wish for, much as Carl had done for NRBQ in the early 1970s. The Headhunters' remake was a modest success, too, reaching the outer limits of *Billboard*'s Hot Country Songs chart. It was the latest cover of the Carl classic, and every bit as honky-tonk-worthy as previous takes over the years by George Thorogood and the Destroyers, Jimmy Gilmer and the Fireballs, and Jim Dickinson. It was one of Carl's most covered originals.

Carl also dabbled in the hospitality business, becoming actively involved in a Jackson restaurant called, fittingly, Suede's, which was partly owned and operated by his daughter, Debbie, and her husband, Bart Swift. (Their first date had been a Carl Perkins concert in 1976.) Carl had invested in several businesses over the years—in the mid-1970s he'd purchased stock in the ArLuE Recording Studio in Jackson, and he'd also invested in the Catfish Cabin restaurant chain in western Tennessee, but Suede's was more personal. The walls of Suede's were decorated with highly collectible Carl memorabilia: a setlist from a 1949 Perkins Brothers show; an aging Micro Frets guitar Carl once used; the first two drafts of "Daddy Sang Bass"—even a membership application for the Carl Perkins Fan Club. As for the food, one satisfied customer described the fare as "good ol' Southern cooking at its finest, the way mama used to do it." The menu featured Tennessee barbecue and ribs, boiled shrimp, fried cheese, broiled gulf shrimp, and more. Whenever Carl dined at Suede's, he'd opt for the catfish, his favorite dish.

Carl's relationship with the surviving Beatles remained strong. In April 1993, he caught up with Paul McCartney backstage at the Liberty Bowl in Memphis, and their subsequent jam session and chat—billed as *My Old Friend* and aired on CMT and released on video—covered a lot of territory. Carl looked a little leaner and a little older after his recent cancer scare, but he was still well turned out, his hairpiece in place, his shirt neatly pressed. Together they jammed "Blue Suede Shoes"—playing it in the Perkins style, not the Elvis way, as the two joked—which led to a conversation about Chuck Berry and a jam of "Maybellene," with Carl on electric guitar and Paul on acoustic. They also discussed "Movie Magg": Carl assured McCartney that the lyric was basically true. "I knew that her dad did have a shotgun behind the door," as he revealed in the song.

They also jammed "Matchbox," one of the three songs written by Carl that the Beatles recorded. "I hear you!" exclaimed Carl as McCartney cut loose on his guitar. Carl explained that he wasn't aware of the 1920s number that was the inspiration. "I didn't know there was a guy named Blind Lemon Jefferson had that song out." And, as Carl disclosed, it was Jerry Lee Lewis, who was playing piano on the session, that cooked up the riff that changed the song from a slow blues to a rockabilly classic.

Away from the camera, Carl and McCartney remained solid friends. When McCartney's son James turned sixteen, Carl sent him one of his classic Fender Stratocasters as a gift—a 1956 Strat, along "with a case I'd dragged all over the world," as Carl recalled. McCartney was so struck by the gesture that he suggested that one day he and Carl get all their kids together in the studio and see what emerged. The next time James McCartney saw Carl, he hugged him and said, "I love my Strat! I'll never get rid of it." Carl was pleased it had found a good home. (In reply, McCartney sent Carl a full-size, guitar-shaped birthday cake.) Guitar giving became something of a ritual, because Carl also sent a six-string to Dhani Harrison, George's son, when he reached his sixteenth birthday, in 1994.

Carl had never forgotten how welcoming the Beatles had been all the way back in 1964, at a point when he genuinely thought his career was all over. And that generosity toward Carl had never ceased—he was always welcome at Friar Park and recalled his time with McCartney at Montserrat in 1981 warmly and often. (A good song had come out of that, too, "My Old Friend," which McCartney, with Carl's approval, continued to tinker with in his home studio.) Carl, of course, also had the Beatles to thank for the steady flow of royalty checks emanating from their recordings of "Matchbox," "Honey, Don't," and "Everybody's Trying to Be My Baby."

Paul McCartney may have said, "If there were no Carl Perkins, there would be no Beatles," but Carl knew that in 1964 the Beatles, too, had thrown him a significant lifeline.

It wasn't only former Beatles that treated Carl with due reverence. On November 10, 1994, Bob Dylan's Never Ending Tour rolled up to the Oman Arena in Jackson. Dylan knew that Jackson was Carl's hometown and reached out, inviting him to the show. That night, during his encore, Dylan brought Carl onstage to rock "Matchbox," the same song they'd performed on *The Johnny Cash Show* some twenty-six years before, when they'd first met. Hometown hero Carl, dressed in working man's denim, with a huge smile lighting up his face, got down to business, playing hard and fast, while Dylan strummed his guitar, keeping out of Carl's way, content to be side man—at one point he even managed a rare broad grin of his own. The audience loved it, clapping along wholeheartedly as Carl and Dylan's guitarist John Jackson traded licks like prizefighters swapping punches. "I'm a Jackson boy / It feels real good to be back home," ad-libbed Carl, and the crowd erupted.

Although Carl couldn't quite match Dylan's schedule of a hundred plus shows a year, the C.P. Express was back on the road and working hard. During 1993, Carl had recruited a new rhythm guitarist, Jerry Elston, who held down a day job as deputy sheriff. He was a good man to have on your side, as Carl admitted: "His bread is made by toting a gun and taking care of the bad boys in Jackson." Over the years, Carl's tight connection with the band hadn't wavered, as he told a writer from *Vintage Guitar*: "There is a deep love with this little group." Carl even confessed to feeling a tad guilty when he flew in business class—on the promoter's dime, naturally—while the rest of the band traveled in coach. "I don't like that," he admitted. Carl made sure that his band were given good rooms in the hotels where they stayed, and ensured they all ate together while on the road. To Carl, the C.P. Express was like a gang, a band of brothers. "If someone jumped on one [of us]," he joked, he'd be confronted by the "whole damn bunch."

Carl's high-profile cameos continued throughout the 1990s. In the fall of 1995, two all-star concerts were staged at the two-thousand-capacity Shepherd's Bush Empire in London as part of Buddy Holly Week, which was celebrating its twentieth anniversary. Carl had toured with Holly a couple of times back in the 1950s and remembered him as "a humble boy, a shy, quiet, likable fellow." He was thrilled to take part in the event. Passing himself off as "just a little Liverpool fan," Paul McCartney joined the ensemble—which included Holly's backing band, the Crickets, as well as Bobby Vee, Mike Berry & the Outlaws, and the Rapiers—for a raucous version of "Rave On," but it was Carl's short set that was the highlight of the two-night stand.

As reported in the autumn edition of *Club Sandwich*, the Paul McCartney newsletter, Carl blazed at Shepherd's Bush. "[He] had the audience in the palm of his hand from the off. As the years pass so this man's stature grows and grows, owing not only to his timeless music but also to his physical domination of the stage." Carl rattled off a jukebox full of classics: "Matchbox," "Honey, Don't," "Turn Around," "Blue Suede Shoes," and "Gone, Gone, Gone," as well as a closing medley that celebrated the music of Chuck Berry, Little Richard, Jerry Lee, and Elvis. "The man is truly a giant of rock and roll," reported the McCartney newsletter, "and he made it all look so easy as he caressed his way through a superb set of songs full of passion and unbridled enjoyment." Backstage, Carl beamed a high-wattage smile. "I had a ball," he said.

But the culmination of this prolonged period of adulation was 1996's *Go Cat Go!*, where Carl—with the help of his current manager Rick Korn, a film and TV producer—brought together a remarkable ensemble of friends and admirers, including Johnny Cash, Willie Nelson, Paul Simon, Tom Petty and the Heartbreakers, Bono from U2, and John Fogerty. And in a masterstroke that no other musician alive or dead could lay claim to, Carl's album featured all four Beatles—Harrison, McCartney, and Ringo Starr played on the record, while John Lennon's version of "Blue Suede Shoes," from 1969's Toronto Rock 'n' Roll Revival concert, was also included. In their own way, these contributions completed the journey that had started way back in 1964, when Carl and the Beatles first met.

Carl was surprised by how smoothly and naturally the project came together. "All I had to do was ask these guys," he told CBS TV host Tom Snyder. After forty years of great music making, Carl still seemed genuinely surprised that so many A-listers were eager to work with him. Away from the studio, he was busy at work on a memoir, also titled *Go, Cat, Go!*, collaborating with *Rolling Stone* writer David McGee.

One of the standouts of the album was "Distance Makes No Difference with Love," Carl's cowrite with George Harrison. Carl had contacted the former Beatle by fax, stating how much he'd love to work on a song with him. Harrison's reply read, simply: *I would love to do a song with my friend Carl Perkins. Love, George. Let me know where and when.* Carl and Valda traveled to Friar Park, where Carl played "Distance Makes No Difference with Love"—another song written for Valda—with Harrison looking on. "Wow, man," he said, "that's a beautiful song."

Valda pulled Carl aside and told him, "You know, Carl, you've got a beautiful thing going with Paul [McCartney]. Why don't you give George the opportunity to sing [that song] with you?"

That was all the motivation Carl needed, and the two friends agreed to work on "Distance" together in Harrison's home studio at his estate. In the end, Harrison played piano, rhythm guitar, and added harmonies, while Carl played a couple of guitar parts and sang. Harrison's signature slide guitar was another feature of the finished track. "I think he really poured his heart and soul into it," Carl told *Goldmine* magazine. In fact, Carl rated it as highly as he did "My Old Friend," his 1981 song inspired by Montserrat and his time with the McCartneys, which he also included on *Go Cat Go!*, now with an added string arrangement from Sir George Martin.

When Carl played "My Old Friend" to Harrison and told him the peculiar story about how he'd accidentally repeated John Lennon's last words to Paul in the lyric, Harrison told him: "If John sent it to you, he sent you a good one."

Harrison gave Carl Ringo Starr's private number in Barbados, and he called and asked if he might consider contributing to the album. Starr sent Carl a live recording of "Honey, Don't" that he'd cut with his All-Starr Band in San Francisco. "You do whatever you want to it," Starr advised Carl from his Caribbean hideaway.

Carl was a big fan of Paul Simon's 1986 album *Graceland*. It was a dual Grammy winner that sold fourteen million copies and introduced much of the Western world to South African music rarely heard, due to the country's oppressive apartheid regime. Carl hadn't met Simon when he reached out to him with the idea of recording together on *Go Cat Go!* What ensued was very much like the time Paul McCartney called Carl's house in Jackson.

"Carl," Valda said after answering the phone, "it's Paul Simon."

"You're kidding," he replied.

"No," she insisted, "I can tell by his voice."

Carl spent a couple of days in New York with Simon and his

son Harper, also a musician, and then they traveled together to Sun. Together they wrote and recorded the lovely, understated "Rockabilly Music" as well as "A Mile Out of Memphis," a juiced-up slice of rockabilly that gave Carl the chance to really bend some strings on his guitar.

Tom Petty, a native of Gainesville, Florida, was another modern master whom Carl admired greatly. Petty was a true rock and roll gatekeeper, who'd nurtured strong relationships with Roy Orbison, Del Shannon—he produced his 1981 comeback album *Drop Down and Get Me*—as well as Roger McGuinn, whom he once famously defended (on camera) against music biz stooges trying to convince the former Byrd to record inferior material. ("I could smoke a joint and come up with a better line than that," snarled Petty, when he heard the lyric. "This is a bad song.") When he and Carl got together for *Go Cat Go!*, they bonded immediately, as Petty later told *Rolling Stone*. "He once told me, 'Tom, I like you so much—if I lived by you, I'd cut your grass.' That warmth and wit came through in his music. He was not the kind of guy to blow his own horn; he was very humble."

Carl and Petty, along with his group, the Heartbreakers, whom Carl rated highly—"they're pickers"—recorded two tracks, "One More Shot" and "Restless." While recording the latter, Petty had taken a restroom break, but when he heard the band playing, he dashed back into the studio, pulling at his trousers and reaching for his zipper. When Carl asked what the heck he was doing, Petty explained that he could hear them from the bathroom and feared missing out on the action. "Man," he said, "I knew it was in the groove!" Petty proved to be correct. Even though they attempted another pass at the track, it was the original that worked best, despite Petty's not playing any guitar. (He was still trying to do up his pants at the time.) When Carl mentioned this to him, Petty shook his head and said, "No, I ain't touching it. I'll sing on it, but *that groove!*" Instead, Carl and the Heartbreakers' lead guitarist Mike Campbell swapped stinging licks. At one point, Carl asked, "Can I pick?" and proceeded to knock off a roaring rockabilly-flavored solo—it was so good, in fact, that when he stopped playing, Petty and his band broke into spontaneous applause. Together, Carl and the Heartbreakers had breathed new life into a Perkins classic, a song that celebrated itchy feet and brought the best out of anyone who recorded it.

Carl had met John Fogerty before; they'd worked together on the *Class of '55* project, Chips Moman's tribute to Memphis. "I had a greater affinity for Carl Perkins [than Elvis]," said Fogerty, "because he was a musician. He played guitar and wrote songs . . . he went right to the middle of my musical soul." But Carl almost blew his chance to record again with the reclusive Fogerty, who came into the studio with the intention of cutting "All Mama's Children," backed by Petty's Heartbreakers.

"Are you kidding?" Carl asked him. "That's the sorriest song I ever wrote."

Fogerty thought otherwise. He said that, as far as he was concerned, "All Mama's Children" was Carl's best song, hands down. Carl wasn't a great fan of the nursery-rhyme lyric but was eventually talked around. Frankly, he didn't want to miss the chance to rock out for a second time with the Creedence legend. The result was another highlight of the finished record, the pair sprinkling a little grit on Carl's cowrite with Cash that dated all the way back to 1956. "John's a great guy," Carl made clear. "We had a good time."

As had been the case with Carl's music since the mid-1970s, *Go Cat Go!* was also a family affair: His boys, Greg, Steve, and Stan played on several tracks, while his daughter, Debbie, contributed lyrics for the title track and "Don't Stop the Music." "She's got some good stuff," Carl said. "She's going to . . . become a really good writer." Reviews for the album were strong. "*Go Cat Go!* is a fun, consistent tribute to his songwriting and sound; it's an album that's breezy and holds up across its 55 minutes and dozen performers," noted the music critic for Biloxi's *Sun Herald*.

Carl filmed a promo video for the album in New Orleans, with a reporter from the *Daily Press* looking on. "At age 64," wrote Tom Piazza, "Perkins is slim and handsome, with sculpted cheekbones . . . an easy smile and a curly, steel-gray toupée, which is the topic of frequent jokes by its owner." Carl laughed with the writer about the days of "Blue Suede Shoes" and how passersby would regularly ask for photos of them stepping on his shoes. "I used to carry a wire brush," said Carl, "so I could reach down and brush them back to life." Just as he said that a bicycle rider slowed down and yelled, "Hey, Carl Perkins! How's it going?" Carl grinned and replied, "It seems like it's rocking right along."

During its creation, *Go Cat Go!* did some miles—Carl undertook several trips to the West Coast and to New York, and a couple of visits to Austin, Texas, in order to bring the songs to life. He also got to work with the best in the business. "I'll look back on it for the rest of my life," said Carl, "realizing that I was helping to put together something that I can truthfully stand and tell the world I'm not ashamed of."

Go Cat Go! was Carl's last studio album.

CHAPTER 19

I never wanted that mansion on the hill with the iron fence around it

Not long after the release of *Go Cat Go!*, Carl celebrated his sixty-fifth birthday. It had been one hell of a ride, especially over the past few years. He'd been inducted into the Rock and Roll Hall of Fame. The C.P. Express was still filling venues and he'd somehow managed to have no less than four Beatles perform on his most recent album. His memoir, *Go, Cat, Go!*, had been well received. ("At its best," observed one reviewer, "the book reads like timeless Southern fiction, with Carl, and his wild-eyed brother Clayton, resembling characters right out of the Snopes family.") And Carl's marriage to Valda, after more than forty years, remained as strong as ever. They now had nine (soon to be ten) grandchildren—Shannon, Carla, Suzanne, Lesleigh, Jay, Chase, Matthew, Jonathan, and Cody—and two great-grandchildren. Thanksgiving dinner had become Carl's favorite family celebration—it was a day that Chez Perkins would be bursting with family, and spirits were always high.

Life was good.

"Today I look in the mirror," Carl said during the 1997 The Nashville Network documentary *Life & Times*, "and the fellow that I see is one of the most blessed human beings that ever walked on this earth." Carl made it clear that he wouldn't have dreamed of swapping his life with any of his peers—be it Elvis, Roy Orbison, Johnny Cash, or Jerry Lee Lewis—despite their bigger commercial success and higher public profiles.

In an interview with *Guitar Player* magazine, Carl laughed about how people would sometimes pull him up and ask, "What happened to you?"

"I went home," Carl would usually reply. "I never wanted that mansion on the hill with the iron fence around it."

"Stumbling blocks are always there," Carl said during *Life & Times*, "but it's what you do with them . . . by playing my music, by having as many friends as I can, by having the same woman for forty-four years and children who are not ashamed to say, 'Carl Perkins is my Dad.' That's . . . the highlight."

Carl's very public role with the Child Abuse Center continued in sync with his life as a musician and proud family man. In 1993, the center was relocated to the former site of Hardeman Music in Jackson, where some fifty years back Carl had bought his first good guitar. Carl was determined to wipe off the remaining mortgage on the building by playing at more fundraisers. "My dream," he told the *Jackson Sun*, "is to burn the mortgage right there onstage." In 1996, Carl helped raise about $75,000 at the Blue Suede Dinner & Auction at Jackson's Civic Center. In 1997, he did his part in raising more than $100,000 at the event, sharing the bill on the night with a local a cappella group, the Fabulous Delacardos.

The auction's chairman, James Allison, promised to erase any remaining mortgage by March 1997. Carl was overwhelmed. "I can't ask west Tennessee for more," he said on auction night. "There's a four-letter word that covers it all: That's love." Carl often provided memorabilia to be auctioned at the auction; one year it was some Beatles collectibles, signed by his friend George Harrison. "To be associated with [the center] and to be able to spread the word about it has just been a phenomenal thing for me," Carl said.

And Carl continued to build rock-solid relationships with his fellow players. Tom Petty, the man who impressed Carl enormously during the *Go Cat Go!* sessions, was playing a series of shows with the Heartbreakers at the Fillmore in San Francisco in late January 1997. Petty asked Carl if he'd like to come along—and perhaps he might also like to get up and *pick a few*. Carl agreed, despite some concern that Petty's audience would be younger than his own, and not familiar with his music. But it was Tom Petty, Carl figured, a man he liked so much that he'd mow his lawn.

Petty stepped up to the mic at the Fillmore on the night of January 25, and spoke with the audience. "He's one of the great rock-and-rollers and was there when it all started. And I think he's had more songs recorded by the Beatles than anybody. He's one of the great all-time guitar players. I want you to put your hands together for Mr. Carl Perkins." The crowd roared when Carl, dressed in black from head to toe and rocking Cuban heels, took the stage. Carl didn't say anything at first; instead, he let his music do the talking as he and the Heartbreakers played "Honey, Don't."

"Thank you, San Francisco," Carl said as the crowd applauded warmly. "I been sitting up here listening to Tom and his great band and they are out of sight." He then led them into "Matchbox." "Play that guitar, man!" Carl shouted above the roar of the crowd and Heartbreaker Mike Campbell duly obliged.

Before playing "Blue Suede Shoes," Carl shared the story he'd told a thousand times before. Even now he was still trying to make sense of the honky-tonker who prized his "suedes" more than his girl. "I thought, you fool!" said Carl. "I could not get it out of my mind."

"Weeeeeelllll," sang Carl—but then he stopped and looked over to Petty. "Tom," he said, with a huge grin, "we started a lot of songs off with that word, didn't we?" Once they did get started, the audience took over on the chorus—all Carl needed to do was look on and smile while playing his guitar, savoring the moment. By the time of "Restless," their last song together, Carl and the band were in top gear, Carl playing his guitar as if it were on fire, leaving Petty and the band in awe. "Now, was that something or what?" said Petty as Carl disappeared backstage. "You never grow old with rock and roll."

Soon after, while speaking with *Rolling Stone* magazine, Petty revealed that Carl had been visibly nervous before their short set. He was worried that the Filmore audience wouldn't recognize him. "They may not know who I am," he said. But Petty set him straight. "Carl," he said, "they're going to know you and love you."

"When Carl hit the stage," said Petty, "he just ripped the room apart. Neil Young was there that night, and he was shaking his head. Carl was that good."

Carl was also in fine form a few weeks later when he was a guest on the *CMT Presents Monday Night Concert* series (which actually aired on TNN), filmed at Nashville's Ryman Auditorium. The host was Ricky Skaggs, the multi-Grammy winner who, as part of the New Nashville Cats, had lifted Carl's spirits when he was recovering from cancer and heard their hit cover of "Restless" on the radio.

The show opened with Skaggs, country player Wade Hayes, and Carl—decked out in hard-to-miss blue suede boots (not quite shoes) and a black-and-white Western-styled shirt—rocking out to "Restless." An onstage Q&A ensued; Skaggs began by asking Carl how his playing style came about. Carl told the story about getting his first guitar as a child, the Gene Autry model that was heavy with paint. He also spoke about his desire to play the Grand Ole Opry, especially given how poorly things had worked out for him at school. "The teachers felt sorry for me and I sang my way through eight grades and finally had to quit and go to work helping my Dad on the farm."

Skaggs mentioned the Beatles, telling Carl, "You really touched those guys." Carl flashed back to that memorable night in London in 1964, when Chuck Berry was a no-show and he spent much of the night fielding questions from the Fab Four. Then Carl played "Matchbox"; even while seated, his legs still jiggled uncontrollably. He followed this with a snippet of "Honey, Don't," continuing the Beatles theme.

Skaggs moved on to Johnny Cash and "Daddy Sang Bass," Carl's biggest hit this side of "Blue Suede Shoes." "A lot of folks may not know that you wrote that," Skaggs admitted.

Wade Hayes then rejoined them, seated on steps at the front of the stage, as Carl talked about the influence Bill Monroe had on his music, before playing a snippet of "Blue Moon of Kentucky." Carl then played some rockabilly licks that neither Skaggs nor Hayes were able to emulate, despite their best efforts. Following that, Carl played "Down by the Riverside" and the audience clapped along— the ever-amenable Carl even "picked a little," on Skaggs's request, as they headed to an ad break.

Skaggs asked Carl asked about the Million Dollar Quartet—how did it feel to be part of such a famous ensemble? Carl insisted that they were a "group of non-jealous people. When someone got a new Cadillac, everyone was so proud for them." Carl recalled one red-letter day in 1957 when Memphis's humble Union Avenue resembled a Cadillac dealership. "There were six new Cadillacs parked down that street in front of that one little door at Sun Records," he said. "It looked like a rainbow."

The show closed with the obligatory jam of "Blue Suede Shoes," the audience clapping so loudly that they almost drowned out Carl, Skaggs, Hayes, and the house band, which included Carl's sons Stan and Greg on drums and bass. By the time the closing credits rolled, the three pickers were at the lip of the stage trading licks, and the audience were out of their seats and on their feet, soaking up every note they played. Carl had won over yet another audience.

CHAPTER 20

Remember Carl Perkins said to you,
"Winners never quit and quitters never win."

In April 1997, Carl had four dates booked in Florida; he was to share the stage with another veteran, Van Morrison. Together they'd recently recorded several songs, including Carl's "Boppin' the Blues" and "Matchbox," during sessions for Morrison's album, *The Healing Game*. But he was forced to cancel at the last moment due to ill health. Not Carl's health, mind you, but his son Greg, who at thirty-six had been told by doctors that he had serious liver damage and might even need a transplant. At the same time, Valda was also at the tail end of a lengthy illness. It was a rough time health-wise for the Perkins family.

Just a few weeks earlier, Carl had given a keynote speech at the annual South by Southwest Festival, a big music industry bash staged in Austin, Texas. (Previous keynote speakers included Rosanne Cash, Johnny Cash, and Kinky Friedman.) When approached about the gig, Carl felt that maybe he wasn't the right man for the job. "Keynote?" he asked his manager Rick Korn. "What's a keynote?" But Carl was talked around, and soon after strode onto the stage at the Austin Convention Center, dressed in a dark pinstripe suit, his guitar at the ready, just in case he ran out of wisdom to share.

Carl's forty-five-minute address—billed as "Chasing That Dream"—was an informal, back-porch chat about such pals as Presley ("This business never had a more special fellow than Elvis") and one of his first heroes, Bill Monroe. Carl made it clear that to his mind, "the first rockabilly song was 'Blue Moon of Kentucky.'" He also joked about looking on as the Beatles did their thing with "Matchbox" in Abbey Road in 1964. "Tears came into my eyes," said Carl. "Then I started thinking of the royalties I'd get, and the tears left my eyes."

Carl also played segments of his songs, including "Honey, Don't," "Blue Suede Shoes," and a song from *Go Cat Go!* called "Quarter Horse." Having given what one observer said was "the best keynote speech in my five years of [SXSW] watching," Carl smiled and closed with this: "Remember Carl Perkins said to you, 'Winners never quit and quitters never win.'" With that, he was gone.

Due to his family's health issues, Carl didn't play a lot of shows during 1997; less than thirty in all. On September 6, just after the twentieth anniversary of Elvis's death, he performed at Graceland, Elvis's stately Memphis mansion, where, apart from his own classics, he also added "Hi-Heel Sneakers," "Mean Woman Blues," and "That's All Right" to his set. Just nine days later Carl plugged in at London's Royal Albert Hall, playing as part of the Music for Montserrat fundraiser. The concert, organized by Sir George Martin, was raising money for residents of the island who'd been affected by a major volcanic eruption earlier in the year. Carl's connection with Montserrat was strong after his time there with Paul McCartney, who was also on the bill, as were Mark Knopfler, Sting, Elton John, and Eric Clapton. The house was very full when Carl, who was to open the show, hit the stage.

Carl looked a little gaunt but seemed to burst into life as he walked into the spotlight, dressed in a pinstripe suit jacket, with a gold crucifix around his neck and his monogrammed guitar strap across his shoulders. "Thank you very much, good evening, ladies and gentlemen," he said, and then proceeded to tell the story about being called at home and invited to Montserrat "by one of the nicest friends I've had since 1964."

Carl spoke about that week back in 1981, during the recording of *Tug of War*, "what a wonderful thrill it was, what a beautiful island it was, and hope it will be when this is all over." Just before Carl sang his signature song, he invited the audience to help him out with the opening. They obliged, their voices echoing around the stately Albert Hall. "Y'all been out rehearsing," Carl said with a smile. "You're great." He and the band tore up "Blue Suede Shoes," and after the final note, Carl turned to acknowledge his fellow musicians as the audience cheered and clapped. It was a fitting farewell.

In early November 1997, Carl was a surprise guest at the one-hundredth-birthday celebration for Jackson resident Alliene Key, a fellow member of the First United Methodist Church. Ms. Key was dining at Suede's with fellow church members when Carl appeared at her table with his guitar and sang for her. "I was in a state of shock," Ms. Key admitted.

But barely a week later, Carl suffered the first in a series of strokes that resulted in his being admitted to Jackson-Madison County General Hospital. (Carl had been hospitalized in early June, undergoing surgery to relieve a blocked carotid artery.) By early December, he was convalescing at home and, as his son Stan told reporters, was expected to make a full recovery. Therapy would help address some problems Carl was experiencing with his balance. But in mid-December, he suffered a third stroke and returned to hospital. Carl's outlook was grim; he was partially paralyzed and was admitted to intensive care. "It's very serious," said Stan. "He's not in good shape now." Carl remained in the hospital and died there on the morning of Monday, January 19, 1998.

Carl Perkins was sixty-five years old.

Carl's hometown of Jackson was in mourning. He was a beloved citizen, one of their favorite sons, an entertainer and a humanitarian who'd contributed a lot to the city. "When he'd make appearances on television," remembered his son-in-law, Bart Swift, "he'd always make sure to mention Jackson, Tennessee, as his home." To which Carl's daughter, Debbie, added: "He was proud to be here and proud to be where he was from growing up." A sign was erected on a billboard near the hospital where he died. It read, simply, REST IN PEACE, MR. CARL PERKINS. Another sign appeared outside Suede's Restaurant: PLEASE PRAY FOR THE PERKINS FAMILY. And yet another read, THANKS FOR THE MEMORIES, CARL PERKINS 1932–1998. Flags all over Jackson flew at half-mast.

"Perkins was there when it happened," reported the *Tennessean* in its obituary. The *Jackson Sun* pronounced Carl a "music man and humanitarian . . . Carl Perkins was more than just a guy with a guitar. So very much more." Johnny and June Carter Cash expressed their deep sorrow in a statement, which read, in part: "Carl was a very close friend for over 40 years, and his musical legacy is certain to prevail forever." *Rolling Stone* magazine hailed Carl as "one of the founders of rock and roll," giving credit to the huge influence he had on such superstars as the Beatles and Eric Clapton.

Carl was a "pioneering rockabilly singer, songwriter and guitarist," Jon Pareles wrote in the *New York Times*. "Mr. Perkins was a quiet, genial, devout man . . . well into his 60s he was on the road, revitalizing even his most familiar oldies with an unmistakable twang." "His was a pure, uncomplicated sort of cool that can't be faked," wrote *Salon*'s Gavin McNett. Perkins should be remembered as "a titan of rock, the likes of whom we may never see again."

Tom Petty remembered his friend in an essay in *Rolling Stone*: "Carl Perkins's songs will outlive us all."

The day before Carl's funeral on January 23, George Harrison, who was recovering from treatment for throat cancer, chartered a plane to fly from Los Angeles to Jackson, where the service was to be held at the R. E. Womack Memorial Chapel on the grounds of the University of Memphis Lambuth campus. The next day, Harrison, his hair worn long, his chin sprinkled with salt-and-pepper whiskers, quietly sat alongside his wife, Olivia, and the faithful and the famous who were gathered at Carl's service, which was broadcast on a local TV network. Hundreds of onlookers lined the path outside the chapel. As MTV News later reported, "All of Jackson, it seemed, had come out to mourn Carl Perkins, the undisputed King of Rockabilly."

Garth Brooks was among the mourners, as were Sam Phillips, Jerry Lee Lewis, Johnny and June Carter Cash, and Lee Rocker from the Stray Cats. Carl's family filled several rows of the chapel. A large section was set aside for the public, and the pews overflowed with friends and admirers, many wearing blue suede shoes in honor of Carl. The turnout was so overwhelming that a separate site had been set up, just across from the chapel, with 250 chairs and a large-screen TV to enable those who couldn't squeeze into the five-hundred-capacity chapel to watch the service.

There were tributes delivered by Ricky Skaggs, Johnny Rivers, Tennessee governor Don Sundquist, and Dr. John A. Jones, a United Methodist minister from Memphis. Ricky Skaggs sang "Silver and Gold" and then Wynonna Judd—who told the gathering that Carl was "the coolest cat I ever met"—delivered a soul-stirring version of "How Great Thou Art." As MTV reported, "it was an astonishing, mesmerizing moment" that brought tears to the eyes of just about everyone in the chapel.

Judd sought out George Harrison in one of the front pews. She had a favor to ask. "George, I don't want to put you on the spot or anything, but is there anything you want to request? Do you wanna come up here and be with us?" she asked. "I think Carl would want that. You gotta sing for your supper, son. Don't be shy."

After a little more prompting from Judd, George slowly rose from his seat and picked up Ricky Skaggs's acoustic guitar, stopping briefly to pat Carl's casket. He hadn't planned on singing and was concerned that Carl's family thought he might be intruding, so he sought them out in the chapel, hoping that he was doing the right thing. ("I smiled at him," Stan Perkins later said, "and it lifted his spirits.") Harrison was unsure if he could actually sing after his recent cancer treatment.

"Well, I think somebody out there must know this," Harrison said from the altar. "It's from Carl's first album. It's been a long time." Harrison, who was joined onstage by the church's choir and members of the gathering, then found his voice, quite literally, and sang "Your True Love." It was a poignant moment, the best possible farewell from a friend to a friend. "Thank you and God bless Carl," Harrison said before returning to his pew. After a final prayer, the service was concluded.

Carl's former bandmate Wes Henley was among the mourners, and he felt that Harrison's impromptu performance changed the mood of the service in a very positive way. "It made it more of a celebration about Carl, rather than a grieving thing." It was exactly how Carl would have wanted his funeral to be.

After the service, Harrison was driven to Carl's home. He found himself drawn to the den, Carl's favorite nook in the house, where such songs as "Silver and Gold," a hit for Dolly Parton, had been written. George noticed that Carl's black guitar was resting alongside an amp. Harrison instinctively reached for the instrument when a family friend intervened.

"What are you doing?" he was asked.

"It's Carl's guitar, I just wanted to put my hands on it," Harrison replied.

"Not today you don't."

Harrison understood perfectly. At times like this, some things were sacred.

Carl was interred at the Ridgecrest Cemetery in Jackson. Alongside his nameplate was the Sun Records logo, which read, most fittingly, "Where Rock 'n' Roll Was Born!" Memorial shows were staged at the House of Blues in Los Angeles. Johnny Rivers and Dwight Yoakam appeared the first night, the Stray Cats the next. All proceeds from the concerts went to the Carl Perkins Center for the Prevention of Child Abuse. George Harrison attended the gigs, and not long after he met with Stan Perkins at the Hyatt Regency on the Sunset Strip, where he was staying. George told Stan that he hadn't been sure if he'd be able to sing at the funeral service; he was still very weak from his radiation treatment. "I did the best I could," he assured Stan.

Carl's son had a gift for Harrison—the guitar that Carl had played during the *A Rockabilly Session* special in 1985, which until recently had been an exhibit at the Rock and Roll Hall of Fame in Cleveland. Harrison was stunned when he presented it to him.

"You're going to give me this guitar?" Harrison asked. "Are you sure?"

Tears welled in his eyes.

"I can't think of anybody I'd rather see walk away with this guitar than you," Stan told him. "It's yours."

Just before his death, Carl had been asked how he would like to be
remembered. He paused before responding, then quoted from a
plaque hanging on the wall of his home in Jackson. It read: "Within
these walls I've written my songs. I've done you right and I've done
you wrong. Let it be said when I'm gone that he smiled and wasn't
ashamed to play." It was a very fitting epitaph.

Epilogue

What Happened Next

1999: During his induction into the Rock and Roll Hall of Fame, Paul McCartney remembered Carl as "a beautiful man," before playing "Blue Suede Shoes," backed by Eric Clapton, Bonnie Raitt, Robbie Robertson, and other luminaries.

Carl's album *Live at Gilley's* was released.

Black Sabbath's version of "Blue Suede Shoes" was released.

2000: Bear Records released the comprehensive *On Top* four-CD set of Carl's music.

2001: George Harrison died from cancer on November 29, aged fifty-eight. He was a smoker, like Carl, and blamed cigarettes for his health problems. He did not perform in public again after Carl's funeral service.

2002: At the Concert for George memorial, Ringo Star performed Carl's "Honey, Don't." "George loved Carl Perkins," Starr told the audience at London's Albert Hall.

2003: Johnny Cash died at the age of seventy-one on September 12. His *American Recordings* collaborations with Rick Rubin won three Grammys and three Country Music Association awards.

Sun founder Sam Phillips died, aged eighty, on July 30.

2004:   Carl was ranked #99 in *Rolling Stone*'s 100 Greatest
        Artists of all Time; Tom Petty wrote the accompanying
        essay. Roy Orbison ranked #37, Johnny Cash #31, Jerry
        Lee Lewis #24, and Elvis Presley #3.

        The Drive-By Truckers recorded a song called "Carl
        Perkins' Cadillac" on their album *The Dirty South*.

2005:   Valda Perkins died on November 15 and was buried
        alongside Carl at Ridgecrest Cemetery. A family friend,
        Doris "Cousin Tuny" Freeman, said, "Carl used to say
        he'd sown his wild oats, but Val helped him collect them.
        There was only one woman in his life, and that was Val."
        Greg Perkins died three days later from cancer, aged
        forty-six.

        In the Johnny Cash biopic, *Walk the Line*, Carl was
        played by Johnny Holiday.

2006:   "Blue Suede Shoes" was added to the Library of Congress
        National Recording Registry collection.

2009:   Steven Perkins died from cancer, aged fifty-three.

2010:   *The Million Dollar Quartet* musical, written by Colin
        Escott and Floyd Mutrux, made its Broadway debut, with
        Robert Britton Lyons in the role of Carl, and ran for 489
        performances. It then opened on London's West End in
        2011.

2013:   The Jerry Lee Lewis Café and Honky Tonk was opened
        on Beale Street in Memphis. A Blue Suede Shoes cocktail,
        a potent mix of vodka and blue curaçao liqueur, featured
        among the drinks.

2014:   Carl's first drummer, W. S. "Fluke" Holland, was honored
        at the Carl Perkins Center in Jackson for his sixty years
        of music making.

2016:   Scotty Moore, Elvis's guitarist and a friend of Carl's, died,
        aged eighty-four, on June 28.

2017: CMT produced the eight-part TV series *Sun Records*, based on *The Million Dollar Quartet* musical. Dustin Ingram was cast as Carl Perkins.

Tom Petty died on October 2, one week after the Heartbreakers' 40th Anniversary Tour ended and just less than three weeks before his sixty-seventh birthday.

2018: Carl was given a posthumous Lifetime Achievement Award at the Tennessee Music Awards.

2020: "Fluke" Holland, died, aged eighty-five, on September 23. In a 2001 interview with *Rock & Blues News* magazine, Holland described himself as "a good old boy who can play a little bit of the drums."

2021: The New York music company Primary Wave purchased Sun Records for a reported $30 million. The sale included nearly six thousand master recordings and the iconic Sun Records logo.

2022: Jerry Lee Lewis, the longest-surviving member of the Million Dollar Quartet, died at the age of eighty-seven, on October 28. At the time of his death, the Killer was living with his seventh wife, Judith Lewis. His final studio album, 2014's *Rock & Roll Time*, featured appearances from Keith Richards, Robbie Robertson, and Neil Young. Two weeks before his death, Lewis had been inducted into the Country Music Hall of Fame.

Bob Dylan wrote about "Blue Suede Shoes" in his book, *The Philosophy of Modern Song*. "Carl wrote this song," noted Dylan, "but if Elvis was alive today, he'd be the one to have a deal with Nike."

2023: The Carl Perkins Civic Center in downtown Jackson continued to host live music.

2023:   The Circles of Hope Telethon, a fundraiser for the Carl
        Perkins Center for the Prevention of Child Abuse,
        marked its fortieth anniversary. The center continued to
        operate across forty counties, working with around four
        thousand children every year, providing essential support
        services. The Blue Suede Dinner & Auction remained
        a banner event on the Jackson social calendar, raising
        approximately $450,000 at its 29th annual gathering in
        February. www.carlperkinscenter.org.

Bibliography

Alabama Journal. "Carl Perkins Billed in Coliseum Show." May 29, 1956.

Angola Herald. "'Blue Suede Shoes' at Buck Lake Ranch." June 13, 1956.

Anthony, Michael. "Carl Perkins sets feet tapping at Union Bar." *Star Tribune*, May 31, 1980.

Arizona Republic. "Music Greats Mourn Loss of Rock Pioneer to Heart Attack." December 8, 1988.

Ayer, Audie. "The Original Rockabilly Is Trying Again." *Daily American Republic*, January 22,1977.

Ayers, Bob. "Mr. Blue Suede Shoes to Return from England." *Jackson Sun*, November 23, 1964.

Ballard, Delores. "Aging Carl Perkins Isn't Staying Idle." *Roanoke Times*, June 28, 1975.

———. "Old Jackson Friends Remember Elvis." *Jackson Sun*, August 17, 1977.

Bates, Don M. "Life Was Hard for Country Singer." *Indianapolis Star*, August 3, 1980.

Battle, Bob. "A Wealth of Memories." *Country Style*, n.d.

Bishop, Nancy. "Carl Perkins' Sound Is Back—and He's Never Left." *Fresno Bee*, June 10, 1983.

Bleiel, Jeff. "Rockin' into the 90s." *Goldmine*, June 15, 1990.

Brown, Mark. Album review: *Go Cat Go! Sun Herald*, January 31, 1997.

Browne, David. "Balding Pop Stars." *Entertainment Weekly*, July 24, 1992.

Buffalo News. "'Jamboree' Opening in Center." December 12, 1957.

Byworth, Tony. "Ol' Blue Suedes Is Back." *Country Music People*, May 1978.

Cajiao, Trevor. "Straight Out of the Honky Tonks." *Now Dig This*, n.d.

Carr, Patrick. "Livin' Legend." *Country Music*, September 1973.

Carter, Maria. "Inside Patsy Cline's Rise to Fame before Her Tragic Death at 30 Years Old." Countryliving.com, October 20, 2019.

Cash, Johnny, with Patrick Carr. *Cash: The Autobiography.* San Francisco: HarperSanFrancisco, 1997.

Cleave, Maureen. "Carl Perkins: Here's the Man to Set You Patting Your Blue Suedes." *Evening Standard*, June 6, 1964.

Club Sandwich. "20th Buddy Holly Week, Thursday September 7, 1995." *Club Sandwich* 75, Autumn 1995.

Coleman, Mark. "Second Annual Rock and Roll Hall of Fame Bash," *Rolling Stone*, March 12, 1987.

Coleman, Ray. *Lennon: The Definitive Biography.* London: Pan Books, 2000.

Commercial Appeal. "Blue Suedes and Beatle Boots Have Found Common Ground." December 20, 1985.

Conner, Thomas. "Go South-West Young Man." *Tulsa World*, March 23, 1997.

Country Music People. Carl Perkins interview, February 1972.

Courier-Post. "Carl Perkins Tops Bill at Steel Pier." September 8, 1956.

Cullison, Art. "Rock'n'Roll Galore—Strand Theater Plays 'Jamboree.'" *Akron Beacon Journal*, December 13, 1957.

Daily Advertiser. "Carl Perkins Recovering from a Stroke." December 7, 1997.

Daily Mirror. "Bet That Proved a Life-Saver." June 8, 1976.

Dalton, David. "Carl Perkins: Let It Bleed." *Gadfly*, July 1998.

Davis, Paul. "We Were Just Doing the Music Our Way." *Country Music People*, April 1977.

DeCurtis, Anthony, and James Henke, with George Warren. *Holly: The Rolling Stone Album Guide.* Straight Arrow Publishers, 1982.

Dellar, Fred. "Chuck Berry Plays His First UK Tour!" Mojo4music. com, May 7, 2022.

DeWitt, Howard A. "WS Holland—Drumming to Stardom." *Rock & Blues News*, February–March 2001.

Donahue, Michael. "Carl Perkins Moving Firms to Memphis." *Commercial Appeal*, November 21, 1985.

Drozdowski, Ted. "Carl Perkins, 1932–1998." *Boston Phoenix*, February 2, 1998.

Edwards, Joe. "Carl Perkins Wants Beatles to Be Influenced Once More." *Forth Worth Star-Telegram*, December 14, 1985.

Eipper, Laura. "After 25 Years Johnny Cash is Looking Ahead." *Tennessean*, February 8, 1980.

Escott, Colin, and Bill Millar. Liner notes for *The Classic Carl Perkins*, Bear Family Records, 1990.

Flanagan, Bill. "Through the Past Brightly." *Musician*, May 1984.

Flynn, John. "Blue Suede Blues." *Courier-Journal*, October 23, 1977.

Fong-Torres, Ben, ed. *The Rolling Stone Rock 'n' Roll Reader.* Straight Arrow Publishers, 1974.

Forte, Don. "Daddy's Home." *Guitar Player*, March 1997.

Frangione, Tom, and Ken Michaels. "Carl Perkins: The Beatles Connection." *Goldmine*, November 6, 1998.

Galipault, Gerry. "Carl Perkins Faces Another Challenge." *Tampa Bay Times*, April 4, 1997.

German-way.com. "Johnny Cash in Germany and His Songs in German." n.d.

Graves, Tom. "Carl Perkins: *Born to Rock*." *Rock & Roll Disc*, July 1989.

———. Book review: Carl Perkins with David McGee, *Go, Cat, Go! The Life and Times of Carl Perkins*. *Washington Post*, June 23, 1996.

Green, Richard. "Johnny Cash, Carl Perkins, the Carter Family, the Statler Brothers: Queen Elizabeth Hall, London." *New Musical Express*, September 25, 1971.

Grow, Kory. "Johnny Cash Guitarist Bob Wootton Reflects on Fabled San Quentin Gig." *Rolling Stone*, April 13, 2017.

Grunwald, Mary. "'For the Abused Children'—Telethon pulls in $41,718 in gifts." *Jackson Sun*, August 19, 1985.

Guerrero, Gene. "Johnny Cash, Carter Family, Statler Brothers, Carl Perkins: Civic Center, Atlanta, GA." *Great Speckled Bird*, February 14, 1972.

Guralnick, Peter: *Careless Love: The Unmaking of Elvis Presley.* Boston: Little, Brown and Company, 1999.

———. "The Million Dollar Quartet." *New York Times*, March 25, 1979.

———. *Last Train to Memphis: The Rise of Elvis Presley.* Abacus, 1994.

———. *Sam Phillips: The Man Who Invented Rock 'n' Roll.* New York: Little, Brown and Company, 2015.

Hensley, Dennis E. "Everybody's Country Rock Hero." *Guitar Player*, n.d.

Herman, Arthur. "Beatles Help Celebrate Carl Perkins Anniversary." *Daily Herald*, December 29, 1985.

Hilburn, Robert. *Corn Flakes with John Lennon.* Emmaus, PA: Rodale, 2009.

———. *Johnny Cash: The Life.* London: Weidenfeld & Nicolson, 2013.

Holdship, Bill. "Perkins, Presley, et al: The Complete Million Dollar Session." *Creem*, June 1988.

Huntsville Times. "Rock'n'Roll Singer Mobbed but Blue Suede Shoes Unhurt." December 16, 1956.

Hurst, Jack. "Carl Perkins, Who Might Have Been Elvis, Is Content to Be Carl Perkins." *Chicago Tribune*, September 28, 1977.

Isler, Scott. "Frontman." *Musician*, August 1992.

Jackson Sun. "Benefit Show for the Family of JB Perkins." November 17, 1958.

Jackson Sun. "Carl Perkins Sings for Birthday Girl." November 9, 1997.

Jackson Sun. "Danny Moss Reappointed Easter Seals Treasurer." March 5, 1980.

Jackson Sun. "Family Weekend: Concerts, Fishing Big Catch at Reelfoot." July 18, 1980.

Jackson Sun. "Perkins Involved in Wreck, No Injuries." August 30, 1956.

Jackson Sun. "Perkins Selected Chairman of Area Cancer Fund Effort." April 22,1976.

Jackson Sun. "Valda 'Val' Crider Perkins Obituary." November 16, 2005.

Johnson, Robert. "Memphis Singer Hurt in Crash." *Memphis Press-Scimitar*, March 22, 1956.

———. "TV News and Views." *Memphis Press-Scimitar*, December 5, 1956.

Johnson City Press. "Carl Perkins' Museum Is Songwriter's Showcase." September 15, 1985.

Jones, Trina. "Musicians Plan Benefit for Abused Children." *Jackson Sun*, July 3, 1980.

Jopling, Norman. "Chuck Berry, Kingsize Taylor & the Dominos, Carl Perkins, the Animals, the Nashville Teens: Finsbury Park Astoria, London." *Record Mirror*, May 16, 1964.

Kansas City Star. "Western Singing Stars in 3 Shows." January 21, 1962.

Kaye, Elizabeth. "The Memphis Blues Again." *Rolling Stone*, November 21, 1985.

———. "Sam Phillips: The Rolling Stone Interview." *Rolling Stone*, February 13, 1986.

Kaye, Lenny. "The Very Large Legend of Carl Perkins." *Guitar World*, July 1982.

Knoxville News-Sentinel. "Singer Wounded." September 25, 1966.

Kyle, Dave. "There When It Happened." *Vintage Guitar*, March 1998.

Langbroek, Hans, and Adri Sturm. *Talking with Carl Perkins*, unpublished, February 27, 1972.

Lavividhair.com. "Did Carl Perkins Wear a Toupée?" April 18, 2022.

Leader-Post. "Opry Show Emphasises Rock, Roll." May 13, 1957.

Lexington Herald-Leader. "Carl Perkins Hospitalized." June 4, 1997.

Lydon, Michael. "Carl Perkins." *Rolling Stone*, February 21, 1970.

———. *Rock Folk*. New York: Dial Press, 1971.

Malone, Bill C. *Country Music USA*. Austin: University of Texas Press, 1985.

Marsh, Dave. "The Million Dollar Quartet." *Musician*, June 1981.

Martell, Tony. "Chatter of Platters." *Times-Tribune*, March 31, 1956.

McGee, David. "I Felt out of Place." *Rolling Stone*, April 19, 1990.

———. "Stars Turn Out for Rockabilly King Carl Perkins' Funeral." MTV.com, January 26, 1998.

McLaughlin, Tom. "'That's Love'—Carl Perkins Celebrates the Generosity of West Tennesseans at Saturday's Fund Raiser." *Jackson Sun*, February 9, 1997.

McNett, Gavin. "Carl Perkins, 1933–1998," Salon.com, January 20, 1998.

McNulty, Henry. "Rockabilly Keeps Rolling Along." *Hartford Courant*, May 18, 1980.

Means, Andrew. "Johnny Cash, Carter Family, Statler Brothers, Carl Perkins: Royal Albert Hall, London." *Melody Maker*, October 7, 1972.

Medina, Teddi. "With Hawaii's Filipino Community." *Honolulu Advertiser*, May 24, 1959.

Mehr, Bob. "Musical Icon, Elvis' Guitarist Scotty Moore Dies." *Memphis Commercial Appeal*, June 28, 2016.

———. "Rock'n'Roll Pioneer Dies at 87." *Memphis Commercial Appeal*, October 28, 2022.

———. "Sun Records, One of the Key Labels in Rock'n'Roll History, Purchased by New York Company Primary Wave in Reported $30M Deal." *Memphis Commercial Appeal*, January 28, 2021.

Mellish, Ilene. "Still Bopping after All These Years." *Melody Maker*, April 29, 1978.

Memphis Press-Scimitar. "Carl Perkins' Hard Luck." July 22, 1964.

Memphis Press-Scimitar. "Police Trail in Night Spots—Impersonator of Singer Reported." March 6, 1956.

Meyer, W Matt. "Auction to Fight Child Abuse." *Jackson Sun*, February 6, 1997.

————. "The Beatle . . . with a Little Help from His Jackson Friends." Harrisonstories.tumblr.com, n.d.

————. "Perkins Suffers Third Stroke." *Jackson Sun*, December 17, 1997.

Millar, Bill. "Boss Blues Bopper: Carl Perkins." *Creem*, July 1971.

Moore, Samantha. "Down on Main Street." *Jackson Sun*, April 25, 1988.

Morrow, Thomas. "He Cottons to Suede Shoes." *Chicago Tribune*, January 17, 1957.

Morthland, John. "Carl Perkins' Family Affair." *Rolling Stone*, February 8, 1979.

Newman, Ralph M,. and Jeff Tamarkin. "Ol' Blue Suedes Then & Now." *Time Barrier Express* 25, July–August 1979.

Nolder, Graham, producer. *Blue Suede Shoes: A Rockabilly Session.* Cinemax: 1986.

Norman, Philip. *John Lennon.* New York: Ecco, 2008.

————. *Paul McCartney: The Biography.* London: Weidenfeld & Nicolson, 2016.

"Ol' Blue Suedes Bops Back." Source unknown, April 1978.

Otteson, Jan. "Carl Perkins Is Back: Rockabilly Lives." *Music City News*, February 1979.

Pareles, Jon. "Carl Perkins Dies at 65: Rockabilly Pioneer Wrote 'Blue Suede Shoes.'" *New York Times*, January 20, 1997.

Partin, Kathy. "Volunteers Focus on Child Abuse." *Jackson Sun*, August 8, 1985.

Patton, Buck. "Carl Perkins at Reelfoot." *Memphis Press-Scimitar*, July 24, 1980.

Perkins, Carl, with David McGee. *Go, Cat, Go! The Life and Times of Carl Perkins.* New York: Hyperion, 1996.

Piazza, Tom. "Originally Rockabilly Back in Public Eye with New CD, Book." *Daily Press*, January 8, 1997.

Premier Guitar. "Bob Wootton: Keeping the Johnny Cash Flame Alive." August 19, 2009.

Pitts, Shawn. "Discovering Carl." *Southern Cultures*, Winter 2017.

Rhodes, Larry. "Like Starting Anew." *Country Style*, May 5, 1977.

Richmond Times-Despatch. "Carl Perkins to Perform Here Today." May 27, 1956.

Roberts, Bill. "Carl Perkins Named ArLuE Head." *Jackson Sun,* December 10, 1975.

Roberts, Jeremy. "Hello and Farewell to Cool Rockabilly Cat Carl Perkins." Medium.com, July 1, 2021.

Robinson, Simon, and Brian Smith. *Boom Boom Boom Boom: American Rhythm & Blues in England 1962–1966.* Easy on the Eye Books, 2020.

Roland, Tom. "Perkins Was There When It Happened." *Tennessean,* January 20, 1998.

Schneider, Richard. "Carl Perkins: The Music Man and Humanitarian." *Jackson Sun,* January 25, 1998.

The Scotsman. "Sir Paul McCartney Was Almost Known by a Different Stage Name." July 25, 2018.

Selvin, Joel. "Carl Perkins Dies at 65—A Patriarch of Rock'n'Roll." Sfgate.com, January 20, 1998.

Setnyk, Jason. "Interview with Johnny Cash Legendary Drummer WS Holland." theseeker.ca, June 30, 2017.

Shaw, Russell. "Legend of Rockabilly Keeps Rollin' On." *Country Music,* January–February 1979.

Shepherds Bush Gazette. "Pop Singer Shot Alert." June 4, 1964.

Shields, Brandon. "Carl Perkins Cared More about Others, Less about Fame." *Jackson Sun,* January 18, 2018.

———. "Remembering Carl Perkins 20 Years Later." *Jackson Sun,* January 18, 2018.

Sholin, Dave. "Born to Rock." *Gavin Report,* July 4, 1986.

Sievert, Jon. "A Rock and Roll Pioneer Heads into the 90s." *Guitar Player,* June 1989.

Stevens, Guy. "Sun Records: Country Meets Rock." *International Times,* May 23, 1969.

Stone Brown, Peter. "Interview: Carl Perkins, October 31, 1978, at the Bijou Café, Philadelphia, Pa." Unpublished, October 31, 1978.

Szolkowski, Roman. "Rockabilly Roots and Blue Suede Boots." *Goldmine,* n.d.

Takiff, Jonathan. "Debts Owed to Perkins." *Philadelphia Daily News*, January 8, 1988.

TBS. *Coming Home: A Rockin' Reunion*. August 1989.

Tennessean. "Carl Perkins' Father Dies." January 22, 1975.

Theroux, Gary. "A Legend in Blue Suede Shoes." *Goldmine*, September 26, 1986.

Thomas, John. "Noise vs Music." *Guthrian*, January 29, 1957.

Time. "Radio: Opry Night." January 29, 1940.

TNN. *CMT Presents Monday Night Concert*. February 1997.

Tribune. "Carl Perkins Hit by Third Stroke." December 18, 1997.

Troedson, David. "Carl Perkins: Blue Suede Shoes and Elvis Presley." Elvis.com.au, November 1, 2015.

Trosene, William K. "Rock'n'Roll Craze Keeps Rolling Along." *Pittsburgh Press*, July 1, 1956.

Weiser, Ron, and Dick Blackburn. "Carl Perkins Interview." *Rollin' Rock*, September 1977.

Whitaker, Sterling. "Remember the Car Accident That Nearly Ended Patsy Cline's Career?" Tasteofcountry.com, June 14, 2018.

Wickline, Larry. "Carl Perkins Not Quite a Superstar . . . but Happy." *Daily Press*, March 27, 1977.

Wooten, Bobby. "The Lost Interview." Radio station KAYO, Seattle, June 16, 1967. (See www.youtube.com/c/SpaGuy for this and other interviews.)

York, Max. "Cash Taping Recalls Past Yules." *Tennessean*, October 19, 1977.

Acknowledgments

A big thank-you to James Abbate, Chloe Aldrich, Ann Pryor, and all at Kensington Books (and to freelancers David Koral, Joe Gannon, and Steven Roman). Technically speaking, this is our second book, but it's the first to be commissioned directly by James, who's been a huge help and a constant source of support and encouragement throughout the entire process. Here's to many more. *Go, cat, go!*

I'd also to thank my lawyer, Ryan E. Long, for his ability to cut through the legalese and get right to the point. And my sincere thanks to Slim Jim Phantom, the coolest cat of all, for his big-hearted foreword; and to Elizabeth J. Rosenthal and C. M. Kushins, for their kind words.

Thanks also to Billy the Spa Guy (www.youtube.com/c/SpaGuy) and Kim Reis from the *Tennessean*, as well as the following photographers: Linda Matlow (and Ellen Morgan at Pix International), Dwight Haldeman, George DuBose, Jim Herrington, Brent Marilyn, Bob Mehr, and George Lange.

Simon Robinson was incredibly generous with his time and advice; thank you, sir, and by proxy, thank you also to Brian Smith, the cofounder of the Carl Perkins Fan Club back in the early 1960s. His book *Boom Boom* (published by Easy on the Eye books) is a remarkable celebration of Brian's great musical taste and his excellent photographic skills. Good health, sir.

Colin Escott, the cocreator of the *Million Dollar Quartet* musical, was also very helpful, as were Robert Hilburn and Ellen Mandel (on behalf of Michael Lydon).

A special thank-you to Dave Booth and all at Showtime Music Production, Inc., who provided me with a wealth of great research material, much of it very rare. My thanks, too, to Emily Di Marco for helping out.

And, as always, huge thanks and big love to my people: Diana, Christian, and Elizabeth.

Index